A FREEBORN PEOPLE

A FREEBORN PEOPLE

*Politics and the Nation in
Seventeenth-Century England*

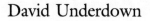

David Underdown

CLARENDON PRESS · OXFORD

1996

Oxford University Press, Walton Street, Oxford OX2 6DP

Oxford New York
Athens Auckland Bangkok Bombay
Calcutta Cape Town Dar es Salaam Delhi
Florence Hong Kong Istanbul Karachi
Kuala Lumpur Madras Madrid Melbourne
Mexico City Nairobi Paris Singapore
Taipei Tokyo Toronto
and associated companies in
Berlin Ibadan

Oxford is a trade mark of Oxford University Press

Published in the United States
by Oxford University Press Inc., New York

British Library Cataloguing in Publication Data
Data available

Library of Congress Cataloging in Publication Data
Underdown, David.
A freeborn people : politics and the nation in seventeenth-century
England / David Underdown.
p. cm.
1. Great Britain—Politics and government—1603–1714.
2. Nationalism—England—History—17th century. 3. England—
Civilization—17th century. I. Title.
DA135.U53 1996
320.941′09′032—dc20 96–5463
ISBN 0-19-820612-7

1 3 5 7 9 10 8 6 4 2

Typeset by Graphicraft Typesetters Ltd., Hong Kong

Printed in Great Britain
on acid-free paper by
Bookcraft (Bath) Ltd
Midsomer Norton, Avon

PREFACE

This book originated as the Ford Lectures delivered at Oxford in Hilary Term, 1992. When I was invited to deliver these lectures I spent a long time deciding what would be an appropriate subject. I had written about royalist conspiracies in Cromwellian England; about the politics of the Long Parliament; and about the experience of my native county, Somerset, in the civil war. Until that stage of my career I had been a more-or-less conventional political historian, but when writing about Somerset I made the now not very remarkable, but then still surprising, discovery that the rural common people had their own politics, which were very different from those of the Levellers and the radical sects, hitherto the main focus of historical interest. And the outlook of the common people, I found, seemed to vary according to the region in which they lived. I pursued this line of investigation in a couple of articles and another book, and as I did so it struck me with increasing force that the two kinds of politics—the élite and the popular—ought not to be kept in separate compartments. It also struck me that if they were to be brought together it would be necessary to bridge the chasm that has so often divided social from political history. For as long as I could remember historians—with notable exceptions like Christopher Hill and Lawrence Stone—had written about the politics of the period before the civil war while paying only routine, perfunctory attention to the social conditions in which those politics were embedded. At the same time social historians were opening up marvellous new vistas through their work on marriage and the family, on gender relations and the experience of women, on the local community and popular mentalities, and a whole host of other fascinating topics—with only the barest passing mention of politics, or even of the civil war, the most significant event of the seventeenth century. We ought surely, as others more eloquent than I have observed, to be trying to bring these two broad areas of history together. In his 1989 inaugural lecture at Cambridge, Patrick Collinson made a compelling plea for study of social history 'with the politics put back'.[1] There is, of course, the inevitable corollary that we should also do political history with the social history restored.

So the relationship between the politics of the élite and the politics of the common people seemed a tempting subject, and as a number of

talented scholars had raised new questions and opened up exciting pos-
sibilities in both areas, it seemed that this might be a good time to try
it. It certainly was an appropriate subject for an historian with my particular experience. And finally, it seemed especially appropriate for someone most of whose career has been spent outside the United Kingdom.
There have been both advantages and disadvantages for me in what
some might see as this transatlantic exile. The disadvantages are obvious:
remoteness from sources, lack of daily contact with fellow specialists,
the experience of constantly having to teach undergraduate students
who sometimes come to British history without even the rudimentary
exposure to the national historical culture that one can presumably still
take for granted in Britain.

Yet there are also some countervailing benefits for those of us who
teach our national history to foreigners. In the first place, we can never
assume that its importance is self-evident, and this can often be good
for us. Whether we are talking about the Groom of the Stole or the
Constable of Batcombe, we have to make the office comprehensible in
terms of the larger culture to people who are in one way or another outside that culture. We have always to ask ourselves why we, or anyone else,
should actually *care* about it. And at a somewhat higher level of discourse, since much of our conversation is with colleagues who specialize
in very different fields, or in disciplines other than history, we are constantly having to explain our own work in broadly comparative and conceptual terms. In the teaching of both undergraduate and postgraduate
students the separation between political and social history—or any other
kind of history—is inevitably less pronounced in America than it is in
Britain. All this encourages a habit of mind that runs against the grain
of specialization as it is practised in many British universities. I am not
suggesting that this is necessarily good or necessarily bad, but at least it
helps to explain why those of us who remain attached to British history
on those far-flung colonial shores may be somewhat more inclined to
cross disciplinary boundaries than we might have been if we had followed our trade in the United Kingdom. It may explain, for example,
why someone might be rash enough to take on a theme as broad as the
relationship between élite and popular politics.

In one respect, however, my own particular experience in the United
States contradicts everything that I have just said, in that it has also given
me advantages that have nothing to do with interdisciplinary breadth,
or cross-cultural comparativeness: because Yale, the university in which
I now teach, has for a very long time been a vigorous centre for the study

of the politics of Stuart England. To start at a fairly trivial level, Yale is situated in a region full of echoes of the seventeenth century. New Haven was founded during the great puritan migration; after 1660 it sheltered three of the fleeing regicides, one of whom—John Dixwell—is buried there; the suburb in which I live is named after John Hampden. Several of my distinguished predecessors at Yale—Wallace Notestein, J. H. Hexter, and Conrad Russell, for example—have in their different ways left indelible marks on seventeenth-century historical studies. To Notestein and Hexter we owe the foundation of the Yale Center for Parliamentary History, one of the great institutional centres for the study of seventeenth-century Westminster. Without the meticulously edited Yale editions of the debates of the 1620s my own work, and that of anyone else seriously studying the political history of the Stuart period, would be immeasurably more difficult. Being able to observe the day-to-day preparation of this great edition has given me more insight into the way politics worked in the seventeenth century than I could have obtained in any other way. My involvement with the Yale Center for Parliamentary History is one more reason why it seemed appropriate to choose as one of the main themes of these lectures a subject that would require me to take another look at those apparently well-worn early Stuart constitutional conflicts.

Living in the midst of the editorial preparation of these parliamentary debates, it would be easy to swallow uncritically the traditional narrative of the Stuart period. It was, after all, from parliamentary debates and suchlike sources that the great Whig masters like Gardiner and Trevelyan constructed their narratives of that contentious century. And historians, we all know, are the prisoners of their sources. The reader will have to judge whether I have driven through this minefield with due care and attention. In the course of this book I shall necessarily have a good deal to say about Parliament, and in particular the House of Commons. This may strike some readers as old-fashioned, flying in the face of an impressive body of recent historical opinion which asserts the insignificance of that body.[2] In these days, when the House of Commons is little more than a rubber-stamp for decisions made elsewhere, it may be natural to think that it was always like that. Historians have often been accused of importing the present into the past, and we ought always to be on our guard against this. But John Pym's House of Commons was not as predictable or subservient a body as John Major's House of Commons; it operated on a different set of procedural conventions, had no party system, and occupied a totally different place in the constitution. So the book will begin by taking yet another look at the early Stuart parliaments.

The title of my first chapter refers to 'two narratives' of the Stuart century, by which I broadly mean, on the one hand the narrative of 'high politics', the politics of parliament and Court; and on the other the narrative of 'popular politics', the politics of the common people. That duality is of course a gross over-simplification, because both narratives are highly problematic: no two historians of élite politics are likely to agree on their narrative, any more than any two historians of the common people will on theirs. But one has to begin somewhere, and they will be my starting-point. After having indicated some of the problems and difficulties of the exercise, I hope to suggest ways in which it may be possible to bring the various narratives together.

The remaining five chapters will consider the two principal levels of the political nation—broadly speaking, the élite and the popular—more or less alternately. We shall first take a new look at the gentry in the forty years or so before the civil wars. We shall observe a political nation partly controlled by the familiar structures of hierarchy and deference, its motives largely explicable in terms of either localism or personal ambition. The narrative for this segment of the gentry is one concerned primarily with government, bureaucracy, state-building. But we shall also encounter another part of the political nation trying to protect its version of the 'ancient constitution', and to defend both local and national rights against the encroaching central state. The narrative here is dominated by politics and contention rather than by deference and consensus.

This will lead into the third chapter, for the dominant themes of popular politics were also concerned with the defence of a traditional, customary order—the popular version of the ancient constitution—against unwanted innovations. Popular politics was conservative, but by no means universally deferential. Ordinary Englishmen, like their superiors, had ways of criticizing contemporary developments that threatened their interests: the increasing use of state power, the excesses of acquisitive individualism, for example. One way in which they did this was through the use of inversion themes—particularly the inversion of status or gender roles—in their rituals of protest. But whether by this means or others, they tended to give priority to an older conception of society which they thought was fast disappearing, a mythical just order stressing the obligations of the rich and powerful to those below them; the extending of hospitality by the rich to the poor; the enforcement of 'moral economy' regulations which protected subsistence; the defence of the ancient birthrights of freeborn Englishmen. Until the civil wars of the 1640s these two kinds of politics, of the gentry and the people, coexisted in relative harmony.

The fourth and fifth chapters will survey the period of the civil wars and the revolution on much the same lines; a review of how the wars affected gentry politics in Chapter 4; a similar journey through some aspects of popular politics in Chapter 5. Previous historians have focused so heavily on the parliamentarians that this part of the book will concentrate more than is the custom on the royalists. Chapter 5 will examine a popular newspaper of the Commonwealth period—a seventeenth-century equivalent of the *Sun*—to see what it can tell us about the popular political vocabulary. Finally, the sixth chapter will review both levels of the political nation after the Restoration, and try to draw the various themes of the earlier chapters together. The reader will quickly realize that the book does not pretend to provide a complete or connected history of the relations between élite and popular politics during the seventeenth century. It should be approached, as it originated, as a set of lectures, a series of meditations upon a central theme. I hope it will encourage others to pursue the questions it raises in their own way.

Throughout the book both spelling and punctuation in quotations have been modernized. The dates given are in the old style, except that the year has been taken to begin on 1 January rather than 25 March.

ACKNOWLEDGEMENTS

It has often been said that an invitation to serve as Ford's Lecturer is the greatest accolade that can be bestowed on anyone who writes on British history, and I naturally begin by expressing my thanks to the electors for the great honour they have done me by this selection. I am even more sensible of the honour because I am, I believe, the first historian to have been invited to serve as Ford's Lecturer while teaching at an American university—or indeed at any university outside the British Isles.[1]

When I left Oxford many years ago the possibility that I might one day come back in such circumstances would have seemed, if it had even occurred to me, laughably remote. To have done so as Ford's Lecturer naturally reminds me of all the debts I owe to those who made it possible. I am, I suspect, among the very few people to have been a pupil of both C. T. Atkinson, who was one of the most conservative men I have ever known, and of Christopher Hill, who was one of the least. From Atkinson, who was superficially terrifying but in fact always kind to those who shared his taste for cricketing and Gilbert-and-Sullivan metaphors, I learnt how to write relatively decent prose. Christopher Hill taught me how to use historical sources, and how important it was not to take at face value the assumption so often made by those in power that they alone were the makers of history. From him I learnt, too, that the best history was the kind that raises questions and opens up new perspectives, rather than the kind that closes them off by insisting that all the answers are now known and settled. In between I was fortunate to have as my college tutor Greig Barr, whose wisdom and moderation in making historical judgements I have always wished to aspire to, even if I have not always been able to emulate it.

I have many other Oxford debts to acknowledge—to Eric Kemp, afterwards Bishop of Chichester, who patiently tried to make me think seriously about the Middle Ages; and to the late Menna Prestwich, whose mark will be on these lectures, as it has been on so much of my work, because she was my tutor in the Commonwealth and Protectorate special subject, and always an inspiring one. Nor can I forget all those who were not formally my tutors, but who nevertheless often taught me as much as if they were—Herbert Nicholas, Hugh Trevor-Roper, and many, many others. And I wish to express my gratitude to the Warden and Fellows of All Souls for electing me to a visiting Fellowship during the two terms in which the lectures were given and the process of revising them for publication was begun.

My thanks are also due to the John Simon Guggenheim Foundation for awarding me a second Fellowship, which enabled me to prepare the lectures in their original form and provided further support during my two terms at Oxford. As usual I have benefited from the courtesy and helpfulness of the staffs of numerous libraries, particularly those of the Bodleian, the Codrington Library at All Souls, and the Yale University Library. I wish to express particular thanks to Maija Jansson and the other members of the editorial team at the Yale Center for Parliamentary History for sharing with me their incomparable knowledge of parliamentary proceedings in the 1620s. Parts of Chapters 2 and 5 were given as lectures at Wooster College, Lewis and Clark College, Marshall University, and Brown University, and as papers at the New England Conference on Renaissance Studies (also at Brown University), and at the Center for Medieval and Early Renaissance Studies at Binghamton, New York (part of Chapter 5, which is also printed in a volume of proceedings at that conference, appears with the Center's permission).[2] I am grateful to all those who made constructive contributions to the discussions that followed. Thomas Cogswell, Mark Kishlansky, and John Morrill have given generously of their time to read the book in manuscript: the inadequacies that have survived their scrutiny are entirely my responsibility. Finally, as always, I wish to thank Susan Amussen for her unfailing help, understanding, and constructive criticism throughout the period of this book's composition.

CONTENTS

ABBREVIATIONS

APC	*Acts of the Privy Council*
BIHR	*Bulletin of the Institute of Historical Research*
BL	British Library
CJ	*Journals of the House of Commons*
CSPD	*Calendar of State Papers, Domestic*
DNB	*Dictionary of National Biography*
EHR	*English Historical Review*
Foster, *1610*	Elizabeth Read Foster (ed.), *Proceedings in Parliament 1610* (New Haven, Conn., 1966)
Gardiner, *1610*	S. R. Gardiner (ed.), *Parliamentary Debates in 1610* (Camden Soc., 1862)
HMC	Historical Manuscripts Commission
JBS	*Journal of British Studies*
KAO	Kent Archives Office
PRO	Public Record Office
1614	Maija Jansson (ed.), *Proceedings in Parliament 1614 (House of Commons)* (Philadelphia, 1988)
1621	Wallace Notestein *et al.* (eds.), *Commons Debates, 1621* (New Haven, Conn., 1935)
1625	Maija Jansson and William B. Bidwell (eds.), *Proceedings in Parliament 1625* (New Haven, Conn., 1987)
1626	William B. Bidwell and Maija Jansson (eds.), *Proceedings in Parliament 1626* (New Haven, Conn., 1991–6)
1628	Robert C. Johnson *et al.* (eds.), *Proceedings in Parliament 1628* (New Haven, Conn., 1977–83)
1629	Wallace Notestein and Frances Relf (eds.), *Commons Debates for 1629* (Minneapolis, 1921)
TRHS	*Transactions of the Royal Historical Society*
TT	Thomason Tracts
VCH	Victoria County History

In the notes, all places of publication are London, unless otherwise stated.

1

INTRODUCTION

COMPETING NARRATIVES OF THE STUART PERIOD

Few historical narratives have been as contested in recent years as the one describing the politics of early seventeenth-century England. When I went up to Oxford during the Second World War the handiest guide to the Stuart reigns was J. R. Tanner's *English Constitutional Conflicts of the Seventeenth Century*, published in 1928.[1] It conveniently summarizes the Whig view of that period: the Tudor inheritance of a powerful crown and a powerful parliament working in relative harmony; the foolishness of the pedantic James I in transforming the acceptable Tudor doctrine of the royal prerogative into the quite unacceptable theory of the divine right of kings; the 'high road to civil war' along which the House of Commons travelled in a series of great constitutional statements, from the Apology of the Commons to the Petition of Right; the 'eleven years' tyranny' that followed the stormy dissolution of Parliament in 1629; and so on through civil war, republic, and Restoration to the final confirmation of parliamentary government after the revolution of 1688. Out of conflict came stability, order, and—eventually, much later—progress towards liberal democracy.

This rosy view of English constitutional history had already been seriously undermined by the time Tanner wrote. The Great War and its aftermath of economic depression and social conflict had made the excellence of parliamentary institutions a bit less self-evident. The Whig interpretation was also being challenged by new intellectual fashions. It was rejected by Marxists, who saw laws and liberties as the ideological superstructure built on the material base of economic processes, the Whigs' great conflict of principle as no more than the reflection of a class struggle which culminated in the 'bourgeois revolution' of the 1640s. During and after the Second World War the rejection of Whig history continued. Many who did not accept the entire Marxian historical scheme nevertheless put more emphasis on economic and social change than on political and constitutional ideas when they tried to explain the revolution of the 1640s. For R. H. Tawney and a whole generation enthralled by him the central explanation was, of course, 'The Rise of the Gentry'. As James Harrington had argued long ago in Cromwell's time, the dissolution of the monasteries and the sales of crown estates later in the sixteenth century had changed the balance of property and had brought a new class to the fore. The political conflicts of the early Stuart period reflected the newly emergent gentry's demand for a political, as well as an economic, place in the sun.[2]

The Whig interpretation was challenged from another direction by Sir Lewis Namier and his followers. In 1929, in *The Structure of Politics at the Accession of George III*, Namier launched a frontal attack on the hitherto virtually unquestioned Whig narrative of eighteenth-century England, arguing that it rested on totally anachronistic foundations. The Whigs, as his ally Romney Sedgwick put it, had criticized George III for 'having endeavoured to imitate the Stuarts when he ought to have anticipated Queen Victoria'.[3] Namier was much influenced by Freud, and thus saw subconscious drives—in his case, primarily for power— as the determinants of political behaviour. So prosopography and the study of interest and clientage groups and of political manipulation replaced the Whig narrative of impassioned ideological debate. Sir Lewis's followers—the so-called Namierites—carried his approach to extremes as they too wrote off lofty ideas like law and liberty as mere rhetorical smokescreens. Most of the Namierites, like their master, were primarily concerned with the eighteenth century, but after 1945 a watered-down version of their project found its way into work on the Stuart century.[4]

In spite of these challenges, until the last twenty years or so residual bits of the Whig interpretation could still be found in most narratives of the seventeenth century. The 'Victorian' assumptions of historians like S. R. Gardiner might be out of fashion, but the broad outline of their narrative, modified in some respects by Wallace Notestein's hypothesis about 'The Winning of the Initiative by the House of Commons', remained secure.[5] To take one memorable example, Lawrence Stone, working in the Tawney tradition, might be more interested in the social forces that produced a rise of the gentry, a decline of aristocracy; might see in Sir Edward Coke's adulation of the common law a certain tincture of lawyerly self-interest, a concern for perquisites as well as principles. Yet his work betrays no doubts about there having been a real conflict between country gentlemen and lawyers on the one side, courtiers and Laudian clerics on the other, over the nature of the constitution, or doubts that the conflicts of the years between 1603 and 1629 were a prelude to the later civil wars.[6]

During the 1970s all this began to change. A new version of English seventeenth-century politics emerged and until quite recently appeared to be acquiring the status of an orthodoxy. In the writings of Conrad Russell, John Morrill, Kevin Sharpe, Mark Kishlansky, and other scholars of great skill and insight a picture of the period was created that would be unrecognizable to anyone whose historical reading had stopped at— let us say—1972.[7] No longer were the economic and social changes of the period 1540–1640—once known as 'Tawney's Century'—regarded as relevant to the revolution of the 1640s. As early as 1973 Conrad Russell reproved Lawrence Stone for having tried to explain 'events which did not happen' (a revolution in 1640), as the outcome of a social process (the rise of the gentry—crisis of the aristocracy) 'for which the evidence remains uncertain'.[8] The civil war, he and others argued, was the result of a series of short-term misunderstandings and mistakes, not of any long-standing social or political dysfunction. It is therefore now possible for Russell to begin his *Fall of the British Monarchies* in 1637, with little prior analysis of either society or politics earlier in the seventeenth century.[9]

The new approach requires us to study the reigns of James and Charles I without benefit of hindsight, without regarding them, in G. R. Elton's well-known phrase, as a 'high road to civil war'.[10] Russell and the others who have done this have found the politics of the period 1603–29 far less confrontational, far more directed towards the achievement of consensus, than the Whigs and their successors had believed. The House of Commons, Russell had argued, was less inclined to speak independently about legal and financial grievances than readers of Notestein's 'Winning of the Initiative' might imagine. Parliament's real business was the production of legislation, much of it of a very routine, localist kind. And the men elected to these early Stuart parliaments—or selected, as Mark Kishlansky would prefer—were incapable of mounting an ideologically motivated opposition to the crown and its ministers. They were not independent spokesmen for their constituencies—their 'countries', they would have said—they were the deferential clients of greater men, of peers and royal councillors. The real locus of politics was the Court: conflict in the House of Commons was so much shadow-boxing, simply an 'extension of court faction', just as it had been in Queen Elizabeth's days. We should devote more time to the House of Lords than to the pathetically dependent Commons. The attempt to impeach the Duke of Buckingham in 1626, for example, seen by the Whigs as a dramatic example of the Commons' initiative, was actually engineered by 'a powerful court conspiracy', rather than by the independent action of enraged country gentlemen.[11]

What, then, was all the fuss about? Why were so many people imprisoned for resisting crown policies in and out of Parliament? Why all the lofty rhetoric associated with the Petition of Right? Why did the Speaker have to be restrained from leaving the chair in that famous scene at the dissolution in March 1629? The problems, we are told, were not the result of social or ideological change, or of any other profound historical forces. Instead, they were provoked by the particular circumstances of the four years after Charles I's accession: by the financial strains resulting from the wars with Spain and France into which Buckingham blundered, and by the adoption by Charles I of an unpopular religious policy, which promoted and rewarded Arminian critics of the Jacobean 'Religion of Protestants'. So the traditional picture of heroic patriots fighting for English liberties appears to have sunk without trace. 'What they were debating', Russell says of the MPs who were drafting the Petition of Right in 1628, 'was civil liberties in time of war', obviously an exercise in political futility.[12]

After 1629, with the ending of Charles I's attempt to govern in alliance with his parliaments, we return, according to this recent orthodoxy, to the normal functioning of early modern government. When peace is made with France and Spain in 1630 the contentious atmosphere that had paralysed recent policy quickly vanished. The emphasis is now on Charles as reformer: on his attempts to restore order after Jacobean chaos, to clean up the Court, limit the sale of honours, make both central and local government more efficient. The greatest triumph of the 'personal rule', on this interpretation, was Ship Money, a fairly assessed and, until 1639, efficiently collected levy, resisted only on technical grounds—the well-publicized constitutional challenge in Hampden's case representing the ideas only of a handful of peers and wealthy gentry. Throughout the early and mid-1630s, the received wisdom insists, there are no signs of significant public discontent: we are in those idyllic, halcyon days of peace and contentment which Clarendon so poignantly recalls in the prelude to his *History of the Rebellion*. England in 1637, Russell assures us, 'was a country in working order', and the state papers of the period are not 'the record of a regime which believed it was sitting on a powder keg'. In a massive recent study Kevin Sharpe concurs.[13]

Government archives are not necessarily the best place to look for evidences of official failure. Still, the interpretation of the period that I

have described is a powerful and coherent one. It has recently been but-
tressed by the argument that the collapse of Charles I's government
was in large part the result of a 'problem of multiple kingdoms'—of his
ruling over three distinct, though closely interrelated states. Attempts
to deal with difficulties in one often had what Russell calls a 'billiard-
ball effect', destabilizing one or both of the others. This approach has
inspired a new way of conceptualizing the civil wars of the 1640s: as a
'war of three kingdoms', part of a 'British' rather than a merely English
revolution, which can only be properly understood if the 'British' nature
of the problems underlying it is realized.[14] The new paradigm—if such it
is destined to become—has much to commend it, particularly at a time
when English historians are increasingly embarrassed by their insularity
and are rightly trying to think of their subject in a less parochial way.
Moving from England to Britain as the unit of study would not get us
into Europe, but it would be a step in the right direction.

But although the 'multiple kingdoms' concept may be a useful one
for historians trying to understand Charles I's difficulties, it is of relatively little help to us in illuminating the subject of this book. In some
respects, indeed, it is a step backward, as it returns us to the relations
between states and kingdoms and élites. 'The commonest causes of
instability in multiple kingdoms', Russell assures us, 'were war and the
distribution of offices': once again we are invited to confine our attention to the behaviour of the rulers.[15] As for 'Britishness', in so far as it
existed, it was an identity of which a few Anglo-Scottish or Anglo-Irish
noblemen, and a much larger number of Protestant settlers in Ireland,
may have been conscious, but of which there are few signs among the
English common people. So although the redefinition of the civil war
as a British one may have useful results, to understand it properly we
should still need to explore the political cultures of the three compon-
ent kingdoms, which were very different from each other, among other
things in the relationships between the political élites and their inferiors.

It may well be that Scottish and Irish historians would approach the
subject of that relationship in their own distinctive ways. But the kingdom under discussion in this book is England, so it is time to leave this
discussion of the latest conceptual framework for the conflict of the
1640s and return to the earlier politics of the seventeenth century. One
problem with much of the recently fashionable interpretation of that
period is that, like Namier's version of the 1760s, it trivializes Parliament's activities, and takes us away from what the participants thought
they were doing, or at least from what they said. It may be Whiggish

of me, but I am inclined to take rather more seriously a body that could so successfully obstruct, as well as advance, royal policies, and not dismiss its debates as mere rhetorical smokescreens. We have been rightly asked to look at the evidence afresh.[16] But parliamentary speeches are part of the evidence, no more biased and subjective than the official papers of the Council, or the correspondence and memoranda of councillors. All these pieces of evidence are texts, and we do not have to be deconstructionists to accept that texts have to be decoded and read critically if they are to tell us anything worthwhile about the pre-textual reality that we are trying to understand.

By marginalizing the parliamentary texts and defining the Court as the only public arena worthy of study, the earlier revisionists were able to depict a political nation that until 1640 was almost universally deferential and harmonious, and then suddenly exploded in rebellion. We might perhaps call this the big bang theory of the civil war. The big bang turns out, appropriately, to be of divine origin. In so far as the resistance of 1640 and 1641 was not purely fortuitous and circumstantial, in this view, it was caused by religion, by Charles I's decision to promote Arminian innovations which divided his subjects and exposed his Court to suspicions of popery. The explosions of Calvinist revolt in Scotland and Catholic rebellion in Ireland compounded the suspicions, and given the problem of governing 'multiple kingdoms', made compromise impossible. David Hume, it seems, was right to put religion at the centre of it all: 'the disorders in Scotland entirely, and those in England mostly, proceeded from so mean and contemptible an origin.'[17]

It will already be clear from this discussion that I have strong reservations about some of the revisionist studies of the 1970s and '80s. These reservations are, happily, not simply those of lone eccentric sitting in historiographical isolation on the far-away shores of a Long Island Sound. Some of them have been powerfully expressed by earlier critics,[18] and more recently by a number of younger historians who, while accepting the most useful of the revisionists' insights, have begun the process of constructing an alternative interpretation which takes into account the conflicting as well as the consensual aspects of the early Stuart decades. Thomas Cogswell, Richard Cust, Ann Hughes, Johann Sommerville, and others have challenged the central assumptions of revisionism and have forced us yet again to look anew at the period. The title of the collection of essays which put some of their conclusions before the public clearly proclaims their approach: *Conflict in Early Stuart England*.[19] Succeeding chapters of this book—particularly the second one—

will owe a good deal to their work, which it will try to extend by attempting a more detailed discussion of the relations between élite and popular politics.

The Whigs and their revisionist successors, whose views I have (no doubt all too crudely) summarized, may differ on many things, but in one respect they are very similar: all tend to write history from the top down. The Whigs wrote from the point of view of the parliamentary gentry and lawyers, and the non-Laudian clergy—the chief elements of the 'political nation' as they defined it. Their revisionist successors have generally adopted either a Whitehall or a provincialist point of view. In the former case they stress the problems and policies of central government, in the latter those of the counties. Very different narrative strategies necessarily result, but whichever narrative is chosen is likely to be primarily concerned with the politics of one or more branches of the élite. Public opinion is the opinion of gentlemen, noblemen, and clerics; the issues that agitated such people were usually connected with the distribution of power and offices. In spite of valiant efforts by localist historians and by some of the revisionists' recent critics to broaden the social area that they are dealing with, the accepted narrative of the seventeenth century still rests on what James Scott has called the 'public transcript', the official record of the dominant élite, of the peers and the greater gentry.[20]

But there is another narrative of the seventeenth century which is very different from those of either the Whigs or their critics, and which focuses far more directly on the experience of the ordinary, non-genteel population. The best-known and most coherent version of this alternative narrative is the one found in much of Christopher Hill's work, though as with the narratives of élite politics, numerous alternative versions have arisen to challenge it, and also to contradict each other. The alternative narrative starts from a very different definition of the political nation from the one used by the Whigs and their critics: one which includes not only the commercial and mercantile classes, but also the 'people' in the usual seventeenth-century sense of that term—the artisans, the independent craftsmen, the yeomen and better-off husbandmen, the groups Hill has somewhat arbitrarily lumped together as the 'industrious sort'.[21] Rural elements of that group (though not the yeomen) were among the chief victims of the sixteenth-century demographic explosion, and the land shortage and price inflation it brought in its wake. Unable to produce enough for the market to take advantage of rising agricultural prices, many of them went to the wall during bad periods like the 1590s and the 1620s. Others, particularly forest and fen dwellers, were pauperized and swindled out of long-held rights of common when the crown decided to unload its forest holdings to reward favoured courtiers and entrepreneurs, or to promote the ecological revolution initiated by fen drainage, in the name of agricultural 'improvement'.

A restive and economically disadvantaged population, according to this version of the narrative, naturally blamed the crown for its problems, especially when, as in the Forest of Dean, the profiteers were well-known monopolistis or courtiers like Sir Giles Mompesson and members of the Buckingham clan. Political opposition was also likely to encompass the more affluent and respectable middling-sort—people who in puritanism had found an ideology that enabled them to rationalize their individualism as godly virtue, and blame the problems of society on the two social groups between whom they were sandwiched—the idle, immoral rich, and the equally idle, ungodly poor. We need not at this point confront in detail the problems inherent in this interpretation, though some difficulties follow from grouping together the beneficiaries of the expanding market economy, the wealthy merchants (many with crown connections) and the lesser folk, many of whom were being exploited by them just as severely as by the courtiers, gentry, and aristocracy. Still, as both Christopher Hill and Brian Manning have shown, it is possible to construct a coherent narrative that explains how on certain issues—monopolies, taxation, religion—both ends of this wider political nation were able to work together before the civil wars, and to ally with and accept the leadership of sympathetic groups among the élite.[22]

The civil wars disrupted this alliance, persuading many of the wealthy bourgeoisie, as they did many of the gentry, that the lower orders could not be trusted. In this interpretation the Levellers and, after their eclipse, the various radical sects which flourished during the 1650s confirm the radicalism of large groups of the common people, and their determination to turn the world upside down.[23] But although the two revolutions of 1640–2 and 1648–9 temporarily succeeded, the hypothetical third revolution—the democratic one of the Levellers and the sects—did not. The gentry and the urban oligarchies closed ranks, first behind Oliver Cromwell as a temporary 'saviour of society', and then behind Charles II as a more permanent one. Much was lost at the Restoration, but the agenda of the more affluent elements of the bourgeoisie was in large part achieved: they gained the less regulated economy they wanted, and a state more closely attuned to their commercial and colonial interests.

But the demands of the lower sort—for a more democratic political order, the establishment of religious toleration, the protection of copyholders and other small landholders—were abandoned. The Monmouth rebellion was the last kick of the old kind of rural radicalism. When the popular cause reawakened later in the eighteenth century it was to be in a largely urban setting.

This version of the narrative of 'popular politics'—one which identifies the aspirations of the common people as essentially radical, directed towards democratic political reform and a more egalitarian society—has in recent years been challenged just as sharply as the Whig narrative has been. One strikingly contrasting version of English social development was presented a few years ago by Jonathan Clark: England was a society based on hierarchy and deference, a confessional 'ancien régime' state, in which there were virtually no fundamental changes at all until the nineteenth century. Without necessarily going this far, other social historians have argued that there were few significant changes in either the class structure or the familial relations of early modern England, and have consequently put consensus rather than conflict at the centre of their descriptions of the period.[24]

Even those historians who, like Keith Wrightson, put more stress on change now emphasize the basic conservatism of the English common people. In this case, though, conflict is not banished from the narrative; indeed, Wrightson has made an important argument that 'social polarization' (an early stage in the process of class formation) was a significant feature of the seventeenth century. He and others have given the numerous grain and enclosure riots of the period much attention.[25] But the objectives of those riots turn out to be much less radical than the ones identified in the earlier version of popular politics. The rioters' primary objective is now thought to be the preservation of a vanished, just order of society, a mythical merry England in which landlords and grain dealers do not cheat or oppress the poor, and in which both monarch and gentry uphold the traditional laws and regulatory structures of the old 'moral economy'. The civil war political group expressing typically 'popular' values is not the democratic Levellers, but the conservative Clubmen; the typical popular manifesto the 1641 *Protestation*, not the 1647 *Agreement of the People*.[26]

As with those of the rival narratives of élite politics, exponents of these two versions of English plebeian politics have differed on many important matters. Yet they have generally adopted a definition of the political nation which is wider than the gentry and aristocracy, and includes a fairly broad spectrum of the total (male) population. My intention in the rest of this book is to explore the similarities and differences between these two broadly defined segments of the political nation—the élite and the popular—and to re-examine seventeenth-century English politics in the light of this comparison. When I use the term 'élite' I shall be talking about the nobility, the courtiers, the country gentry: those who participated in, or directly influenced, the government of shire and kingdom. When I use the term 'popular' I shall be talking about people of lower status: yeomen, husbandmen, craftsmen, small urban householders. All these lesser people were owners of property, and were thus part of the political nation in ways that the increasingly numerous vagrants and landless poor were not. But their participation in government was confined to the performance of inferior (though locally important) offices such as constable, churchwarden, and overseer of the poor, except when they rioted, petitioned, or as freeholders voted in parliamentary elections.

There was no absolute divide between the élite and 'the people', but a spectrum on which a good many intermediate positions existed. Characterizations of élite and popular depend to a considerable extent on the viewpoint of the beholder. William Whiteway of Dorchester would have been thought one of the common people by a great nobleman like the Earl of Suffolk; many of his fellow-townsmen (members of the Pouncey family, for example), would assuredly have regarded him as one of the élite.[27] Yet in spite of these difficulties of definition, the two constellations—the élite and the popular—are usually easily recognizable during the seventeenth century. We might almost think of them, in Disraeli's famous phrase, as 'two nations'.

In this book, however, I shall argue that the political cultures of the two nations were much closer to each other than is commonly supposed, particularly in the first part of the seventeenth century. During and after the civil wars this began to change. The radical forces unleashed by the war destroyed the gentry's confidence that their inferiors shared their priorities. There was a sharper separation between the two political cultures: this process might be seen as part of the more general polarization of élite and popular cultures that some historians have observed in these years. That separation was reflected in language and metaphor. There were always differences in the political vocabularies used by the gentry and the common folk (or by those addressing them); those differences became more pronounced as time went by.

We come, then, to the subject of popular culture. How to define it is no easy matter, for it is certainly a mistake to posit a simple, binary distinction between the worlds of the élite and the popular. Peter Burke has defined the sphere of popular culture as that of 'the unlearned, the non-elite, the people . . . who did not know Latin, who were not members of the king's court or the Inns of Court, and who could not afford to visit a private theatre or buy many books'. This is a useful working definition, but it raises some problems, if only because the people Burke is referring to obviously did read, or listen to, *some* books.[28] There has recently been a good deal of scepticism about the whole concept of popular culture, particularly in so far as it rests on the binary model I have referred to; Bob Scribner in particular has argued that we should return to the notion of a single culture with multiple subcultures. And as Carlo Ginzburg has pointed out, we cannot use 'popular literature' (whatever we may mean by that term) as if it was a transparent expression of popular values: much of it was written by members of the literary élite with the conscious aim of influencing opinion. On the other hand, it is equally simplistic to dismiss it as nothing more than part of the process of imposing cultural hegemony by a governing class: if it was written simply as propaganda, with no effort to engage with the linguistic, metaphorical, and value systems of its intended readership, it was not likely to get very far. My approach to this problem owes something to both Ginzburg and Scribner. There is, I am sure, a reciprocal, interactive relationship between the different levels of the larger, common culture, which is visible in both literature and popular rituals.[29]

Instead of the binary model it is more useful to think about popular culture and politics, as both Burke and Scribner have proposed, in terms of a spectrum. We make distinctions between different classes and status groups, and it is surely reasonable to accept that each group had its own subculture. Obviously there *were* different cultural levels. The illiterate labourer did not inhabit the same cultural universe as the minister (probably a university graduate) who preached to him on the sabbath, or the squire who governed him as lord of the manor and JP, and who was affected by at least some rudimentary elements of polite culture. But before we can fully apprehend these differences we need to step back from the historiographical, conceptual, and theoretical issues which have so far framed our discussion. These involve intellectual constructs of our own times, and we cannot avoid them. But we should also keep in mind that the main responsibility of the historian is to try to enter, to the extent that any late twentieth-century person can, the minds of our seventeenth-century subjects. First of all, we need to consider at some length the relevant parts of the common culture, particularly those parts which were most closely related to our central theme: the connections between élite and popular politics.

People of all levels shared, or were exposed to, a common stock of familiar ideas and metaphors about household and commonwealth: the patriarchal state, the body politic, the divine origins of monarchy and hierarchy; together they formed an all-embracing ideology of order. To say this is not to assume an uncontested intellectual system of the kind depicted by E. M. W. Tillyard more than fifty years ago. It was an ideology that served the interests of people in authority—not only those of the monarchs, bishops, lords, and gentlemen at the top of society, but those of every father of a family or master of a farm or business, however small. But repeated incantation did not mean that everyone obeyed every aspect of the ideology unquestioningly and all the time; the system had its chinks and its points of stress in both gender and class relations, and some elements of it were certainly more honoured in theory than in practice. Yet this was a system of beliefs to which most people subscribed, or were expected to subscribe; it was supposed to be systematically transmitted to a large popular audience by parents and teachers, and above all by the clergy in their sermons and by the process of regular catechizing. At the centre of it was the patriarchal family. Patriarchal authority was assumed to be 'natural', and disobedience to it among the worst of sins. Ordained as it was by God, it was inevitable that the devil should constantly try to undermine it: the symbolic power of patriarchy as the foundation of society is dramatically clear in the story that before he became one of the disciples, Judas had murdered his father so that he could marry his own mother.[30]

One impressive source of patriarchal imagery was the King himself. It is well known that James I's writings and speeches are drenched in patriarchal metaphors: the King as father, the King as husband, both versions recalling the duty of obedience on the part of children or wife. Family portraits of royalty provided visual reinforcement of the message.[31] In 1614 Sir Walter Chute spoke of James's 'motherly' affection for the House of Commons, but normally it was Parliament or the country that was assigned the feminine, subordinate role; in the same Parliament William Hakewill referred to 'our dear mother the commonwealth'. Husbands and wives were supposed to agree and 'live quietly' together, and if they did not somebody had to be blamed for 'disuniting those that should be married together, the King and people'. John Winthrop was sufficiently unhappy about the King's government of the church to escape to Massachusetts. Yet he too based his authority as Governor on the familial metaphor: once the people had accepted a king or any other kind of magistrate, they must do as any good wife did, and obey, 'whether he frowns, or rebukes, or smites her, she apprehends the sweetness of his love in all'.[32]

This was not a matter that divided puritans and non-puritans, whatever we may mean by those terms. Protestants of all stripes emphasized the duty of obedience. Catholics were dangerous precisely because, as Sir Richard Grosvenor put it, they destroyed 'the seeds of loyalty and religion'. Their teachings made children 'disobedient to their parents', wives 'unconstant to their husbands', and both 'disloyal to their prince and country'. Yet there was, of course, a problem: what if kings, or parents, commanded things which were contrary to the laws of God? It was a particular problem for the Stuarts' Protestant subjects, taught as they were that God required obedience to lawful authorities, but that obedience to His will must come first. Thomas Beard offered the most widely accepted solution. Both 'law and reason' required children to be submissive towards their parents, and because rulers were as fathers to their people it was similarly required that 'all subjects perform that duty of honour and obedience to their Lords, Princes, and Kings, which is not derogatory to the glory of God'. 'Not derogatory to the glory of God': even the Elizabethan 'Homily on Obedience', the most widely circulated text on the theory of order, accepted that one limitation. If king, magistrate, or father commanded 'any thing contrary to God's commandments', the Christian should refuse to perform it. But this still did not justify active resistance; the subordinate must then passively accept whatever punishment authority chose to inflict. Sir Robert Filmer, the most thoroughgoing of English divine-right theorists, allowed even less scope for resistance. Whatever sins monarchs committed, resistance to their authority could never be justified: subjects should obey and leave it to God to make an equitable distribution of rewards and punishments in the hereafter.[33]

Similar games could be played with the next most popular political metaphor, the body politic, and here again the analogy tended naturally to uphold the authority of the monarch/head. James I was almost as fond of comparing himself to the head of a body as to the father of a family. In 1610, for example, he did so to justify his collecting impositions without the consent of Parliament: 'to take from the body and give to the head is proper, for the body cannot be sustained without the head.[34] But this metaphor could also be turned upside down, as it was by the preacher at Suffolk assizes in 1630 who warned of the dangers of 'the head receiving all the nourishment, and causing the other members to fail and the whole man to die'.[35] And there were other, more subtle ways in which the metaphor could restrict royal prerogative. An MP in 1610 spoke of Parliament as 'the pulse of the commonwealth, which shows life or death', and in 1625 Speaker Crewe likened the ancient, fundamental laws to the 'sinews' which held 'the body of the common-wealth' together. In either case the King would be well advised not to damage the organs in question.[36]

What these and other metaphors of this kind have in common is the idea of a superior—monarch, father, husband, head, sea-captain—who commands; and subordinates—subjects, children, wife, body, crew—who obey. But in most such discussions of authority and subordination those subordinates were not thought to be entirely without rights. Political language was used to reconcile what at first sight might appear to be incompatibles: authority and liberty. The English gentry never tired of congratulating themselves on their good fortune in living in a polity which enabled them to achieve this agreeable compromise. Thomas Hedley made the point as clearly as anyone during the great debate over impositions in 1610: 'this kingdom enjoyeth the blessings and benefits of an absolute monarchy and of a free estate'. Liberty and sovereignty were not opposites, but twins—again the familial analogy—in being mutually sustaining. James I used the same metaphor, though for him the twins were 'law and prerogative'.[37]

Familial metaphors, Susan Amussen has reminded us, were as well known to people lower down the social scale as they were to Parliament-men. The lessons of authority and obedience were regularly prescribed as the basis for the well-ordered family, as well as being almost auto-matically transferred to the wider political arena.[38] The powers of hus-bands over wives, of parents over children, of masters over servants and apprentices, were routinely upheld by clergy, magistrates, and others in authority. There were those who thought that parents did not do enough to ensure the obedience of their offspring. Why is it, John Northbrooke asked rhetorically in 1579, that England contained 'so many adulterers, unchaste and lewd persons, and idle rogues?' The reason, he decided, was the 'naughty, wanton, and foolish bringing up of children by their parents'.[39] No doubt he exaggerated, and certainly fathers were ready enough to enforce their authority if children or subordinates challenged either sexual or social hierarchies. When a servant eloped with Sir Edward Ludlow's daughter, Ludlow sent a party of his dependants galloping after them to beat the servant up. Edmund Crase, a young tailor in Somerset, foolishly boasted of the familiarities permitted him by the lady of the house when he was employed to make clothes for the children of a JP, John Jennings of Churchill. Jennings told his servants to get Crase drunk, and then joined them in flogging him to within an inch of his life. Patriarchal authority included both sexual authority over a wife, and social authority over a subordinate. 'A man', a Dorset preacher explained in a sermon at about this time, 'hath a more proper and peculiar interest in his wife than in any other commodity.' No doubt Jennings would have agreed.[40]

The analogy between the family and the state ensured that political debate was often conducted in language that made plentiful use of gendered metaphors. Legitimate authority, rationally exercised, was, almost by definition, and certainly by analogy, masculine. Chaos, disorder, and revolt, on the other hand, were equally commonly associated with the feminine. So, at least for some people, was tyranny: to obey a tyrant 'further than necessity forceth', the Canterbury MP Thomas Scott declared, was 'to lie with a whore, or to commit adultery', because a tyrant was 'no husband or king'. Assumptions of this kind were based on a familiar stock of ideas inherited from medieval times and from the Renaissance, which infused both the religious teachings of the church and the propaganda of the state. Woman in the abstract could be either saint or devil: the Blessed Virgin or the temptress Eve. If they accepted the role defined for them by the church women would be chaste, docile, and submissive, content to 'live in quiet' and dutifully provide healing and nurturing for their parents, husbands, and children. But it was a constant struggle for them to do this because they were by nature irrational, unable to control their passions and their tongues: women were so sexually voracious, so subject to emotional and physical instability, so intimately involved with the mysterious processes of birth and death.[41]

Male fears that women were stepping out of their proper spheres and turning the world upside down are as old as literature itself. But they became particularly prevalent during the second half of the sixteenth century, thanks in part, perhaps, to the unusual concentration of women as regents or monarchs, whose reigns, like those of Mary Stuart in Scotland, Mary Tudor in England, and Catherine de Medici in France, led to both personal or public disorder and bloodshed.[42] Before he knew how acceptably Protestant a ruler Elizabeth was going to be, John

Knox's trumpet blasted the monstrous regime of feminine government, while Philip Stubbes and numerous other moral reformers were soon proclaiming the danger to the social order represented by women's appetite for luxury and ostentation in dress and appearance. Admiration for Elizabeth did not prevent historians from Holinshed to Camden from expressing great distaste for the ancient Britons' confusion of gender roles, exemplified by their allowing women a prominent place in both war and government. Holinshed's compilers could admire the heroic Boadicea's bravely nationalistic speech at the outset of her rebellion against the Romans, yet their narrative soon presents her authority as by definition unnatural, and thus inevitably cruel and barbaric. Only the happy success of the masculine, disciplined Romans could have brought Britain out of savagery and into the rational mainstream of Europe. The dangerous contemporary analogies that might be drawn from a Roman victory over a British queen seem to have been insufficient to overcome antiquarian distaste for female rule.[43] Strong and independent women invariably brought chaos and confusion upon those around them, and Elizabethan and Jacobean drama contains countless examples of the disasters that such as Lady Macbeth and the Duchess of Malfi left in their wake.[44]

Women were also commonly associated with the satanic, to which their lack of rational defences made them fatally vulnerable. It is well known that during the period between Elizabeth's accession and the civil war prosecutions for witchcraft in England reached their zenith. This does not necessarily mean that witchcraft beliefs were any stronger or more widespread than they were before or after these dates, but the frequency with which supposed witches were prosecuted indicates that people in authority were unusually alarmed by the dangers they presented.[45] The most frightening feature of witchcraft was that it turned the whole world upside down. Under satanic influence, women (and at least 80 per cent of witchcraft accusations were against women) were stepping out of their properly submissive sphere by trying to control their own and their neighbours' lives, reacting to real or imagined slights or more generally to the deprivations and oppressions from which they suffered, by taking revenge through their knowledge of spells and incantations. The plot of Heywood and Brome's *Lancashire Witches* (1634), in which local witches invert the hierarchical social relations of a hitherto harmonious community and inflict satanic disorder on their neighbours, is a striking expression of the conventional view. The objective of witchcraft was, ultimately, the subversion of divine order. 'Take away kings, princes, rulers, magistrates, judges, and such estates of God's order', the 'Homily on Obedience' intoned, and

no man shall ride or go by the highway unrobbed; no man shall sleep in his own house or bed unkilled; no man shall keep his wife, children, and possessions in quietness; all things shall be common; and there must follow all mischief and utter destruction, both of souls, bodies, goods, and commonwealths.[46]

But the devil had other agents besides the foolish women he might seduce into witchcraft. In a period when millenarian expectations were widespread, and when many people anticipated the imminent, violent culmination of the great cosmic conflict between the forces of good and evil in Christendom, it was also natural for English Protestants to regard their Catholic enemies as agents of Satan. It was equally natural to fuse the two threats—to think of Catholicism, like any other sinful infection, as being associated with witchcraft. Sir Richard Grosvenor deplored 'the enchanting and bewitching of our papists at home'. Rome, a London minister declaimed, was 'the mother of spiritual fornications, magic, sorcery and witchcraft'. If the Catholic menace was being spread by enchantment, what could be more natural than to assume that women, the weaker, less rational sex, were being recruited as its agents? 'Pride and madness are of the feminine gender', Thomas Adams asserted. Women, King James and many others agreed, were particularly likely to be seduced into recusancy. The consequences could range from simple disobedience to husbands to tragic violence. A woman at Acton, Middlesex, murdered her own children after she had been won over to Rome by 'a witchcraft begot by hell and nursed by the Romish sect'.[47]

At the heart of this entire system of beliefs lay the assumption, commonly made by people of all degrees, that God had created an ordered universe. That universe, when it was working properly (which manifestly it did not always do), required the proper, responsible exercise of power by those in authority in family, community, and kingdom; and the respectful performance of the duty of obedience by those below them. It assumed a stable society and a stable economy; an unequal, but nevertheless just distribution of access to essential resources like land and food. Any serious departure from that just, stable order—any major sign of disobedience by wives, children, or subjects, but also any unjust invasion of customary popular rights— inevitably aroused fears of a 'world turned upside down'. 'Where there is no right order, there reigneth all abuse, carnal liberty, enormity, sin, and Babylonical confusion', the 'Homily on Obedience' warned. Satan and the Pope were naturally the usual suspects. After the discovery of Babington's plot in 1586 the St Paul's Cross preacher was told to warn his hearers that the intentions of the plotters were to kill Elizabeth and bring in Spanish forces, 'whereby the land might be overrun, heaven and earth confounded, and all things turned topsy-turvy'. Almost forty years later, the subtitle of an anti-Catholic pamphlet speaks of 'The World Turned Topsy-Turvy by Papists'.[48] As we shall see many times in this book, the image of an inverted world was regularly used at both ends of the social spectrum, by gentry and commoners alike. And equally regularly, it produced a search for scapegoats, for the culprits who had instigated this satanic process of disorder and inversion.

In the early seventeenth century both English society and state seemed to be threatened by a combination of many different forms of disorder —by the consequences of excessive population growth (particularly apparent in the exploding numbers of ill-disciplined young people); by economic dislocation, poverty, and unemployment; by divisions over religion and government; by doubts about the survival of national independence in a Europe disrupted by bitter religious war. It is therefore not surprising that people of all social levels sought scapegoats for the multiple anxieties which afflicted them. And given the vocabularies available to them, it is also not surprising that they formulated the explanations for their misfortunes in languages and metaphorical structures of inversion. These images of inversion were at once political and highly gendered. Historians have all too often separated the political tensions of the early Stuart period from the concurrent anxieties about society and gender relations. It is surely worth attempting to explore some of the connections between them. The interaction between these and the other political concerns of the English gentry during the reigns of the first two Stuarts will be the subject of our next chapter.

2

'ITCHING AFTER POPULARITIE'
GENTRY POLITICS BEFORE 1640

The political landscape described by many recent scholars of early seventeenth-century England is one in which consensus is more visible than conflict, deference than independence, the manœuvres of courtiers and aristocrats of more account than the posturings of Parliament-men. The historians who have contributed to this interpretation pay rather more respectful attention to the makers of policy than to its critics, in Parliament especially. As in those famous studies of eighteenth-century politics by Sir Lewis Namier and his followers, early Stuart parliamentary debates are now sometimes seen as little more than ritualized rhetorical exercises.[1]

It would be absurd to try to revive the discredited Whig narrative. But when I read the sources for the 1603–29 period I find a very different scene from the one depicted in much of the recent historical literature. One of the most striking things about the 1620s is the intensity of political feeling that grips so many people, from MPs to minor country gentry—and as we shall see in the next chapter, people below that level as well. The deferential, apathetic kingdom that it has recently been fashionable to describe is not one that I recognize either in Parliament or outside it. And, as I have already pointed out, I am not alone in this: Thomas Cogswell and Richard Cust have shown us a political nation far more exercised than some historians had imagined by the Spanish Match and the Forced Loan respectively.[2] The gentry's lively interest in parliamentary affairs is repeatedly evident. They devoured letters with the latest news from Westminster, and we may well infer from the frequent anxious adjurations to recipients to burn them that far more such letters were written than have survived. It was dangerous to report political matters: in 1626 Sir John Wynn was advised that he could get much of the news 'at the secondhand with greater safety than may be written'. Yet in spite of such fears, in 1626 a Westminster scrivener was selling copies of the Commons' Remonstrance even before it had been presented to the King, and when Eliot compared Buckingham to the Roman favourite Sejanus it led to a run on Roman histories at the booksellers. Cust has demonstrated how widely news was disseminated in the 1620s, and although it may have circulated less rapidly in the earlier part of James I's reign there was a good deal of interest even then, as the number of surviving 'separates' of important parliamentary speeches shows.[3] 'Libels' —manuscript verses commenting (usually adversely) on public figures —were already freely passed around during Salisbury's ascendency. At least a score had been dispersed on the Great Contract discussions, the Earl complained in 1610, and some of them, he admitted, 'look for a Tiberius or Sejanus', though he does not seem to have been as alarmed by the allusion as Charles I and Buckingham were when Eliot used it in 1626.[4]

These preliminary excursions into parliamentary politics should not mislead the reader into thinking that I minimize the importance of the politics of the Court. On the contrary, we cannot understand one without the other. The Court was where power resided, and Englishmen of all sorts and conditions immersed themselves in the sticky waters that led to favour there. Newsletters and other correspondence show the eternal fascination of gossip about 'who's up, who's down', and with the tedious games of boot-licking and palm-greasing required of courtiers who wished to attract, or retain, a patron. Gerald Aylmer's *King's Servants* gave us a marvellously detailed picture of the court bureaucracy; Linda Levy Peck has reminded us of how corrupt the game became in the early seventeenth century—or at least how the stricter standards of probity now demanded made it seem so.[5] It may help us to understand the perceptions of the Court held by its critics if we take one of its members as an example, and examine his activities in detail. I do not suggest that he was necessarily typical of the middle-level bureaucrat of his day, but enough features of his career conformed to a commonly held stereotype to make him worth pursuing up the ladder of advancement. He may also be useful to us as a reminder that crown policies required the support not only of great councillors and bishops, but also of the lesser men who actually implemented them.

My sample courtier comes from Cawston in Norfolk. Sir Edmund Sawyer was a product of that familiar phenomenon, the rising yeoman class. His father was one of those 'parish notables' familiar to us from Keith Wrightson's work, who came to local prominence in the later years of Elizabeth's reign, helping to run his village with paternalist efficiency, drawing up lists of the poor with meticulous care, and conscientiously organizing the distribution of grain during the dearth of the 1590s. He had connections with powerful county families: he may have done surveys for the Wyndhams at Felbrigg; he certainly leased land from Sir Henry Hobart of Blickling, Attorney-General and Chief Justice of the Common Pleas under James I.[6]

It was evidently the Hobart connection that launched young Edmund Sawyer in the bureaucracy. By 1607 he was described as 'gentleman'—as his father now also was—and by then or soon afterwards he had begun a career in the Exchequer, in which he rose to become senior Auditor. He also speculated extensively when crown lands came on to the market, both on his own account and as agent for others; he has recently been described as 'perhaps the greatest of the early seventeenth-century agents and certainly the most successful financially'. As we might expect from the son of a father who kept such obsessively careful records, Edmund had strong views on administrative efficiency, making numerous recommendations for the improvement of Exchequer procedures.[7] In 1617 he married the daughter of a gentleman from Berkshire, one of the counties in which he was already dealing in crown property. As he would soon be bringing his bride to Cawston, he told his father, it was important to finish the rebuilding of the family's house 'as handsome as conveniently you may'. Edmund would send down a decent bed and bedding, and would buy anything else needed to give his wife and her grand relations 'the like entertainment I have had with them'. The old house and its furnishings, good enough for a former Norfolk yeoman, were not smart enough for an upwardly mobile office-holder and his posh in-laws.[8]

Sawyer soon turned his back on his local origins completely. He was knighted in 1625, and by the time his father died two years later Sir Edmund had bought the manor of Heywood in White Waltham, Berkshire, where he continued to live. In characteristically businesslike fashion he rigorously enforced manorial custom when it was in his interest to do so, extorting arbitrary entry fines and aggressively exploiting his own pasture rights, but showing much less interest in paternalist survivals like the lord's traditional duty of paying for a dinner for the tenants. The tenants claimed to have suffered worse from him than from any previous landlord. Soon after his father's death he sold the little Norfolk estate to Sir John Hobart. 'I am little acquainted with the country', Sir Francis Bacon once admitted. That was to be his undoing, as it was to be Sawyer's.[9]

In 1624 Sawyer was returned as MP for Windsor, and in 1628 he sat for Berwick-on-Tweed. While that Parliament was in session he was appointed a Master of Requests, and there was talk of his becoming Chancellor of the Exchequer: clearly he was a man on the way up.[10] But there were dangers for courtiers in the 1620s, especially in a parliament-time. Sawyer's only recorded intervention in the Commons on a policy matter in 1628 occurred on 11 April, when he spoke in favour of more speedy collection of the subsidies. On 17 May, however, he was denounced as the back-stairs author of a proposed revision of the Book of Rates which would have increased the crown's income from impositions by about £100,000 a year. 'Methinks the King may easily make it double', he is alleged to have said: all they had to do was to make 'one shilling two shillings throughout the whole book'.[11] His defence that he 'did nothing here but by the King's command' simply got him into worse trouble. Everyone knew that the monarch could do no wrong, and it did not help when Charles confirmed that everything had indeed been done by his command. Sir Edmund's most foolish move, however, was to try to organize a cover-up, by urging a customs farmer who was giving testimony not to reveal anything about their conversations. When this came out the Commons promptly expelled him, declared him ineligible for re-election, and put him in the Tower.[12]

No one spoke up for Sawyer when the motion was made to imprison him. He swore that he 'wished that he were hanged' if he had been responsible for the impositions proposal, and this provoked cries of 'a good motion!' Sawyer was a conscientious administrative reformer, genuinely trying to make royal government more efficient and put it on a sounder financial footing. But he had few connections outside the Court, and he had refashioned himself as a Berkshire knight through office, not birth. 'I have ever hated . . . men that have raised their estates thus', Sir Dudley Digges reflected; men who advanced themselves 'by the ruin of the commonwealth'. And the sins of one generation could easily be visited on another: fifty years later Sawyer's lawyer son was sneered at as a man of 'as ill a reputation as his father'.[13] The same sort of antagonism was directed at newly sprung-up peers. When Dudley Carleton was made a lord in 1626 an MP complained that he 'had not a place to be made Lord of', and had been elevated simply to help make a 'party' for Buckingham in the upper House.[14]

Sawyer was promptly released when Parliament was adjourned, and he had many more years of service to the crown ahead of him, both at the Exchequer and as the King's man in Berkshire. Busy as ever on administrative reforms that would benefit the crown, in 1638 he was painstakingly inspecting household accounts from as far back as 1526, looking for book-keeping irregularities.[15] Historians are right to insist on the complexity of the Court/Country relationship: many people had a foot, physically or mentally, in both. But there were enough careerists like Sawyer who conformed to the stereotype of the courtier as the ambitious social climber, supporting arbitrary courses in order to advance himself, to give it plausibility.

For most of the gentry in their country houses the Court was a remote, dimly perceived abstraction. The politics that really mattered to them took place in their localities—in discussions of assessments, the militia, the Forced Loan, the impressment or billeting of soldiers, or in old-fashioned power struggles for personal pre-eminence, sometimes fought out in parliamentary elections. In the past few years we have become increasingly aware of the reciprocal relationship between national and local politics. As we have been so often reminded, MPs were at the intersection of Court and Country, transmitting national policy to the localities, but also conveying local grievances to the government at Westminster. 'We sit here as dutiful subjects to the King', Sir George More reflected in 1626, 'and as faithful servants to the commonwealth.'[16] Enough has been written on this subject to make it unnecessary to pursue the subject in detail, but it is the essential background to the national politics which we shall consider in the rest of this chapter.

Let us do, then, what we have so often been urged to do: escape from the hallowed walls of Parliament into the world of ordinary, or almost ordinary, Englishmen. We might do worse than begin with a story set in the most ancient of all English cathedral cities. Soon after the opening of Parliament in 1628 troops arrived in Canterbury and had to be billeted. Well-meaning city officials bustled about: all propertied householders, they decided, should take one or two soldiers, according to their means, or pay four shillings a week for their maintenance. A Canterbury magistrate was in London soon afterwards and proudly reported his brethren's actions to one of the city's MPs, a gentleman named Thomas Scott. Here is Scott's account of the conversation that followed:

He asked me how I liked this. You have done, said I, like fools and knaves. Like fools and knaves? said he. Yea, quoth I . . . why did you meddle with that with which you had nothing to do? . . . The King, said he, commanded it. Abused, said I, by the Duke [of Buckingham]. Kings may and do err, and in such cases it is the subjects' duty not to do against right and his Majesty's and the people's safety, but humbly to inform and petition his Majesty.

As a Parliament-man Scott was exempt from billeting. But he had strong views on the subject. Billeting, said Scott,[17]

is against the liberty of a free Englishman and gentleman and of a parliament man, and intended by the Duke to do us a mischief. For to what other use can Irish popish soldiers . . . serve? They, together with the [reiters], popish and Arminian and Maynwarian faction, and the rogues whereof this city and the country is full, must help set up popery and the excise and, as some of them do already give out, cut the Puritans' throats.

Scott has often been dismissed as an unrepresentative firebrand, and even Peter Clark's more favourable account of him shows that he was prone to fits of paranoia.[18] But in fact his views were more widely held in 1628 than some have supposed, even if, in Parliament at least, they were usually expressed more discreetly: people often said a lot more in private than they did in public. Scott was one of those middling-level gentry so thick on the ground in Kent, a grandson of no less a person than Sir Thomas Wyatt, leader of the 1554 rebellion against Mary Tudor's Spanish marriage.[19] He sat in both the 1624 and 1628 Parliaments, but never seems to have opened his mouth. If we had only the parliamentary record to rely on, we might imagine that Scott was one of those allegedly apolitical country members whose silence indicates either parochialism or detachment from the affairs of the kingdom. The robust independence of his writings refutes this assumption. We may well wonder how many of the silent majority, sitting enthralled (or intimidated) by the selfconfident rhetoric of articulate leaders such as Coke and Eliot, shared his prejudices and enthusiasms.

Many of Scott's ideas were utterly familiar commonplaces—the birthrights and privileges of freeborn Englishmen, their right not to be taxed or imprisoned without due process of law. By the later 1620s he, and many who thought like him, saw these ancient liberties being menaced by a sinister conspiracy in high places. At its heart was the Duke of Buckingham, plotting, they thought, to promote Arminianism as a cover for popery, and to use Irish troops and German mercenaries (reiters) to suppress Parliament and all who wished to defend the ancient laws. The Duke, they feared, would find plenty of support among the 'rogues'— the disorderly adherents of the traditional festive culture which godly magistrates of their type were trying to stamp out. The aim of the 'Dukists', Scott says in another place, is 'to settle the excise and mass' on the kingdom. 'Popery and arbitrary government', those staples of English political rhetoric for more than a century to come: the conjunction between them is already in place.[20]

There is no reason to believe that the ideas of members of the House of Commons differed in any essential way from those held by the gentry outside its doors. King James certainly did not think so. The quotation in the title of this chapter is from a speech he made in Star Chamber in 1616, and it concerns Justices of the Peace. 'In every cause that concerns prerogative', the King complained, reforming JPs 'give a snatch against monarchy, through their puritanical itching after popularity'. He also warned Parliament-men against their tendency to 'press to be popular'.[21] We should note that James was not using the words 'popular' and 'popularity' in the modern sense of being well liked, but in the sense of pertaining to a government based on popular sovereignty. Some of his councillors had similar worries. Since the beginning of the reign, Lord Chancellor Ellesmere reflected in 1610, the 'popular state' had grown 'big and audacious', leading to many 'contemptuous speeches against the King's regal prerogative and power'. Naturally he did not see this development as part of a high road to some inevitable future conflict, but he did observe that it was 'commonly seen that the waters swell before a boisterous storm'. Ellesmere exaggerated, of course; he was only the first of a succession of Stuart councillors to equate any assertion of parliamentary independence with 'popularity'. But his fears are none the less indicative of a changing political atmosphere.[22]

In and out of Parliament, early Stuart gentlemen repeatedly insisted that a popular government was *not* what they wanted. 'I take God to witness', said Samuel Lewknor in 1610, that it was 'no affectation of popularity' that moved him to speak on the subject of the people's grievances.[23] Their ideas about government were shaped by that cluster of familiar assumptions discussed in the last chapter—the analogy between the state and the patriarchal family, or between the state and the human body. The consensual implications of metaphorical structures of this kind are obvious. Historians who have taken the linguistic turn, and even those who have not, can easily accept the notion that political beliefs are shaped by the vocabularies in which they are articulated.[24] But there was another political language available in early seventeenth-century England, one that enabled men like Thomas Scott to think about politics in way that was very different from that of the Stuart kings and their councillors. That alternative was the language of the 'Ancient Constitution': the idea that there had existed since Anglo-Saxon

times a body of peculiarly English rights and liberties, enshrined in the
Common Law and in parliamentary statutes. The lawyers, naturally,
were the most enthusiastic about it. 'No other state is like this', Sir
Edward Coke boasted: '. . . We have a national appropriate law to this
kingdom. If you tell me of other laws [Roman law, for instance] you are
gone.'[25] In fact it was usually Coke who was gone, off on one of his
dense and (to us) indigestible lists of precedents, which no one could
produce better than the former Lord Chief Justice.

Coke's legal expertise may seem intimidating, but there were others in
these parliaments—Selden, Littleton, Hakewill, for example—who were
almost his equals. None of them doubted that, as Sir Dudley Digges
put it, 'the laws of England are grounded on reason more ancient
than books, consisting much in unwritten customs . . . so ancient that
from the Saxon days . . . they have continued in most parts the same'.
He then proceeded to trace their origins from the laws of Ethelbert.
When Coke could not pluck precedents out of his head other members
found them in the records in the Tower or in the library of Sir Robert
Cotton. 'Here is an old manuscript, *De Modo Tenendi Parliamentum*', Sir
John Eliot mused after doing some research on the voting of subsidies:
'I can find no such precedents as these [the ones being urged by the
Privy Councillors] in it.'[26]

Eliot could find no precedents for voting subsidies under royal and
conciliar pressure, but he could find plenty for the subjects' liberties. The
most glorious feature of the ancient laws, he and his colleagues agreed,
was that they protected liberty and property—property from illegal exac-
tions like the Forced Loan, and liberty from violations like the arbitrary
imprisonment of the loan resisters. These issues had been central to
English political debate ever since the great row over impositions in
1610. Nicholas Fuller had put the matter bluntly in that year: 'the King
cannot lay a charge upon the subject's goods without his consent.'[27]

It is necessary to spend so much time on these admittedly platitud-
inous ideas because of the recent tendency to dismiss them as rhetorical
bombast, behind which the 'real' business of politics—the infighting of
courtiers and great men—was concealed. I should be the last to deny
that there was plenty of courtly infighting, or that it affected those who
were the clients or allies of noblemen like Buckingham and Pembroke.
But those clients and dependants were never more than a small fraction
of the members of the House of Commons, or of the political nation
outside it, so the political culture of the majority, the gentry, should not
be written off as irrelevant. Why should we accept one set of rhetorical

conventions—the ones emphasizing subservience and deference—rather than another—the even more common set which emphasized independence and liberty?

They may sometimes have exaggerated their uniqueness, but seventeenth-century Englishmen did genuinely believe that they possessed rights that set them apart from people in other countries. 'The greatest happiness of the subject and honour of the King', Sir George More declared, was 'that he rules over free men, not bondmen.'[28] This kind of xenophobia is almost tediously familiar: we have all encountered the stock figure of the English yeoman who, as an MP put it in 1626, 'would beat ten of the slaves of France'. Sir Dudley Digges drew on a different experience of foreign parts for his version: 'In Muscovy one English mariner with a sword will beat five Muscovites that are like to eat him.' The King's men could also sometimes make the continental comparison. But the most insistent on their Englishness were those who spoke the language of liberty. Eliot regularly proclaimed his 'true English heart' and appealed to 'our ancient English virtue, that old Spartan valour'.[29]

Spartan valour was obviously a masculine virtue. The gentry's political vocabulary was full of such gendered images. Critics of James I's foreign policy and his extravagant court saw in both a decline from the—paradoxically—manly virtues of Queen Elizabeth's days. Around 1610 the youthful Prince Henry and his circle of Protestant militants had adopted Arthurian imagery, perhaps as a covert criticism of James's pacific outlook. A decade later concerns about the King's alleged subservience to Spain were deepened by his attachment to the infamous 'Spanish match'. Long after the marriage scheme had been abandoned, Eliot was still deploring his countrymen's neglect of the 'martial powers'.[30]

Gendered language was not confined to the Court's critics. Even a royal servant like William Trumbull could speak approvingly of the Commons' alternative policy—military support for the protestant Frederick and Elizabeth of Bohemia—as a 'vigorous and masculine' one. In 1626, after war had come, Sir Robert Harley (still a courtier) identified 'the effeminateness of this kingdom and riotous excess' as the chief causes of the recent failure at Cadiz. Another of Buckingham's allies, the Yorkshireman Sir John Savile, agreed: 'ease makes us effeminate.' So the Duke was not necessarily the target of these charges; indeed, after his angry return from Spain in 1623 he had assiduously presented himself as the chief exponent of the 'masculine' war policy.[31]

These anxieties had originated years earlier, and we shall hear more about them in the next chapter. The murder of Sir Thomas Overbury in 1614, when the Earl of Somerset's secretary had been poisoned in the Tower at the instigation of the Earl's new wife, Frances Howard, and her confidante Mrs Turner, had provoked a spate of pamphlets denouncing the degeneracy of the Court—revealed in sexual and other kinds of corruption, in the popularity of masculine styles of dress (much favoured by Mrs Turner) among women, and of effeminate, foreign styles among men. Our minds, the old soldier Barnaby Rich declared in 1617, 'are effeminated, our martial exercises and disciplines of war are turned into womanish pleasures and delights . . . we are fitter for a coach than a camp'. Ten years later Englishmen were still being urged to shake off their 'soft effeminacy and wantonness'.[32]

Moralizings like this had been part of the staple fare of puritan re-formers at least since the 1580s. But they had special resonance in Stuart England when they were coupled with evocations of the glories (often grossly misrepresented) of Queen Elizabeth's reign. Nostalgia for Eliza-beth, David Cressy reminds us, was often a way of uttering coded criti-cisms of the Stuarts.[33] Not always very discreetly coded:

> Where are those spirits that in woman's reign
> Sacked Ca[diz] and into terror struck all Spain?

an anonymous versifier asked in 1624. 'Where now is Essex, Norris, Raleigh, Drake?', John Rhodes demanded after the Isle de Rhé fiasco three years later.[34] No great skill was needed to crack the code when Gloriana was invoked in the House of Commons. Elizabethan victories were the yardstick against which the failures of the 1620s were judged, and, Eliot and his friends liked to argue, were the result of the mutual love between her and her subjects, and the confidence that people had in her councillors. She 'governed by a grave and wise counsel', Sir Francis Seymour declared, 'and never rewarded any man but for desert'—it did not require much insight to know that his subtext was an unspoken comparison with Buckingham, no longer the hero he had appeared to be in 1624. But Elizabeth had also prospered, Coke and Phelips both pointed out, 'because she cleaved to God'—to a Protestant God, of course. The Duke's friends naturally did not relish these comparisons: Eliot says that 'the glories of that princess were like basilisks in their eyes'.[35]

Stuart policies, both at home and abroad, lacked the masculine, protestant vigour demanded by men who warmed themselves with romanticized memories of '88. 'Come, let us to the wars again', a popular ballad urged, soon after the outbreak of the Thirty Years War, appealing to the example of the Elizabethan heroes who had fought 'for God and his Gospel'. The myth of the 'elect nation' may have been less prevalent in this period than once was thought, but there were still plenty of people who believed that God had given England special responsibility to defend the godly cause against the Roman Antichrist. Paranoia about the Catholic menace remained as widespread as ever in the 1620s.[36]

There was a growing tendency at Court to label holders of such beliefs as 'puritans' and thus by definition disloyal. Their defenders retaliated by accusing the Arminians, now basking in royal favour, of smearing 'dutiful and honest subjects', thus dividing King and Parliament, and of proposing to the King 'designs that stand not with public liberty'.[37] Worries about clerical influence had been visible long before the rise of the Arminians in the 1620s. 'Have we not sermons made every day to rail upon the fundamental laws of the kingdom?' an MP asked in 1610—the best road to preferment, he feared, was 'to tread upon the neck of the common law'.[38] Thomas Scott soon labelled his clerical enemies 'kinglings', opposed to all 'true liberty'. In 1614 the Bishop of Lincoln, Richard Neile, denied that the Commons had any right to debate impositions, and warned the Lords that they would hear only 'undutiful and seditious speeches' from the Lower House. There was an immediate outcry in the Commons; Neile was 'worthy to have his head set up at Tower Hill' one member suggested. What made matters worse was that people like Neile had such easy access to the King. 'They would do ill offices in private that had done this so publicly', Sir Dudley Digges warned, while another member complained that 'things were snatched out of this House and carried to the King to no good intent'. Always suspicious of clerical absolutists, in 1625 the Commons objected to having one from Oxford foisted on them as their preacher.[39]

Soon after the accession of Charles I the 'winds were turned', to use Eliot's phrase, against old-fashioned Calvinist protestantism and in favour of the new Arminian beliefs. But the Commons continued to complain about them. The committee which considered Richard Montagu's 'factious and seditious' opinions denounced his *Appello Caesarem* as 'a great encouragement of popery'. The general conclusion, as one MP put it in 1629, was that 'an Arminian is the spawn of a Papist'.[40] Arminians were held to be dividing church and kingdom by creating a 'factious party', of which Buckingham was the patron, to support such 'oppressions' as the Forced Loan: popery and arbitrary government again.[41]

Not so long ago the polarities of Court and Country provided a comfortable conceptual anchor for historians of early modern England. Nowadays most of us are more suspicious of binary models of politics and society. People from the upper echelons of the political nation inevitably had a foot in both camps (if indeed they were camps), or were themselves inwardly divided, their outlook part Court, part Country. Parliamentary criticism of the Court, we have been told, often came not from 'country' members, but was stirred up by one Court faction against another. Yet as Stuart Clark has shown, thinking in binary opposites was an almost universal habit of mind in the seventeenth century, and this makes the recent revival of the Court/Country model by Richard Cust and Ann Hughes rather more persuasive. Country gentlemen *did* blame the Court's extravagance and corruption for many of the kingdom's ills. 'The cause of his Majesty's wants', said Sir James Perrott, was 'imposed by himself [through] the great pensions he gives.'[42] And not only pensions. Corruption, we have been reminded, was not a straightforward moral issue. Yet its obvious prevalence at James's Court seriously undermined the confidence of gentlemen outside the charmed circle within which the benefits of place and patronage so agreeably circulated. The elaborate masques put on at the marriage of the royal favourite, Robert Carr, to Frances Howard were 'a means to make the Chequer poor', a Northumberland gentleman complained: 'at last the poor subject shall pay for all.' 'Pompous vanities', Walter Yonge complained when he heard that Buckingham had spent £4,000 on a banquet for Charles I and his queen ten years later.[43]

And the language of Court and Country was so thoroughly familiar, a veritable mode of discourse, a literary genre: all those dialogues of courtiers and countrymen, all those pastorals contrasting the honesty and simplicity of the country with the viciousness and corruption of the Court. Some of the best of it, of course, was written by courtiers. It provided ammunition for invective—in some quarters the epithet 'courtier' was regarded as actionable.[44] Whatever their own motives may have been, parliamentary orators in the 1620s knew that they were appealing to people who had made the Court–Country dichotomy the very core of their politics. Digges wanted Charles I to rely on 'the honest country knights and burgesses', not, by implication, their opposites.

'Courtiers . . . and other like implements', Thomas Scott thought, ought to be barred from Parliament; if they were not it would lead to 'slavery and ruin'. 'An honest man, but a courtier', he says of one acquaintance: it was almost a contradiction in terms. Of all the 1620s Parliament-men, Sir John Eliot was perhaps the most wedded to this kind of thinking, and it provides a constant refrain in his speeches. But he was only one among many who used it.[45]

There was always the danger of eliding one polarity into another: Court and Country into King and people. Not that the gentry openly blamed the King for the misdeeds of his Court—it was always his advisers who were at fault. Their whole system of political ideas made it essential for them to believe this. When Wentworth says, 'I speak truly for the interest of the King and people', or Phelips protests, 'If we were to choose a government, we would choose this monarchy of England above all governments in the world', we can be sure that they mean it. However, they were not always sure that their loyalty was reciprocated. Phelips thought he knew why: 'Let him be accursed . . . that by any course seeks to divert the King from his people. We come with loyal hearts. His Majesty shall find that it is we that are his faithful counselors.'[46] We, not they: them and us. Sides are being taken. Courtiers are misrepresenting the motives of loyal countrymen. A newsletter reporting the dissolution of the 1625 Parliament speaks of 'the king and his party'. People in the countryside could also see what was happening: the Dorchester diarist William Whiteway noted that the dissolution occurred 'with great dislike of both sides'. Three years later Sir John Rous complained that out of fourteen members returned for Suffolk seats in 1628, ten were 'courtiers'.[47]

Language of this kind suggests that the divisions involved something more than a simple breakdown of communication between centre and localities, but that they had an ideological dimension.[48] Some courtiers were thought to favour policies which threatened the very foundations of the Ancient Constitution. There had been the row over Cowell's law dictionary, *The Interpreter*, in 1610—the Commons described its definitions as undermining the very 'power and authority of the parliament'. Cowell's defenders, it was reported, sought to 'extenuate his fault for the valuing of themselves with the King'.[49] When, in 1614, James threatened dissolution if the Commons did not immediately vote supplies, Sir Thomas Roe feared that this would be 'the ending, not only of this, but of all parliaments'.[50] Hyperbole, no doubt; yet later parliaments continued to worry about their liberties. In 1626 Sir Nathaniel

Rich claimed that there had been more invasions of parliamentary liberties under James than in any previous reign.[51]

People were looking uneasily (or sometimes, enviously) across the Channel and noting the decline of representative assemblies. The King of France, Carleton professed to believe, was 'at liberty to do what he list', and Sir Roger Owen agreed that 'by power of edict [he] never calleth parliaments'.[52] It was surely no coincidence that just at this time Edward Grimeston published his translation of Pierre Matthieu's *History of Lewis the Eleventh*. In contemporary political discourse Louis XI repeatedly appears as the archetype of tyranny.[53] 'We are the last monarchy in Christendom that retain our original right and constitutions', Phelips declared in 1625, and four years later Eliot was still going on about a Court plot 'to bring a Spanish tyranny amongst us'.[54]

Every Parliament had its favourite buzzwords. In 1626 the buzzwords were 'new counsels': a term picked up from the Court to signify the authoritarian policies to which Charles I and his advisers claimed they were being driven by the Commons' obstructiveness. On 20 April the King warned the House that if they did not vote supply within five days he 'must be driven to change his counsels', and this threat was several times repeated. On 12 May Carleton ominously mentioned other countries where 'monarchy is changed by new counsels', the turbulence of representative assemblies having forced kings to adopt 'another form of government'. The implied threat—to the very existence of future parliaments—was passed over at the time because the House had more pressing business (the arrest of Digges and Eliot) to attend to, but when the matter came up again three weeks later there was a great uproar. One member wanted those who advocated 'new counsels' to be declared traitors; another said that 'we were born free, and must be free if the King will keep his kingdom'. This was going too far and the Commons sent him to the Tower. But there were no concessions on the main issue; the Commons firmly condemned the collection of tonnage and poundage without parliamentary consent, and blamed it on the 'new counsels'. After dissolving Parliament to save Buckingham from impeachment, Charles did indeed resort to the 'new counsels', with results that Richard Cust has so admirably analysed: the Forced Loan was a qualified fiscal success, but a public-relations disaster.[55]

Buckingham was blamed for the Loan. But the Loan was not the only source of the widespread hatred of the Duke, a hatred that historians have never entirely explained. It may help us, perhaps, to understand the outlook of people from both levels of the political nation—élite and popular—if we explore that hatred a little further.[56] In order to do so we need to return to the theme of inversion.

Between 1626 and 1628 Buckingham became the focus of all the searing fears and anxieties that so violently gripped his contemporaries. One of the most acute of those fears was of malign feminine influence in high places, to which the favourite was thought to be particularly vulnerable because of his numerous female Catholic relatives. Women who stepped out of their properly submissive place, it was thought, threatened to turn the whole world upside down, to make it a prey to satanically inspired forces of disorder and inversion.

Male dislike of rebellious women was nothing new, but a succession of recent Court scandals had reinforced it and given it immediate political relevance. Salisbury's sexual improprieties, combined with his physical deformities, were regarded by his enemies as unmistakeable signs of political and financial corruption.[57] But the really serious decline in the Court's reputation occurred only after the Earl's death in 1612. First came the unsavoury proceedings which enabled Frances Howard to annul her previous marriage to the Earl of Essex so that she could marry the royal favourite, Robert Carr. Then followed the revelations about the subsequent poisoning of Carr's secretary, Sir Thomas Overbury, which the Countess and her friend Mrs Turner were found to have plotted. There was much dark talk of witchcraft: Mrs Turner, it was alleged, practised 'sorcery and enchantment', and used malign charms to make Essex impotent. A succession of sorcerers, including the well-known Simon Forman, had been consulted, and the Countess was also said to have asked a 'wise woman' about ways of killing the unfortunate Earl. Mrs Turner was executed for the Overbury murder, but the Countess, along with her new husband, now created Earl of Somerset, was pardoned by the King. The Howards, hitherto the dominant faction at Court, suffered further damage when the Earl of Suffolk, Frances's father, was found guilty of large-scale corruption, for which his wife (also thought to be an 'enchantress') was largely blamed.[58]

The Howards were not the only court family to be involved in such scandals. Lady Roos, daughter of the Secretary of State, Sir Thomas Lake, charged her husband with incest with the Countess of Exeter, his grandfather's young wife, and was in turn accused of incest with her own brother. Lady Hatton and her husband, Sir Edward Coke, got into an unseemly public brawl over Coke's (eventually successful) attept to marry off their daughter to Buckingham's brother, Lord Purbeck. We shall see in the next chapter how these episodes were processed in the popular mind; even to the gentry they seemed to exemplify the malevolent power of women, exercised through sexual intrigue and the use of poisoning, sorcery, and witchcraft. Such assumptions had an obvious scriptural foundation. Giving judgement in the Exeters' slander suit against the Lakes, James compared Secretary Lake to Adam, his wife to Eve, and their daughter, Lady Roos, to the serpent. But they also had more immediate political implications. By now, John Chamberlain reported, the King was 'in a great vein of taking down high-handed women', and after Lake's dismissal ordered his Secretaries 'not to impart matters of state to their wives'.[59]

The fears of independent women, and more specifically of witches, seem to have reached a peak in the decade of the 1620s. Witches did not have to be women, of course. John Rhodes described the Spanish ambassador Gondomar, with his allegedly malign influence over James I, as 'that witch, whose charms enchanted us'. The language may have been metaphorical, but when similar charges were made against Buckingham they were meant to be taken literally. The Duke was repeatedly accused of access to the black arts of magic and poisoning, both through his mother, the Countess, and his servant, Dr John Lambe, the sorcerer who was to be lynched on a London street in 1628, shortly before Buckingham himself was assassinated. Buckingham's sister-in-law, Lady Purbeck, was alleged to have used 'powders and potions' against her husband and possibly against Buckingham himself; it was rumoured that she had a wax effigy of the Duke, who was sufficiently worried to consult Bishop William Laud about it. Lambe was one of Lady Purbeck's favourite sorcerers until Buckingham lured him into his own employment. The Duke was also accused of having an 'enemies list' which included noblemen who had offended him: the Marquis of Hamilton and several others who were on it died in allegedly mysterious circumstances. Some thought that the Duke's purpose was to remove opponents of his pro-Catholic policies: was there anyone left 'unslaughtered or unpoisoned', Rhodes asked rhetorically in 1628, to resist the headlong rush to 'Spanish thraldom'?[60]

The most sensational charge, which figured prominently in the 1626 impeachment proceedings, was that Buckingham had hastened the death of James I by administering a plaster and a treacle posset made by the Duke's mother. Buckingham himself gave James the drink, and the plaster was applied on his orders by a Catholic doctor who was not one of the King's appointed physicians. Suspicions about the role of

Buckingham and his mother were not, it should be noted, simply concocted after the event by the Duke's enemies in Parliament; both the Earl of Kellie, writing from Court a few days before James died, and the Venetian ambassador, on the day of his death, had already taken note of them.[61] The Countess's access to evil black arts seemed all the more credible because she was a Catholic recusant (so, at different times, were Buckingham's wife, brother, and sister), and thus automatically suspected by Protestant Englishmen of being an agent of the Roman Antichrist. Thomas Crosfield, an Oxford don of moderate opinions, expressed the common belief: Fisher, the Jesuit who had converted her, ruled the Countess, and 'she the Duke, he the King'. Purbeck, Buckingham's brother, made no secret of his opinions. Smashing a window at Wallingford House in 1622, he waved his bloody fist at people passing in the street and shouted 'he was a Catholic and would spend his blood in the cause'.[62]

Buckingham's supposed association with the forces of evil did not end there. Dr George Eglisham, the royal physician who first went public with the poisoning charge, also accused him of using 'enchantments' and of 'frequent consultations with the ringleaders of witches'—people like Lambe, in other words. On 12 June 1626, the day that the King and Buckingham were believed to have decided to abort the impeachment proceedings by dissolving Parliament, there was a great thunderstorm in London, apparently accompanied by a tornado—a 'tempest whirling and ghoulish'—which opened the graves of some of the victims of the previous year's plague epidemic. The day was long remembered as the 'terrible Monday': some thought Dr Lambe had caused it, and a gentleman was reported to have said that 'one of the Duke's devils did arise' in it.[63] To our rational modern ears these stories sound absurd and historians have generally ignored them. But in the seventeenth century even educated people subscribed to a system of beliefs which required constant supernatural interventions in human affairs, and took them perfectly seriously. It was not thought at all ridiculous, for example, for a country vicar to be charged in the Court of High Commission with being 'a professor of the Art Magic', his speciality, apparently, having been the 'charming of pigs'.[64]

Witchcraft, recusancy, the murder of the previous sovereign: these crimes of Buckingham and his circle were used to buttress the more familiar political charges. The initial parliamentary attack on him, in 1625, had been provoked by naval mismanagement, though there were also complaints about his 'multiplicity of offices' and consequent monopoly of patronage.[65] Proceedings against the Duke completely dominated the 1626 Parliament, and charges of increasing gravity were introduced: his incompetent conduct of war and diplomacy; the vast accumulation of gifts and lands by his family; his corrupt sale of titles and offices; his encouragement of Catholics.[66] But the poisoning accusation was surely the most astonishing: no higher charge could have been brought against a royal minister than that of complicity in the murder of the previous King. Recent efforts to portray Buckingham as the victim of a Court conspiracy are not inaccurate in themselves. Dr Turner and some of the other leaders of the original parliamentary attack were indeed Pembroke's men; the Duke's own client, Conway, dismissed the accusations as coming from 'that wretch Turner . . . that slave'.[67] But Turner's connection with Pembroke, and the elaborate parliamentary manœuvrings which followed his intervention, should not obscure the almost paranoid hatred of the Duke that was shared by a large segment of the 'political nation'.

The Duke was saved by the dissolution, but the pursuit was resumed in 1628 as soon as the King had given his assent to the Petition of Right. 'You all wish the Duke of Buckingham's fall', Thomas Scott had assured his Canterbury neighbours earlier in the year; the Duke, 'whom . . . all the realm suspects to have poisoned King James'.[68] Almost equally violent language was soon being heard at Westminster. On 5 June, after the King had ordered the Commons not to cast any further aspersions on the government, Coke defiantly named Buckingham as 'the cause of all our miseries'. There was a chorus of approval: the Duke 'would make us all slaves'; his friends were 'papists and atheists'; he was sending soldiers 'to cut our throats'. Such language once again brings Thomas Scott closer to the mainstream than he is usually thought to be. Benjamin Valentine wanted to vote the Duke 'the common enemy of the kingdom'—'of all Christendom', Richard Knightley proposed to add. The question was just being put that the Duke was 'an enemy to the state' when the Speaker arrived with the King's order to adjourn.[69]

The gentry's fear and hatred of Buckingham was made plain both in and outside the House of Commons. Once again Pierre Matthieu was enlisted: two separate translations of his life of the favourite Sejanus were published in 1628. And in at least one anonymous libel the Duke was explicitly identified with the tyrant Louis XI, whose biography, it will be recalled, Matthieu had also written. There had been nothing like this since Wolsey's time, and now, thanks in part to the wide circulation of manuscript libels and ballads, there was a much better-informed political nation than there had been in the sixteenth century.[70] Earlier royal ministers, as Pauline Croft has recently shown, had also been the targets of libels, but even those attacking Salisbury had lacked the virulence of the ones aimed at Buckingham, and the worst epidemic of them had occurred only after the Earl's death.[71]

Buckingham had enjoyed a brief period of popularity after the breakdown of the Spanish Match, but this was only a minor interruption to the flood of bitter denunciations levelled against him in parliamentary debates, pamphlets, and above all in the libellous verses so popular in early Stuart England. Their wide circulation is attested by the frequency with which they crop up in the diaries and commonplace books of the period.[72] The Duke's upstart origins, his ravenous appetite for gain for himself and his kinsfolk, his sexual habits, military incompetence, connections with papists and Arminians, and his supposed Spanish sympathies, were all remorselessly attacked. 'Spanish gold, alas, finds rare denial', John Rhodes reflected, but Buckingham was also pro-French, paradoxically, embarking on wars with both continental superpowers only in order to destroy his own (Protestant) country. At the Isle de Rhé, 'disloyalty, not fortune, lost the day', Rhodes thought, and he went on in undistinguished verse to enumerate all the crimes for which the favourite deserved punishment:[73]

> . . . poniards, poisons, swords,
> With plaisters, potions, witchcraft, coining Lords,
> Corrupting, selling justice; wasting treasure
> In oyster-voyages and seats of pleasure.

Most of the libels are from Charles I's reign, but a few date from the early 1620s and contain what were soon to be familiar charges. One introduces the Sejanus analogy, and notes the Duke's corrupt sales of offices, while another associates this practice with the whole Villiers family. 'Hark how the wagons crack | With their rich lading', the anonymous author says, going on to ask: 'Will you an office get? | Then you must come buy it.' The same libel includes some leering verses on the family's sexual promiscuity, reporting an alleged affair of Buckingham's mother with the Lord Keeper, Bishop Williams, and the use of the Villiers women to connect the Duke with the old nobility—'They get the devil and all, | That swive the kindred.' It also contains allegations of homosexuality against other courtiers, though (perhaps surprisingly) not against Buckingham himself. But other libels noted how the Duke influenced people by his 'Ganymedian looks', and coded references to

Buckingham's relationship with James were common. Thomas Scott had certainly heard them and may even have thought that the Duke was also Charles's lover; in one place he describes him as Charles's 'Gaveston'.[74]

The Court, to be sure, was the source of many of the libels, but courtiers well knew what the country's attitude to Buckingham was. One asks

> Why did this knight, and that rich squire,
> Who did their kingdom's good desire,
> The voices of their shires to gain,
> Free open houses now proclaim?

The answer was clear: they were celebrating because they thought Buckingham was leaving the country and so there would soon be a parliament. Alas, the poem continues, 'The Duke's returned, these hopes are vain'.[75] Buckingham had his defenders, of course, but the libels put out by Court scribblers appear to have aroused less interest than the critical ones. We find the scandalous verses in the commonplace books of a Dorchester merchant and a Cambridge wit, for example, and in the diary of a Suffolk minister.[76] A mock epitaph composed after the Duke's assassination was a particular favourite:

> I that my country did betray,
> Undid that King that let me sway
> His sceptre as I pleased; brought down
> The glory of the English crown;
> The courtiers' bane, the country's hate,
> An agent for the Spanish state;
> The Romists' friend, the gospel's foe,
> The church and kingdom's overthrow . . .

The gentry could not openly acclaim the Duke's murder—as the next chapter will show, it was a different matter for the common people— but many did so in private. Felton, the assassin, gave two different accounts of his motives: one, that he had been passed over for promotion and was owed £80 in arrears of pay; the other, that he had been moved to murder Buckingham by reading the Commons' Remonstrance of 14 June, in which the Duke was named as 'the principal cause' of the evils besetting the kingdom. Felton said that this convinced him that by killing the favourite 'he should do his country great service'. Perhaps he had also heard reports of speeches like Edward Kirton's on 5 June: 'The Duke is an enemy to the kingdom, and so to the King; and I hope every good subject will before long draw his sword against the enemies of the King and kingdom.' Did the firebrand Scott ever say anything more inflammatory? It is a measure of how far things had gone that the House quickly excused words that so closely bordered on an invitation to assassination or even rebellion, resolving that Kirton 'did not exceed the bounds of duty and allegiance'.[77]

Thomas Scott had long since wanted Buckingham brought to account for 'poisoning King James, and those other treasons and murders whereof he is accused'. So he naturally commended Felton and saw Buckingham's death as a providential deliverance; it was followed by a change in the weather, which became 'fair and seasonable beyond expectation'.[78] A few libels deploring the assassination appeared, but to judge from the popularity of the ones that applauded Felton as a hero, Scott's views were widely shared. 'The Duke is dead, and we are rid of strife', one versifier began hopefully, going on to argue that Felton's act was justified because Buckingham had avoided a lawful trial by parliamentary impeachment. Numerous mock epitaphs listed the Duke's vices and commended the assassin. 'Live ever, Felton', one ended, 'thou hast turned to dust, | Treason, ambition, murder, pride and lust.' King and kingdom had been 'set at liberty' by the murder, one libel suggested, while another thought that it was now possible to reunite Charles and his subjects, previously divided by the Duke's evil counsel.[79]

The parliamentary gentry attacked Buckingham so violently because their assumptions made it unthinkable for them to attack the King. The doctrine of the 'evil councillors' became their principal justification for doing in practice what they could never do in theory: demand that the King change his government. Buckingham was repeatedly charged with having used 'misinformations' to maintain his control over a supposedly helpless monarch. The King could do no wrong: if wrong was done by the King's command, it could only be because he had been misinformed before he gave that command. As Eliot put it in 1626, 'no act of the King can make him unworthy of his kingdom'; such an idea would be 'against the tenet of our religion'.[80] The argument was brilliantly designed to ensure that whatever actions the Commons took, even ones that the King thought hostile, were in fact expressions of the deepest loyalty. 'If anything fall out unhappily', Phelips complacently reflected, 'it is not King Charles that advised himself, but King Charles misadvised by others and misled by misordered counsel': by the likes of the Duke or Sir Edmund Sawyer, in other words.[81]

So a good many of the gentry, both in and outside of Parliament, shared Thomas Scott's conception of politics. Parliament, Coke declared was 'the ancient birthright of the kingdom'. Even Magna Carta, Thomas Hedley announced in 1610, was simply a 'restoring and confirming' of older liberties.[82] The Charter was regularly invoked, but it could no longer be taken for granted. 'Is it now held inconvenient to speak for confirmation of that Charter which our ancestors got with much sweat and blood?', Sir Thomas Beaumont demanded in 1610.[83] Even less could it be taken for granted in 1628 after the Forced Loan and the imprisonment of the loan resisters. 'Until of late', William Coryton asked rhetorically, 'who dared violate Magna Carta?' Hence the need to restate those threatened liberties in the Petition of Right. 'What we have done', Sir Walter Erle declared, 'is only for the liberty of the subject, and it is no new thing.' They had been sent to Westminster by their countries, another member reflected in language that Thomas Scott could have used, 'to save them and ourselves from being slaves'.[84]

But although it was unthinkable to attack the King directly, the 1620s debates were marked by increasing violence of language, and the Commons seem to have been increasingly willing to excuse it. When More suggested the possibility of tyranny in 1626 the House sent him to the Tower with Elizabethan promptness.[85] But when in 1628 Kirton seemed to threaten rebellion if Buckingham was not removed, they quickly decided that he meant nothing disloyal. 'We must either lay the fault upon the King or the Duke', Coke reflected, and as the former was impossible, everything had to be piled on the Duke's shoulders.[86] Defending himself in 1625 from critics of the French marriage, Charles deplored the speeches of 'malicious men' who had hinted that he was 'not so true a keeper and maintainer of the true religion that I profess'.[87] Some of these 'malicious men' remembered Charles's elder brother and felt that things would have been very different if he had lived to succeed James. Thomas Scott was one of them: in 1628 he was still commemorating 'the day of noble Prince Henry his nativity'.[88] But open criticism of the King remained taboo. The only recorded instance of it in the Commons in 1628 occurred in a debate on the charges against Buckingham on 5 June, when Hugh Pyne said, 'I think we can hardly tax the man in question without blaming a greater power'. Pyne was a notorious radical who had been in serious trouble a few years earlier for saying that Charles was 'as unfit to rule as his shepherd', and it is astonishing that no action was taken against him. It may be that hardly anybody heard him—during his speech the members' attention would have been fixed on the Speaker, who was just entering the House with the message adjourning them until the next day.[89]

Scott may have been unusual in the intensity of his political passions, but there is plenty of evidence that they were shared, sometimes in less virulent form, by others of his class. Many people, of course, dutifully intoned the ideal of harmony. The Commons, Sir Edwin Sandys piously claimed in 1610, wished to say nothing 'that toucheth the sweet harmony of state'.[90] Courtiers were even more likely to invoke the consensus ideal, as Carleton did in 1626 when he regretted 'that we talk in this House in sides'.[91] Few, probably, would have agreed with Eliot when he praised 'variety of opinions', or argued that 'by debate and reasoning pro and con truth comes to light'.[92] Yet noisy and disputatious practice all too often disrupted the prescribed harmony. Things had been particularly bad in 1614: there were 'murmurings' during speeches, a member was 'hissed at' when he wanted to cave in to James over impositions, and the chairman of a committee was threatened with assault. Sir Herbert Croft likened the House to a cockpit.[93] There may have been slightly more decorum in the 1620s—except in 1629, of course—but this was not because MPs were afraid of divisions. There was a striking incident in 1626 when the Commons divided over a motion to ask the Lords to imprison the Duke pending the hearing of the charges of treason against him: 'The no yielded; but the yea would not accept it, desiring to be numbered.' A vote of 225 to 106 violated the conventions of consensus and unanimity, but it also sent a stronger message than a confused medley of voices.[94]

The dramatic scenes that preceded the 1629 dissolution, when the Speaker was restrained from leaving the chair while Eliot's three inflammatory resolutions were carried by acclamation, should now be easier to understand. A lot of people shared Thomas Scott's conviction that there really was a threat to English liberties, and to the Elizabethan Protestantism on which they had been raised. It may seem difficult to grasp why, after all this, Charles I's personal rule should have aroused so little open opposition. One currently popular explanation is that the country gentry were less restive than the verbal posturings of their parliamentary spokesmen would suggest, and that the personal rule represented the normal functioning of seventeenth-century government in peacetime. Charles was in many ways a reforming king, and after 1629 even former critics of the Court like Sir Robert Phelips actively enforced his policies in their counties. In general, Kevin Sharpe has argued, the gentry's reactions to the administrative reforms 'ranged from grudging to enthusiastic'. Sharpe regards Ship Money as 'the great success story' of the decade, and concludes that 'the absence of vocal protest remains remarkable'.[95]

It is certainly true that there were few public protests by the gentry against the personal rule. We should not expect very many in the absence of a parliament, the only acceptable forum in which national grievances could be voiced. Country gentlemen like Phelips had always believed that it was their duty to carry on the King's government in their shires, whatever happened in Parliament. As we have seen, even during a parliament-time people had to be careful what they said, and were inclined to burn their correspondence.[96] Seventeenth-century Englishmen were brought up to believe that obedience to lawful authority was ordained by their religion; and monarchy, after all, still reflected their patriarchal assumptions. The end of the wars with France and Spain in 1630 removed the financial and military pressures that lay behind much of the conflict of the 1620s, while the migration to New England siphoned off some of the most active opponents of the crown's religious policies. And finally, Buckingham was gone: until 1640 there was no obvious scapegoat on whom everything could be blamed.

All this is undeniable, and it is undoubtedly true that most of the conflicts that are visible in the 1630s had more to do with religion than with secular issues. The religious conflict ranged on one side those who were resisting Laudian liturgical innovations and the ungodly Book of Sports, and on the other, those who wished to define all critics of Laudian policies as seditious 'puritans'. In 1634 and 1635, John Rous noted, there were many verse libels in circulation attacking both the 'orthodox' (that is to say, the Calvinists), and the 'new churchmen', or Laudians.[97] But there is much evidence of continuing hostility to Laudian ceremonies, and of growing suspicions of Catholic infiltration in both Church and government. No doubt those firmly attached to such beliefs were a minority, but they were a large and influential one, and they can only be regarded as 'puritans' if we accept the Laudian redefinition of the term to include virtually everyone who disagreed with the Archbishop's policies. As Esther Cope's study of the personal rule reminds us, it is a mistake to separate religion and politics at any time in the seventeenth century, particularly in a decade like the 1630s when increasing numbers of people were coming to believe in the existence of a sinister 'popish plot' against English liberty and independence.[98]

Even in the absence of Parliament there was widespread concern about the direction of affairs. Victor Morgan has shown that there were worries about the claims to a virtually uncontrolled royal prerogative even in the universities, not normally places to look for courageous criticism of Whitehall.[99] It is true that, as Sharpe, John Morrill, and others have shown, there was very little open opposition to Ship Money on grounds of principle before Hampden's case in 1637. But the proliferation of rating and other procedural disputes has been widely noted, and many historians now agree that a protest about assessments was the natural tactic for sensible people to adopt when they had increasingly serious private doubts about the legality of the rate as levied. It is interesting that even at the time of the early writs, diarists tended to record instances of opposition to the tax rather than the allegedly more general acquiescence.[100] Hampden's case may not have been typical, but the trial aroused enormous public interest—Sir Thomas Knyvett could not get in even though he had been queuing since early morning—and there was a huge demand for copies of the judges' opinions. Similar 'multitudes' had attended the Star Chamber trials of Prynne, Burton, and Bastwick a few months earlier, and there had been the same demand for news about them.[101]

So the current of religious discontent was easily reconnected to politics when the personal rule ran into serious trouble in 1637. I find it hard to believe that many people had ever disconnected them. The example of Sir Robert Harley—until 1635 Master of the Mint, but by then also a real 'country-house radical'—shows how inextricably interwoven the divine and the secular spheres still were. In 1633 Harley's notes for family prayers included petitions for 'an happy meeting in parliament'; for the continental Protestants whom England had abandoned (he prayed especially 'for a worthy general to succeed the King of Sweden'); for the suppression of popery and Arminianism; for those 'gone out of the land' [to New England]; and for other highly political causes.[102]

But the gentry of the political nation still believed in monarchy, and some of them were undoubtedly disturbed by what they saw as the turbulent, perhaps even seditious, behaviour of some MPs in 1628 and 1629, and by the evidence of even more widespread discontent outside Parliament. Thomas Hobbes was sufficiently alarmed by the tide of opinion to produce a new translation of Thucydides in order to warn against the dangers of popular government, and against those who 'swayed the assemblies, and were esteemed wise and good commonwealth's men' because they advanced 'the most dangerous and desperate enterprises'.[103] A few years later Sir Roger Twysden noted that many of his neighbours in Kent thought Parliament 'much to blame' for what had happened before the dissolution. Another Kentish gentlemen was so shocked by it all that he felt impelled to refute the dangerous heresies of those who were still 'itching after popularity'. He was related to Thomas Scott by marriage, had certainly met him, and in the cosy social world of the Kent gentry he must have heard enough from Scott and from others like him to cause him to fear that the very foundations of his world were threatened. By 1632 Sir Robert Filmer had written his famous *Patriarcha*, with its subtitle: *The Natural Power of Kings Defended against the Unnatural Liberty of the People*. Only recently has it been discovered that this classic monarchical tract was written, not in reaction to the collapse of kingly power in the civil war, but in a panic fear of popular government after the events of the 1620s.[104] It is time to look more closely at the 'unnatural liberty of the people' that Filmer so much dreaded.

3

CUSTOM AND INVERSION
POPULAR POLITICS BEFORE 1640

The hatred of Buckingham, almost universal among the English gentry outside Court circles in the 1620s, was shared with equal fervour by many of their inferiors. So also were several other elements that we have found in the politics of the élite: the respect for ancient custom, the anxieties about social and gender instability, the intense suspicion of Catholics and fears of popish conspiracy. This was a shared political culture, but as we shall see, some features of it were even more deeply ingrained in the outlook of the common people than in that of the gentry: the use of metaphors of inversion, for instance. But before we turn to the particular features of the commoners' response to public matters before 1640, we ought to pay some attention to the more general context of popular politics.

Earlier in this book I expressed some reservations about making too sharp a distinction between élite and popular culture. But we should not throw the baby out with the bath-water. Some cultural forms obviously did belong to the élite, others to the plebeians. Levels of literacy affected access to printed culture. If he chose to, the university-educated minister could read anything from a Latin treatise to a street ballad; the illiterate labourer had access only to the ballad, and then only if it was read aloud by somebody else. Even when they required no particular level of education, some activities were appropriate for the rich, others for the poor. 'It is not fit that clowns should have these sports', said James I in 1610, calling for stricter game laws. When Robert Dover organized his 'Olympick Games' on the Cotswolds a few years later he was trying to rebuild a unified community, but he was careful to provide different sports for different classes: fencing and horse-racing for the quality, shin-kicking and wrestling for the plebs.[1]

The gentry did not need Robert Dover to remind them of their cultural superiority. It was part of the air they breathed, and it determined their attitudes to many other matters besides rural sports. The law, for example: in 1626 an MP moved that the prosecution of certain types of offenders should be 'by men of quality and not by the ordinary jurors of small value or judgment'. A given level of wealth and education was appropriate to any status or occupation. It was thought particularly reprehensible when a Welsh bishop gave livings to 'unable and unworthy men'—decayed tradesmen, a footman and groom, a sexton, an officer of the ecclesiastical court. Complaints about a parson's disorderly living in the 1630s included the charge that he kept company with 'beggars, tinkers, bedlam men, and all sorts of people'.[2]

Some were more fit to govern than others, and even the aristocracy's fiercest critics knew this. Thomas Scott might wish to see wider political participation by the honest Canterbury tradespeople, but he also believed that 'drovers, brewers, tiplers, and base mechanics' ought not to hold civic office. He wanted a 'puritan parity' in the church, by which he meant a drastic reduction in the authority of bishops, but he indignantly denied wanting an 'Anabaptistical parity', which would mean undermining the authority of civil magistrates, in the state.[3] Sir Edward Coke was equally insistent on the sanctity of hierarchical relationships. Much of the disorder in James I's household, he thought, was caused by 'ministers who from a shop leapt presently to the Green Cloth': he meant the former Lord Treasurer, Sir Lionel Cranfield, of course.[4] Then as now, people blamed the educational system for whatever was amiss. The Earl of Northampton thought 'nothing so hurtful to the commonwealth as the multitude of free schools', which gave young men ideas above their stations. They 'neither will be soldiers, nor prentices', the Earl complained, but 'either run over sea or go up and down breeding new opinions'.[5]

Social differences were naturally translated into differences of culture. Visible markers like dress helped to define the individual's status. As a Parliament-man, the clothier John Noyes had to attend the investiture of the Prince of Wales in 1610. He was amazed by all the cloth of gold, the expensive lace and embroidery sported by his richer colleagues, and felt, he said, 'like a crow in the midst of a great many of golden feathered doves'.[6] That was the point: he was meant to. These differences inevitably included differences in political culture. This does not mean that there was an absolute social divide, or that the common people—and in particular the smaller propertied householders—had nothing to do with high politics. But there were some important differences of emphasis between the politics of the two levels of the political nation.

When the lower orders thought about politics they thought about taxation, billeting, and impressment; but they also thought about more local matters. Contests for place and patronage could be fought just as fiercely around the parish pump as in the royal Court. To the particip-ants, the stakes in a struggle over access to town lands at Malmesbury, a new charter at Leeds, the town clerk's place at Blandford, or the rights of the freemen at Dorchester might seem just as high, and might gener-ate just as much passion, as one at Whitehall over the appointment of a gentleman of the bedchamber.[7]

Issues of this kind were of concern primarily to urban householders. But some aspects of popular politics were of concern to virtually every-one. People of all classes, in country as well as town, treasured their customary rights of access to basic resources like land and food, and were likely to take action when those rights were threatened. Much has been written about food riots in early modern England, and we need only recall a few salient points about them.[8] In the typical riot of the kind described by numerous modern historians rioters would seize the grain, appealing to the now frequently ignored legislative prohibitions against such shipments in times of dearth. Their targets were usually not the local producers or landowners, but the middlemen thought to be responsible for the shortage. 'Take heed how they do oppress | The poor that God obey', a ballad urged corn-hoarders during the bad years of the early 1630s: 'God will not let these long alone that do him wrong.'[9] Elizabethan and early Stuart grain riots reflect the widening gulf be-tween those elements of the middling sort who were by now adopting the values of the market economy, and their poorer neighbours, who still remained attached to the ideals of custom and good neighbour-hood: the values of the 'moral economy'.[10]

Much the same pattern is visible in the typical anti-enclosure riot. When tenants were at odds with their landlords over illegal enclosures or violations of rights of common, the first step was a lawsuit, paid for out of a common fund. If this failed there might be threats against the landlord or his agents, minor or symbolic violence against property— the killing of sheep, the burning of ricks or barns. Finally, if the sense of injustice was still strong enough, full-scale riot might erupt, with the destruction of fences and the occupation of the land allegedly taken unjustly by the landlord.[11] At Frampton-on-Severn in 1610 Lord Berkeley tried to enclose land near the river on which the inhabitants claimed rights of common. About 100 people collected, Berkeley's steward records, 'whereof some threatened death . . . others struck the work-men, others filled up the ditches, others chased the justices' horses up and down the grounds'. Twenty years later John Williams, leader of the 'skimmington' rioters in the Forest of Dean, threatened violence, even against the King's officers, if they 'entrenched upon his liberties'.[12] Enclosure rioters, like grain rioters, were protecting a traditional way of life threatened by innovation, and this was just as much the case in the riots against drainage, disafforestation, and mining projects as it was in enclosure riots in the more traditional arable regions. When their lands were being ruined during the coal boom of the early 1600s, the Tyneside copyholders used both legal and direct action against the coal-owners, appealing, David Levine and Keith Wrightson have written, to 'custom, consent, reasonable dealing, and hostility to the exercise of an arbitrary absolute power'. This is not so very different from the expectations of the gentry when they thought about the affairs of the commonwealth.[13]

These grass-roots conflicts ranged against each other adherents of two opposed political, economic, and ecological systems. The protesters saw themselves as the defenders of ancient rights and customs guaranteeing mutual subsistence. But to the drainers and enclosers they were simply obstructionist nuisances: 'ignorant and froward men who had rather live a poor and lazy life than a rich and industrious one', as Charles I's Council said of opponents of Lincolnshire drainage schemes.[14] Their appeals to ancient custom were treated with arrogant contempt. In 1609 the crown's agents in Kingswood Forest dismissed such stratagems as those of 'a company of silly country partially affected inhabitants . . . who cannot speak of above sixty or seventy years, a weak proof'.[15] When it suited them a few eminent defenders of the Ancient Constitution might try to protect the customary rights of their poorer neighbours: Oliver Cromwell as 'Lord of the Fens' in the 1630s, Sir John Wray in Lincolnshire, and Sir Robert Phelips in Somerset are well-known examples. But only when it suited them. Casting around for a way to settle the King's revenue without burdening men of property, in 1625 Sir Edward Coke recommended 'the enclosing of waste grounds . . . the King having thirty-one forests, besides parks', that he could thus exploit. Sir Dudley Digges put forward similar proposals. That the forest-dwellers would lose their common rights did not seem to bother them.[16]

So in these matters both the King and his critics were among the innovators, though it was the King who sponsored the biggest projects that threatened the traditional way of life of the forest- and fen-dwellers. Not surprisingly, there were outbursts of seditious talk, especially at times of high food prices and depression. Memories of Kett's rebellion —the 'camping time'—still lingered at the end of Elizabeth's reign in Norfolk and other eastern counties. The gentry of the clothing districts also worried about the likelihood of disorder. There were 30,000 men within ten miles of his house in Yorkshire, Sir John Savile told the Commons in 1626, 'who, if they have not relief shortly, will take it where they can get it'.[17]

Most of the seditious talk was profoundly conservative, full of nostalgic invocations of a vanished past, and appeals to the universal myth of the absent, just king. In 1607 the Warwickshire rebels told the JPs that they had acted 'out of no undutiful mind to his Majesty', and asked them to intercede with him for redress of their grievances. This was a useful protective device, a strategem comparable to that of the parliamentary gentry when they declared that the King could do no wrong and that everything must therefore be blamed on his councillors.[18] But it was more than a protective strategy when commoners appealed to immemorial right, to an ancient custom, written or unwritten, that to them was as sacred as any charter or parliamentary statute. A famous example is the Mowbray Deed at Haxey in the Isle of Axholme, which guaranteed the commoners their rights of pasture in perpetuity. Kept in a box in the church, beneath a stained-glass window depicting the original grant by Lord Mowbray, it had the same iconic character as Magna Carta had for the lawyers and gentry.[19]

All this is familiar ground, but we need to be reminded of it if we are to stop putting élite and popular politics into different compartments. When the gentry had grievances they could have them expressed in Parliament by identifiable spokesmen. When the commoners protested they had to find their own leaders, and invent names for them: Captain Cobbler, Captain Poverty, and Captain Pouch in earlier rebellions, for example. The Gillingham Forest rioters in 1628 simply borrowed military ranks: 'the colonel', 'the captain', and so on.[20] In Braydon and Dean Forests the leader—or leaders: it was a triumvirate in Braydon—called themselves 'Lady Skimmington', or 'Captain Skimmington'. In Essex in the 1580s there had been no mythic leader, but there had been millenarian expectations of one: the return of 'one that was dead', after whose appearance 'sorrow and care shall be almost past'. Some of these leaders may have emerged less spontaneously than the rioters pretended. On one occasion in the same county some discontented weavers planned to 'get a mad knave and set him on horseback, and to begin at Bocking town's end, and so to Braintree and Coggeshall . . . and to cry "They are up! They are up!", and then people to get to the churches and ring "Awake!"'[21]

With or without mythic leaders, popular resistance was often carefully organized, especially if members of the élite gave a legitimizing nod or wink. When Lord Poulett was obstructing the enclosure of Neroche Forest in Somerset, he got his ranger to tell people that if the King's commissioners did not satisfy their complaints they should appeal to the courts or to Parliament. The ranger called a protest meeting and had it announced in the neighbouring churches on Sunday after morning prayer. All 'such as would stand against the disafforesting' were urged to attend, and on the appointed day a crowd of some two or three hundred assembled. They agreed to 'put their purses together' to prevent the enclosures, and send emissaries to London to start legal action. The methods used in Neroche—public meetings announced in the parish churches—were not very different from the ones used by potential candidates in the preliminary manœuvrings that sometimes preceded parliamentary elections. In Cornwall in 1628 Sir John Eliot and William Coryton sent circulars to the parishes, which were read after service on Sunday, urging freeholders to be present at the poll and by implication to vote for them. In both cases the strategy assumes the existence of an already politicized public.[22]

Historians are now beginning to accept that a considerable section of the public below the level of the élite had by this time become politically conscious. This was certainly clear in 1623, when people of all classes joined in the wild celebrations that greeted the Prince's return from Madrid after the failure of the Spanish Match. The two most vividly remembered public events of the early seventeenth century were the Gunpowder Plot and the October 1623 rejoicings. A local scribe at Symondsbury in Dorset usually recorded in his chronology only variations in the weather and their impact on the harvest; the Prince's return from Spain is the only political event he listed.[23] Gentlemen and commoners shared other triumphs; at the time of the Petition of Right, for example. There may have been some element of élite sponsorship of the celebrations that greeted the King's assent to the Petition: when his reply was reported to the Commons, Sir John Maynard moved 'to make bonfires all over the town', and the House rose so that members could spread the glad news. But even if they were not entirely spontaneous, the celebrations were certainly popular. Some of the revellers thought that they were celebrating because the Duke of Buckingham had been sent to the Tower, and boys tore down the scaffold on Tower Hill, saying that 'they would have a new one built for the D[uke]'.[24]

An incident at Windsor is a good example of the interaction between élite and popular politics. When they heard that the King had given way over the Petition the town's inhabitants made a bonfire outside the castle gate. The Laudian Richard Montagu, who was both a canon of Windsor and a royal chaplain, came hurrying out to investigate. On discovering the purpose of the celebration he told the townsfolk, 'they should answer it', warned them not to ring the bells, and tried to stamp out the flames.[25] Montagu dramatically personifies the dispute that was ranging the King and a considerable segment of the Commons on opposite sides; already under attack in Parliament, on the very day that the incident at Windsor was reported to the House he was elected Bishop of Chichester. His rage at the bonfire—was it perhaps deliberately put there to provoke him and other residents of the castle?— demonstrates the Court clergy's total lack of understanding of the strength of popular opinion, and their well-founded fear that the lower orders could no longer be controlled.

Montagu was not the only cleric to be upset by the public mood. The much more moderate John Rous was distinctly uncomfortable when his Suffolk neighbours muttered against the government. No great admirer of Buckingham, Rous still condemned the libellous verses against him: 'thus foully will the vulgar disgrace him whose greatness they hate.'[26] Some of the opinions Rous heard from his middling-sort acquaintances were certainly shocking. In the summer of 1628 disquiet about royal policies had caused indiscreet people, he noted, to 'be incensed, to rove, and project'. There was even a 'secret whispering' that the King might be overthrown and replaced by his sister, Elizabeth of Bohemia. When the new prince, the future Charles II, was born Rous heard 'glances of jealousy', inspired, he thought, by some puritans 'disallowing of the king and queen's match'.[27]

Rous got his 'country intelligence' from all the common sources that, as Richard Cust has shown, helped to spread political news: corantoes for foreign affairs, proclamations, occasional reports by MPs, political ballads, and general gossip.[28] Charges by the judges at the assizes, and the sermons of prominent clergymen were also occasions for the dissemination of news and propaganda. In 1625, when Charles I was on his way to Plymouth to inspect the fleet that was preparing to sail for Cadiz, he stopped at Bruton, where the Bishop of Bath and Wells, Arthur Lake, preached on the text, 'Let God arise and let His enemies be scattered'.[29] The subsequent military failure suggested that God had not after all arisen, and not far away at Hooke, in Dorset, a local parson soon got into trouble for preaching that 'the land was not governed by justice but by bribery and extortion' (he was echoing the charges that were beginning to circulate against Buckingham), and that God's anger at this had been shown in 'the late repulse' at Cadiz.[30]

The ideas expressed by people below the élite, when we can hear their voices, thus do not seem very different from those of their superiors. A list of grievances in Sir Edward Conway's papers, 'drawn from the observation of the people's speeches' early in James I's reign, included many of the same complaints the King was hearing from the gentry: high taxes, excessive royal bounty to favourites, judicial corruption, and— something especially disturbing to 'the simple Gospellers', Conway reported—the pursuit of a pro-Spanish foreign policy instead of an alliance with the Protestant Dutch. Others besides the gentry thought James's kingship lacking in proper masculine vigour, and made unfavourable comparisons with his predecessor; a 'jeer' making the rounds in Essex referred to 'King Elizabeth and Queen James', an Anglican cleric later recalled. James was cold and remote during his public appearances, 'not delighting in popular salutations', Conway's informants complained, and they naturally recalled 'that the manner of their late Queen was otherwise'. Most disturbing of all, it was said that James 'purposeth to alter our manner of government and that fault be found with our Common Law'.[31] This rough correspondence between élite and popular political ideas continued at least until the civil war.

The similarities were not confined to the expression of grievances. Almost everyone believed in patriarchal order in the family, and thus by analogy in monarchy—the rumblings that so disturbed John Rous might indicate a desire to replace one monarch by another, but not to destroy monarchy itself. There was plenty of room for monarchy under the Ancient Constitution, but many people still rejected exalted theories of royal prerogative. Thomas Scott and some of his Canterbury neighbours certainly did, and at Barnstaple in 1629 people were asking pointed questions 'concerning the rights and prerogatives of Kings'. The gentry were not alone in appealing to law and custom when they felt abused: nobody thought it strange when a Dorchester butcher, conscripted for the Isle de Rhé because his family were at odds with the town's governors, vehemently protested about the injustices of the impressment system.[32] And nobody thought it strange when ordinary people protested at having soldiers billeted on them, with little expectation that they would ever be paid for the privilege. In 1628 complaints about billeting poured in from every county in England, and in many places there was organized, sometimes violent, resistance.[33]

Certainly no one thought it strange when people protested at what they regarded as oppressive or illegal taxes. This kind of resistance has been described as 'a luxury for the gentry', and it is true that the gentry usually took the lead. They orchestrated opposition to the 1614 benevolence, though in some counties where the JPs agreed to contribute they then had difficulty collecting the money: many people would contribute only 'in a parliamentary way'. When another benevolence was demanded in 1622 such protests as occurred came primarily from the gentry and a handful of peers. Although the example set by such powerful people was important, it is clear that by the later 1620s resistance cut across class boundaries. Trying to collect the 1626 Free Gift, the Gloucestershire JPs reported that they had received the almost universal answer: 'That they humbly submitted themselves and their estates to be disposed of by his Majesty, by way of parliament.' No doubt this was the answer the JPs wanted—they may have dictated it themselves—but it is highly unlikely that the people they were pretending to consult would have disagreed with it.[34] The frequency with which punitive impressment had to be used against the 'inferior sort'—150 Loan resisters were conscripted in Gloucestershire alone—also shows how widespread opposition was at this level. The commonly professed willingness to subscribe if taxes were voted in a 'parliamentary way' confirms the convergence of attitudes between the gentry and their inferiors.[35]

In 1625 an MP observed that illegal taxes had always 'bred tumults and commotions'.[36] There was little resistance to the admittedly ludicrously under-assessed parliamentary subsidies, whereas any exaction of questionable legality—the Loan, tonnage and poundage after 1628, Ship Money in the 1630s—invariably provoked a chorus of protest. The story of Ship Money is too well known to need repeating—the early placidity, the later open resistance, the tendency throughout for people to try to avoid paying on technical grounds, questioning specific assessments rather than following Hampden in challenging the levy's constitutionality. But the collection of Ship Money, like the enforcement of any other kind of law, ultimately depended on the consent of the governed. By 1639 people were refusing to pay, boycotting auctions of distrained cattle, and rescuing constables arrested for non-co-operation. Joan Kent quotes a high sheriff who ruefully admitted that even the bravest constable 'dare do nothing but what the parish allow of'.[37]

Once again we observe the convergence of interests and outlook between the gentry and the lesser folk. Some years ago Richard Cust and Peter Lake drew attention to an important speech by Sir Richard

Grosvenor in 1624, in which he urged the Cheshire freeholders to take
an active part in public affairs. Grosvenor, they suggested, wanted to
encourage 'the fullest popular involvement in the machinery of politics'
because he assumed that the commoners' priorities would be the same
as those of the local gentry. The majority at all levels of Cheshire society
were violently opposed to popery and to the Spanish Match, just as a
few years later they were angered by the Arminians and the Duke of
Buckingham.[38]

The grievances of the 1620s—billeting, impressment, arbitrary imprisonment, and prerogative taxation—could in the end be righted only in
Parliament. This surely explains the widening interest in parliamentary
affairs during the decade, and why John Rous, for example, was so
often embroiled in political arguments during these years. In a conversation in November 1627 his companions (evidently minor gentlemen
or yeomen) 'fell upon old discontents, for the parliament being crossed,
expenses, hazard of ships, etc', in a way that shows that they had been
following public affairs quite closely.[39]
   Similar signs of popular political involvement can be seen in some,
though not all, parliamentary elections. It is difficult to generalize about
the electoral politics of the 1620s, but in some places at least national
politics were beginning to intrude. It was the practice in many counties,
Mark Kishlansky reminds us, to secure prior agreement among the gentry
and then present the candidates to the freeholders for formal approval.
But this custom was becoming harder to sustain. There were still peers—
the Earl of Derby in Lancashire, Pembroke in Wiltshire, and Warwick
in Essex, for example—who could get their clients or allies elected. But
in many other counties the gentry had established effective control. The
boroughs were more easily managed, but a strong body of opinion was
offended by attempts to maintain aristocratic control. The nomination
of members by letters from magnates, Serjeant Montagu declared in
1614, was 'the only way to bring in servitude'. Thomas Scott agreed:
'free parliaments', he said, 'cannot long continue if the freedom and
right of elections be violently or deceitfully taken from us.'[40]
   The general drift of Commons' decisions in disputed elections, Derek
Hirst has argued, was towards a broadening of the franchise. 'The
commonality ought to have a voice', the House voted in a typical case.[41]
The cumulative impression given by these decisions is that Sir Richard
Grosvenor was not alone in believing that the freeholders and subsidy-
men who comprised the bulk of the county electorates had much the

same outlook as the gentry: that they too were against arbitrary imprisonment, unparliamentary taxation, and the toleration of 'popery and Arminianism'. To empower such men was for MPs like Grosvenor the best way to protect the shared liberties of the Ancient Constitution. In a debate on the election at Great Marlow in November 1640, Sir Simonds D'Ewes—certainly no radical firebrand—announced 'that the poorest man ought to have a voice, that it was the birthright of the subjects of England'. Parliament-men were to sing a very different tune a few years later.[42]

This does not to mean that Court influence was negligible—even in 1625 it could get members elected in populous shires like Kent—and a determined high sheriff could still control an election, especially if he was directed by one of the local magnates, as was the case in Dorset a year later.[43] In 1628 this kind of manipulation was more difficult; it was easily defeated in Essex, for example. And there are signs of more populist electioneering methods, as by Coryton and Eliot in Cornwall. Their appeal to the people was based on what their enemies described as 'their pretence of suffering for their country' in resisting the Loan, and it was brilliantly successful.[44]

The most divisive issue, for the common people as well as for the gentry, was religion. But the nature of the division depended as much on where you lived as on anything else. There were places where the middling sort responded with enthusiasm to the call for godly reformation—in towns like Banbury, Dorchester, and Gloucester. There were others where there was greater division, as in Salisbury and other cathedral cities. And there were places where the godly made little headway, as in towns in and on the edge of custom-bound, culturally traditional farming regions —places like Sherborne, Blandford, and Bruton.[45] Religion differed from constitutional issues because it was less clearly a matter of custom—or if it was a matter of custom, because people so often disagreed on which side the weight of custom stood. Was the customary position that of the defenders of ritual practices in and outside the church; of the bowings at the name of Jesus, of the kneeling to receive communion, of the churchale and the revel feast? Or was it that of their godly critics, who could equally plausibly claim to represent the traditions of the Elizabethan church, uncorrupted by Laudian innovation? 'Long usage', Sir Henry Slingsby reflected, was the key to popular acceptance, and it was not always clear what the longest usage was.[46]

But although it may not have been absolutely clear in religious matters, it was much clearer with regard to politics and the constitution: the 'popular' position was almost invariably the customary or traditional one. Long usage: 'such time whereof the memory of man is not to the contrary, time out of mind, such time as will beget a custom', so Thomas Hedley explained it in 1610. As he pointed out, customs were usually confined to 'certain and particular places'—the custom of the manor, of the parish, of the county. But all of them came together and were subsumed in the Common Law, 'the custom of the realm'.[47] The rights and liberties of the Ancient Constitution which the gentry were defending against Buckingham could easily be equated with the birthrights of freeborn Englishmen of lesser status.

And however sharp the religious divide in 1640, it does not overcome the distinct smell of political alienation that is also noticeable in many parts of the kingdom. Even in 1625 the Great Yarmouth Common Council had refused to elect the courtier Sir John Suckling because they were worried that he might 'incline rather to the King than to the subject'.[48] It is easier to sum up popular attitudes as negatives rather than as positives. Most people were suspicious of Court corruption and extravagance; were ferociously anti-Spanish, as the joyous celebrations of October 1623 demonstrated; and were fervently anti-Catholic. In the 1630s they became increasingly hostile to bishops; not necessarily to episcopacy as such, but to its Laudian variety. There is much evidence for this, from the sympathetic crowds attending Prynne, Burton, and Bastwick during their journey into exile, to the numerous verse libels circulating during the Bishops' Wars. In 1637 Laud was informed that 'the preciser faction' in Dorset were having some success in convincing people that the new liturgy printed for the Scottish church included 'sundry notorious points of popery'.[49]

This does not mean that public opinion was predominately puritan in any sense in which we might use the term. Judith Maltby has argued persuasively that a moderate (non-puritan, non-Laudian) Prayer-Book Protestantism was in fact the consensus position of the English laity in the early seventeenth century.[50] And all over England there were defenders of conservative culture—of maypoles, churchales, and bear-baitings—who were conformable Protestants though certainly not puritans. Supporters of moral reformation thought such people easy pickings for popish evangelists: Lewis Owen denounced an Augustinian friar, a former actor, who had been sent into England in the 1620s to make converts among 'balladmakers, players, tobacconists, and tinkers'.[51] But the libels attacking puritan sexual hypocrisy and cultural oppressiveness were just as common as those on the other side: they surface in Wells, Bridport, Dorchester, Stratford-upon-Avon, and other places. 'Christian liberty', one of them sneered, was simply an invitation to have 'all things made common', so that 'each man may take another's wife'. Like this one, several libels circulating in the 1630s welcomed the godly's departure across the Atlantic: 'I wish Old England forth may spew | That they may sovereign in the New', one recommended.[52]

Libels and ballads appeared on both sides of many issues. In 1610 James I complained of 'the common printing and dispersing of traitorous and seditious books and of profane and scurrilous pamphlets and libels', and called for legislation to suppress them. The Earl of Salisbury was at that time a favourite target.[53] Every major political development—the execution of Sir Walter Ralegh, the Spanish Match, the impeachment of Buckingham—produced its crop of libels, some primarily aimed at an educated readership, others more popular. Sung in taverns and handed around at fairs, they were, Attorney-General Heath declared in 1627, 'the epidemical disease of these days'. He was speaking in Star Chamber at the trial of three fiddlers who had been singing ballads attacking Buckingham at various places in the London area.[54] Ballad-singers were often first with the news, sometimes even ahead of it, as happened in 1623 when some of them celebrated a premature report of the return of Prince Charles from Spain; the singers were imprisoned, but they had merely anticipated the event by a few weeks.[55]

As we have seen, Buckingham's unpopularity united a large segment of the gentry; it also did much to politicize their inferiors. The allegation that he had poisoned King James was widely dispersed and given the usual gendered twist by the emphasis on the role of his recusant mother. In Suffolk, John Rous heard 'strange rhymes and songs' about the Duke in March 1628, and soon rumours were spreading that he had been sent to the Tower; similar stories were heard when the King accepted the Petition of Right.[56] A visiting Scotsman named Melvin, misled, he afterwards claimed, 'by the report of the common people . . . into the vulgar error of the time', gives us a glimpse into the rumour mill in London in the spring of 1628, which even included stories that implicated Charles in the murder of his own father. Melvin saw the Duke's crimes as presaged by earlier events: Prince Henry, he asserted, had been poisoned by Sir Thomas Overbury, who had then been silenced in his turn by being murdered in the Tower. Now, in 1628, Buckingham (advised by 'Jesuitish Scotchmen'), wanted Parliament dissolved, after which he and the King

'with a great army of horse and foot would war against the commonalty'.
With England engulfed in civil war, the Spaniards would then invade—
'for this kingdom is already sold to the enemy by the Duke'. The government took Melvin seriously enough for Secretary Conway to examine
him and for Attorney-General Heath to draw up the indictment against
him, but in spite of his confession a King's Bench jury obstinately refused
to convict him. The authorities not surprisingly remained alert when
Melvin's allegations continued to circulate, and the Attorney-General
was still investigating them in the autumn.[57]

The assassinations of 1628—first of Buckingham's astrologer-sorcerer,
Dr Lambe, and then of the Duke himself—provide some further clues
to the political outlook of many commoners. Lambe's role as a conjuror
or witch—as a source of evil and satanic disorder—made him a subject
of even greater fascination at the popular than at the élite level. Lambe
had been imprisoned some years earlier for bewitching Lord Windsor,
and in 1624 he was convicted of the statutory rape of an 11-year old girl;
he was also said to have supplied Buckingham's estranged sister-in-law,
Lady Purbeck, with 'powders and potions' to use against the Duke
himself. However, Buckingham may already have been consulting him
too by this time, and he appears to have got the sorcerer a pardon in
return for a promise to enter the Duke's service.[58] Lambe had for a long
time been addicted to dangerous dabbling in state matters. He had
claimed to have secret information about the Gunpowder Plot, and
years later an old servant recalled his predicting that James I would not
die a natural death; it was lucky for Buckingham that she did not come
forward when the poisoning accusations were being investigated. He
was also said to have prophesied in 1626 that Buckingham would have
only two more years of power. Lambe's influence over the Duke was
soon being publicized in the libels. After the disastrous Isle de Rhé
expedition one of them pointedly asked why could not 'thy Lambe's |
Protection safeguard thee from the French rams?'[59] The sorcerer was
said to be providing the favourite with strange 'philtres to incite | Chaste
ladies' loves to give his lust delight'. Lambe, one ballad clearly aimed at
a popular audience declared, was 'the devil of our nation':

> For such a wicked wretch
> In England hath liv'd seldom.
> Nor never such a witch,
> For his skill from Hell came.[60]

Lambe's murder by a London mob after he had been attending a play
with one of his 'minions' was widely seen as a warning to the Duke.

'If his master were there, they would give him as much', some of the attackers were said to have shouted. A paper found on a post in Coleman Street bore a similar warning: 'they intend shortly to use him worse than they did the Doctor.' 'Let Charles and George do what they can, | The duke shall die like Doctor Lambe', another libel warned: it was still circulating in Suffolk in September, weeks after the Duke had been assassinated.[61]

We have already noted the spate of mock epitaphs that Buckingham's murder provoked, and their wide circulation. These were not the only signs of popular rejoicing at his death, and of approval of the murderer, Felton. John Vicars, the ultra-puritan minister at Stamford, asked his flock to pray that the King too might rejoice in the death of 'that wicked Achan'. When Felton was being taken to London on his way to the Tower there were fears of demonstrations in his favour, and of a possible rescue attempt by 'sailors and people by the way'. Unpaid and mutinous sailors were particularly hostile because Buckingham had been involved in violent scuffles with them at Portsmouth, and had had some of them hanged: their friends naturally vowed revenge. Some demonstrations did indeed occur during Felton's journey to London; at Kingston-upon-Thames a woman shouted 'God bless thee, little David' (Buckingham, obviously, being Goliath). The Duke's funeral was held at night to reduce the danger of unseemly outbreaks, but even so there were shouts which the Venetian ambassador thought sounded 'more like joy than commiseration'. An escort of the London trained bands, ordered to 'trail their pikes and beat dolefully', instead 'beat up again with courage and shouldered their pikes'.[62]

All this might suggest that there were no real differences between the outlooks of the two levels of the political nation that we are considering. Even in the enclosure riots discussed earlier in this chapter there are features that remind us of the politics of the élite: the emphasis on law and tradition, for example. The political culture of both groups was shaped by the legitimizing force of custom. Custom sanctioned the rights of access of countrymen to common land, as well as the right of Parliament to give its assent to lawful taxes. At the other end of the spectrum, Parliament showed its familiarity with the old world of custom by sometimes inflicting punishments resembling the shaming rituals so common in popular justice. When in 1621 the monopolist Sir Francis Mitchell was sent to the Tower, he had to walk there through jeering crowds, placarded (like a whore) with a paper declaring his offences, rather than going by water in a way more fitting for a gentleman prisoner. In the same year two bailiffs who had arrested an MP's servant were sentenced to ride backwards through Cheapside, 'with their faces to their horses' tails'.[63]

In spite of these similiarities, the lower orders did have their own ways of looking at politics, and a somewhat different vocabulary. Popular actions were more likely than those of their betters to incorporate festive elements. The enclosure riot was often preceded by a ritual procession led by pipes and drums and banners, and followed by a celebration with cakes and ale. In much the same way schoolboys sometimes had their feasts to accompany the rebellious 'barring out' rituals that Keith Thomas has described. Popular uprisings sometimes started during a time of festive celebration, as in 1549 in Norfolk, when Kett's rebellion began with a riot at a festival commemorating St Thomas Becket. Seventeenth-century fen riots were touched off by football matches, while in one Lincolnshire village in 1616 the annual Rogationtide procession was diverted into an attack on hedges recently planted by the lord of the manor.[64]

Popular disorders were also likely to involve women as well as men. It has often been observed that women played a prominent role in both enclosure and grain riots, and that male participants frequently disguised themselves as women. There is nothing particularly surprising about this: villagers generally accepted that women had a responsibility to share in the defence of communal rights. In a dispute over a common at Acton, Middlesex, in 1616, the women took their turn at 'watching', to keep out cattle belonging to the inhabitants of Willesden, who also claimed the land. For the authorities the fact that women often played leadership roles was another, more disturbing, matter, and severe punishments were inflicted when it happened and things got out of hand. A well-known case is that of Ann Carter, hanged for her prominent part in the riots at Maldon, Essex, in 1629.[65]

Some of the punishments were less savage but more symbolic. At Datchet, near Windsor, in 1599 the women involved in some enclosure riots were sentenced to be ducked in the cucking-stool, the men fined and made to stand in the pillory 'bareheaded and in women's apparel'. The actual violence does not sound very serious: rotten eggs were thrown at a bailiff, women used cartwheel grease to blacken the face of one of the new landlord's servants, and said that if his master had been there they would have 'christened him' with the ladle one of them was carrying. This suggests that a skimmington was in prospect, for it was from that implement—the skimming ladle—that the ritual got its name.[66] One interpretation of inversion rituals of this kind, popular with judges and other male authority figures, was that the men were trying to escape detection, simply 'hiding behind the skirts of the women', who would be likely to receive lighter punishment because of their natural frailty. In 1608 the Southampton magistrates could not believe that women grain rioters had acted on their own initiative, and blamed the town clerk for having 'animated them'.[67]

It is easy to see why the authorities disliked these riotous customs: they involved deliberate transgressions of divinely sanctioned gender codes which even the rioters normally took for granted. Moralists denounced the satanic influences which led to cross-dressing, and which caused women to step out of their natural spheres to take on both the styles of dress and the activist roles which properly belonged to men.[68] Cross-dressing was frequently held to aggravate other offences against order. In a charivari at Wells against a puritan constable, one of the participants rode on horseback in women's clothes, carrying a spinning wheel, to ridicule the unpopular officer. In his complaint to Star Chamber the constable drew attention to the disorders then erupting in the Midlands—the year was 1607—and suggested that the Wells incident ought to be firmly dealt with because it was part of a general breakdown of law and order.[69]

Some of these incidents remind us that the élite and the populace used somewhat different metaphorical systems and political vocabularies. When they thought about violations of their rights, commoners, to a far greater extent than their superiors, did so in a language that repeatedly stressed the evils of a world turned upside down, and made regular use of metaphors of inversion. Given the assumptions that were routinely made about the correspondences between the public and the private spheres, it is not surprising that in the popular vocabulary those metaphors were frequently based on distinctions of sex and gender. The skimmington is a classic example.

I have argued elsewhere that there is a direct connection between the domestic form of the skimmington—in which the inversion of gender roles in marriage is held up to public shame—and the public form, as in the riots around 1630 in Dean and Braydon Forests, led by the mythic Captain or Lady Skimmington.[70] All that we need to note at present is that both forms became especially frequent precisely when fears of a breakdown of obedience in family and state were most acute. The 'crisis of order' of the period 1560–1640 generated widespread male alarm about many different kinds of disorder: women, young people, and social inferiors were all perceived as unusually rebellious. People at the lower end of the social scale shared some, but not all, of these fears. Many lower-class men were certainly concerned about unruly women, and were active in prosecuting witches, putting scolds in the cucking-stool, and taking the initiative—sometimes in defiance of authority—in shaming masculine women and their feeble husbands. They also wor-ried about insubordination by servants or apprentices. But the just, stable social order was equally likely to be threatened from outside the community by people who violated the norms of neighbourly conduct: the enclosing landlord, the rapacious grain dealer. Concern about such matters cut across political and religious loyalties. The Gillingham For-est rioters were largely immune to puritan influences. But the godly inhabitants of Dorchester seem to have been just as sympathetic to their cause as their much less puritan rural neighbours.[71] In such cases localist feeling and support for ancient custom clearly had more force than religion.

As we saw in the previous chapter, the gendered habit of mind—the association of a particular national policy with 'masculine virtue', for example—came naturally to the gentry. It came even more naturally to the commoners. Women's involvement in such popular collective actions as grain and enclosure riots might be tolerated or even welcomed. And in spite of the prevailing value-system, some women took at least an occasional interest in public affairs. When bailiffs came to distrain the property of Ship Money refusers in one Northamptonshire village, a local diarist reports that 'the women assembled and some men and affrighted them, there was much running with forks and cowlstaffs'. Some women were encouraged by their husbands to be politically aware. Thomas Scott's wife had certainly mastered the essentials of the anti-Court argument in 1628. She refused to accept the soldiers the Canter-bury magistrates tried to billet on her and gave them good arguments, Scott says, 'of her own mother wit, or remembering what before the parliament I and other men had talked'.[72] She was a woman of high status, married to an MP, but other Canterbury women also seem to have been unusually politically conscious. A few years earlier, when Buckingham passed through the city on his way to Dover, there was a riot in which the wives of unpaid soldiers attacked his coach, a ballad reports, 'with knitting needles and with ladles, | Spits, fireforks and legs of cradles'. Once again the ladle, the implement used in the skimmington, is high on the list of weapons.[73]

But there were limits to the public tolerance of this kind of behaviour. People of all classes feared chaos and disorder, and women were commonly thought to be the agents through which the forces of darkness did their work, because they were less controlled by reason than men. Besides being typically inclined to scolding and witchraft, they were also more attracted than men to dangerous forms of religious extremism. King James expressed the common view when he regretted 'how busy many be who . . . go about to seduce poor simple women, and how they prevail'.[74]

Mysogynist complaints by men about women have a long history, and it has already been noted that they were expressed with unusual intensity in the early seventeenth century. Women seem to have had a particularly bad influence on the universities, Robert Bowyer reported:

Who knoweth not how the manners of young men are corrupted and drawn from their studies by the ordinary sight and conversation with women: who knoweth not how covetous heads of houses are to maintain, prefer and provide for their wives and children: who knoweth not how much women prevail with their husbands to the overthrow of learning, discipline, yea and of the colleges.[75]

Some blamed the Court of High Commission's permissiveness. The court, it was alleged in 1610, allowed women excessively generous separation allowances, 'to the great encouragement of wives to be disobedient and contemptuous against their husbands'.[76]

What men in the early seventeenth century most feared was the disorder implicit in women's refusal to accept the submissive role in the family that convention assigned them. This could cause disruption from the highest to the lowest levels of society. One of the many ballads from James I's reign poking fun at cuckolds adopts a more serious tone on the subject of female authority:

> But when the sole commanding
> Amongst the females fall,
> For want of understanding
> They commonly mar all.

> Nor doth alone the City
> Such precedents afford;
> In Court, the more the pity
> Some ladies play the lord.

The consequence, needless to say, was likely to be religious apostacy (as in the women of Buckingham's family):

> And then to be in fashion,
> She turns Catholical—
> Oh vile abomination,
> The Pope can pardon all.[77]

The literary controversy that began with the publication of Joseph Swetnam's *Arraignment of Lewd, Idle, froward and unconstant women* in 1615 has received a good deal of recent attention.[78] It might perhaps be argued that Swetnam's work, and that of his detractors, was not written for a popular audience—the frequent use of classical allusions, among other things, might support such a view. Once again we encounter the difficulty of defining 'popular'. Swetnam's readership was probably much the same as the one for which many of the libels mentioned earlier were written—a readership that included the wits and idlers of London, the young gentlemen of the Inns of Court and hangers-on around White-hall, but also the more literate apprentices and journeymen in the City, the sort of people who often attended the public theatre, and who in 1624 thronged to Middleton's highly political satire, *A Game at Chess*. They were not the really poor, but neither were they universally drawn from the privileged and well-born. Annabel Patterson has drawn atten-tion to the socially mixed character of theatre audiences in Shakespeare's time, and the same point could be made about the readership of libels and pamphlets. Swetnam's audience spanned both the élite and the popular, but he was probably aiming somewhat more at the lower than the upper end of the spectrum.[79]

The Arraignment was inspired by the Overbury affair—as we have seen, the greatest of the numerous Jacobean Court scandals. Swetnam's denunciations of female inconstancy and duplicity, vanity and extravag-ance, greed and voracious sexuality, were especially directed at Frances Howard, the new Countess of Somerset, and her friend Mrs Turner. During the trial the women of the Howard family quickly became tar-gets of popular hatred: after the Somersets had been pardoned a mob chased the Queen's coach, 'railing and reviling', on the mistaken impres-sion that Frances and her mother, the Countess of Suffolk, were inside. They were not alone in arousing such animosity. When Lady Roos was being taken to the Tower after her conviction for slandering the Exeters, it was reported that she too was 'cursed horribly by the people'. A libel described her mother, Lady Lake, as 'a bitch of Court, a common stinking snake'.[80]

Swetnam's work played on these feelings, and it was sensationally popular—ten editions by 1637—provoking a flood of rejoinders, both pro and con, during the next few years. The controversy about women's moral failings soon focused on styles of dress, particularly the masculine ones which women were adopting at this time, and the 'feminine' ones which some courtiers were also starting to wear. In her scaffold speech Mrs Turner penitently rejected the whole 'wardrobe of court vanities', but she had been one of the main promoters of the masculine style (starched yellow bands and cuffs were her particular trademark), and the Countess, in her low-cut 'French doublet', one of the most prominent trend-setters. She had enslaved her new husband, one critic of the Court declared, by the use of 'yellow bands, dusted hair, curled crisped, frizzled, sleek skins, opened breasts beyond accustomed modesty'. And the dangerous new fashions were spreading into circles outside the Court. 'Yellow bands', Barnaby Rich declared in 1619, 'are become so common, to every giddy-headed gallant, and light heeled mistress, that methinks a man should not hardly be hanged without a yellow band.' A year later the clergy in their pulpits and the ballad-singers in the streets were still denouncing 'the insolence and impudence of women', and their immodest fashions.[81]

When the pamphleteers denounced wicked women they were also denouncing other public evils which James I had not reformed—or had tried to do so only belatedly, as when he issued a proclamation against the masculine fashions in women's dress. They were denouncing Court extravagance and immorality, which James had done so little to curb. They were denouncing unhealthy, sinister foreign influences which the new styles of dress symbolized. In 1621 an MP complained that young men were spending more on 'roses and shirts than all their fathers' apparel was worth', and wanted a law passed against 'that fantastical change of French, Spanish, German [fashions], and sometimes mixture of them all together' which had so corrupted English virtue. An attack on Spanish fashions could easily be read as an oblique denunciation of James I's pro-Spanish foreign policies.[82] Coded criticism of James can be found in many places in the pamphlets. Swetnam and other popular authors denounced the prevailing effeminacy, the lack of martial vigour which the new styles reflected. 'A man triumphs at wars, but a woman rejoiceth more at peace', Swetnam declared—and it was well known which James rejoiced in. 'Where are the tilts and tourneys?' and other masculine recreations of former times, the author of *Haec Vir: Or the Womanish-Man* demanded. Englishmen had abandoned the arms that used to 'shake all Christendom', and were sunk in 'softness, dullness, and effeminate niceness'. They had even taken up shuttlecock—a girl's game if ever there was one.[83]

Complaints about male degeneration did not end with James I's death. Prynne's attack on long hair—*The Unloveliness of Lovelockes*—was published in 1628, and contains the same kind of moralizings as those of his Jacobean predecessors. Young men had become 'womanish not only in exility of voice, tenderness of body, levity of apparel, wantonness of pace and gesture, but even the very length and culture of their locks and hair'. Martin Parker pursued the same theme a few years later in his ballad, 'Knavery in All Trades':

> Our men are effeminate,
> Which all their manhood disgraces,
> And makes our foes of late,
> To jeer us to our faces.[84]

However, critics of the mysogynist Swetnam could find plenty of examples of martial valour among women to throw at him, and once again the contrast between their behaviour and that of King James must have been obvious. A pamphlet entitled *Ester hath hang'd Haman* listed the usual biblical examples, but also Boadicea, who 'defended the liberty of her country against the strength of the Romans . . . and made them feel that a woman could conquer them who had conquered almost all the men of the then known world'. The favourable view of Boadicea shows that this pamphlet was not directed to an élite readership: to the educated, Boadicea personified feminine, and therefore barbaric and unregulated, resistance to the rational, masculine order the Romans represented. Inevitably, though, the pamphlet ended with Queen Elizabeth, 'a pattern for the best men to imitate'.[85]

The pamphleteers were not simply criticizing James's feeble foreign policy. They were arguing, as many others were arguing at about this time, that their entire world was out of joint. In 1621 the anonymous author of a pamphlet called *Muld Sacke* produced a long list of ills that needed reforming, blaming them all on worldly churchmen, hypocritical puritans, plotting Jesuits, usurers, and so on. Many of these evils he (or she) thought were the result of the growing debasement of public virtue by the values of the market-place. *Mule Sacke* denounces 'the improving of lands, racking of rents, destruction of ancient hospitality, and oppression of poor farmers and tenants'. The masculine styles of female dress, the author of *Hic Mulier* declared, were especially attractive to social upstarts, though contradictorily they also seem to have been invented by noblewomen to make their inferiors look ridiculous. But in either case the connection between gender inversion and social inversion is clear.[86]

All this, *Haec Vir* suggests, can only be reformed when men abandon their effeminacy in both dress and behaviour, and women their masculine styles. As in the circumstances of female assertiveness which provoked the skimmington ritual, women have stepped out of their customarily submissive place only because men have allowed them to do so. *Haec Vir*'s female character ends the argument by calling on men to be 'men in shape, men in show, men in words, men in actions, men in counsel, men in example', and the hitherto effeminate man agrees: 'Henceforth we will live nobly like ourselves.' It does not require much imagination to translate this into a commentary on James I's policies and the moral failings of his Court.[87]

There was, then, a shared culture which linked all sectors of the political nation through such broad clusters of ideas as the Ancient Constitution, anti-popery, and Protestant nationalism, and through shared enemies like the Duke of Buckingham. But certain aspects of that common culture seem to have been stressed more strongly at the popular than at the élite level: notably those parts of it connected with issues of gender and inversion. Before the civil war the resemblances between the two cultures may have been more significant than the differences. As we shall see in the remaining chapters of this book, this was to change after 1640. In both politics and culture it is hard to escape the inevitably commonplace conclusion that the civil wars and revolution of the mid-century formed a great watershed.

4

LIBERTY AND PROPERTY
THE POLITICAL NATION AND THE
ENGLISH REVOLUTION

The historical meaning of the violent events that occurred in mid-seventeenth-century Britain remains as fiercely contested as ever. Did they amount to a revolution, a rebellion, a civil war, a 'war of three kingdoms'? From the days of Hobbes, Clarendon, and Ludlow, historians have endlessly debated the subject, usually revealing as much about their own political prejudices as about the historical situation they are describing. Was this one of the great revolutions of the modern world, somehow connected with great impersonal forces like capitalism, liberal individualism, or religious toleration? Or was it simply the fortuitous result of a series of accidents, just a bit of bad luck? The disagreements have recently become more profound than ever, and it is now fashionable to call the whole notion of an English 'revolution' into question. Conrad Russell has given his collected essays on the period the dismissive title, *Unrevolutionary England*.[1]

The problem arises in part from the short duration and ultimate failure of the revolution (or whatever we choose to call it). Any explanation of why a revolution (under some definition of the term) occurred between 1642 and 1649 gives us little help when we go on to ask why that revolution failed and there was a Restoration in 1660. Yet we need, surely, to understand *both* the revolution and the Restoration. It may help us to do this if we retrace our steps to the beginning of 'the troubles'. This may not be as easy as it sounds. For when, the reader may well ask, *did* the troubles begin? Was it with the outbreak of the strife over the new Scottish liturgy, in 1637? Or was it somewhat earlier, soon after 1625 perhaps, with the crown's adoption of 'new counsels' in the state and Arminian innovation in the church? Could it have been (for, hush, there may still be secret Whigs among us) on the arrival of James I in his new kingdom in 1603, bringing his newfangled notions of divine right? Perhaps we ought to go all the way back to the 1530s, to the divisions over religious matters introduced by the Protestant

Reformation? Or even to that same remote period because, as some have suggested, that is when English society began to refashion itself through the 'rise of the gentry', with all the strains and stresses in the body politic that followed?

No book of this length can possibly disentangle the complex choices that these (and no doubt other) alternative explanations require. Some concessions have to be made to the brevity of human life, and besides, our subject is not the causes of the British whatever-it-was. The only sensible procedure is to return to the actual subject of the book, the relationship between élite and popular politics, which we first began, the reader will remember, in the reigns of the first two Stuarts.

In an earlier chapter we surveyed the politics of the gentry in the 1620s. Looking back on that decade from the perspective of the civil-war years, we are likely to suspect that the sense of alienation from Court and government that gripped many members of the political nation in the earlier years must have had *some* relationship to the collapse of the monarchy in the 1640s. Yet it soon becomes obvious that there is no necessary correlation between the behaviour of individuals in the two periods. People who opposed the Duke of Buckingham in the 1620s did not necessarily fight for Parliament twenty years later. Once again we need to distinguish between the long and the short term. The long-term, structural problems of the English monarchy, in both church and state, existed in both periods. But in the short term, during the years 1640–2, the political map was completely redrawn.

To appreciate how completely it was redrawn, let us take an example from the west country. The two most active and influential leaders in Dorset politics in the 1620s were Sir Walter Erle of Charborough and Sir John Strangways of Melbury, both of them immensely wealthy and respected figures from the very highest level of the county hierarchy. They had their differences on local affairs: Erle's friends were bitter about Strangways's unscrupulous manipulation of the 1626 county election, for example. But on national politics their views were very similar. Both were active in Parliament in the impeachment proceedings against Buckingham, and were struck off the commission of the peace in consequence. They were also by far the best-known of the resisters of the 1627 Forced Loan in Dorset. They were both imprisoned for this, and when they got out and were again elected to Parliament in 1628 they promptly renewed their earlier attacks on the crown's (and Buckingham's) arbitrary policies. After these shared experiences neither, surely, could have imagined that within fifteen years they would be ranged on opposite sides in a civil war. Yet they were, Strangways as the effective leader of the royalist party in Dorset, Erle as the commander of Parliament's local forces. Before it was all over both were imprisoned yet again—Strangways by Parliament in 1645 and on several later occasions, Erle more briefly by the Army in December 1648. The contrasting political paths followed by the two Dorset knights usefully exemplify the divisions among the English gentry in the 1640s and '50s. A full account of élite politics during the Interregnum is beyond the purpose of this chapter; it will instead take the form of a meditation on certain important themes that may help us to understand the period better.[2]

Before we proceed, however, some further words of caution are in order. We should not exaggerate the differences in the way the various levels of the political nation viewed the conflict that was engulfing them. The earlier chapters have shown that I am more impressed by the similarities of élite and popular political cultures than by the differences between them. People of all classes listened to the same ballads, and sang them to the same tunes. The popular song 'Hey then, Up go we!' was written early in 1642. Within a few months, in July, we find the Marquis of Hertford parodying it in a letter to the Queen which shows how familiar the jingle had already become at Court. Their enemies would soon be defeated, Hertford assured the Queen, and 'Hey then, Down go they!' A few weeks later a ballad-singer in The Bear at Exeter was entertaining an audience that included both gentlemen and commoners with songs lampooning the Five Members and other Roundhead leaders. Satirical songs like these and the well-known 'God a-mercy, good Scot' were available to people of all classes when they rubbed shoulders in the inns and taverns. The Cavaliers, of course, had all the best tunes: that of 'When the King enjoys his own again' was borrowed for several other popular songs, including one appropriately titled, 'The World is Turned Upside Down'. In the 1650s seditious Cavalier ballads were sung everywhere from the houses of the gentry to The Black Boy tavern in the Somerset village of Ashcott.[3]

Yet during this period ballads provide us with somewhat less straightforward clues to public opinion than they do in earlier times. Although some of the ballads of the 1620s were written by or for members of Court factions, most of the ballad-writers of that decade were producing their wares for money. To turn a profit they had to be attentive to their market, and to respond to their audience's assumptions and prejudices. So they did during the 1640s, to be sure; but at the same time ballad-making became a branch of party propaganda. There were now two alternative, competing markets. The ballads and popular pamphlets can still be used to uncover the political languages and metaphorical systems of the period, and perhaps the opinions of the individuals who collected them, but it would be rash to cite them as evidence for any general shift of opinion from one side to the other. It is not clear how civil-war ballad-writers were paid for their work. Most of them were still, apparently, free-lance authors, in it for the money; but they were also being recruited and used as propagandists by the two sides.[4] The sheer numbers of new ballads, which proliferated far beyond the output of the 1620s, suggests that we have entered a different world.

The propaganda war, Joyce Malcolm reminds us, reveals the assumptions and expectations of both sides. In their sermons, pamphlets, ballads, and newsbooks, the royalists were primarily concerned with the opinions of the gentry. They routinely sneered at the allegedly plebeian origins of parliamentarian officers, denouncing them for their supposed intention to bring in democracy, anarchy, levelling of degrees and distinctions of rank. Malcolm draws attention to the 'mocking, aristocratic tone' used by the royalist *Mercurius Aulicus*, a tone clearly recognizable in the paper's account of Goring's defeat of a small Roundhead force led by an officer named Wansey. The motto on Wansey's colours was 'For Lawful Laws and Liberties', a tautology which offended *Aulicus*'s purist author, John Berkenhead, and which he sarcastically dismissed as 'full of wit and judgement'. Wansey was a pious watchmaker from Warminster, his humble origins making him, the royalist Sir Edward Walker observed, 'a person of equal quality with many of the rebels' officers'.[5]

During the war royalist ballad-writers occasionally adopted a popular voice for satirical purposes, as in Alexander Brome's 'The Clown's Complaint', written in a bogus Devonshire dialect.[6] But although some of the grievances they denounced (the excise is an obvious example) were shared by gentry and commoners alike, royalist authors generally regarded the populace as 'the clowns', and the parliamentarian cause as fatally tainted by the plebeian origins of many of its leaders. Even the famous Cavalier conviviality, the familiar call not to 'think on tomorrow, | But tipple and laugh while we may', was an expression of class attitudes, an assertion that puritan killjoys were by definition contemptible people of lower rank, the proverbial brewers and draymen.[7]

The Cavaliers' scorn for the people is repeatedly evident in their writings. A 1648 ballad, 'The Anarchie, or the Blest Reformation', argued that claims of popular support for Parliament need not be taken seriously

because the Roundhead cause was fatally tainted by its appeal to women
and the disorderly:

> Come clowns, and come boys,
> Come hober-de-hoyes,
>   Come females of each degree;
> Stretch your throats, bring in your votes,
>   And make good the anarchy.
> And 'Thus it shall go,' says Alice;
>   'Nay, thus it shall go,' says Amy;
> 'Nay, thus it shall go,' says Taffy, 'I trow;'
> 'Nay, thus it shall go,' says Jamy.

Each stanza ends with a confusion of discordant voices—of women,
Welshmen, and Scots, all obviously marginal people. 'Who can expect |
Ought but division' from the commons, the anonymous author demands:

> These popular pates reap naught but debates,
> From that many round-headed beast.

In the end, of course, the rabble are easily converted back to monarchy,
and Tom and Ralph, Doll and Moll (the names from the Celtic fringe
have now significantly disappeared), all join in happily toasting King
Charles.[8]

By 1648 the royalist propagandists had learned from their predecessors' mistakes, and were trying to reach a more socially diverse readership, an effort that I shall pursue in more detail in the next chapter. But
ballads continued to be published that must have been above the heads
of any but an educated reader. One from March 1660 celebrates the
downfall of the republicans, sneering that

> Scot, Nevil, and Vane,
> With the rest of that train
> Are into Oceana fled.

A few lines further on the author refers to the Rota Club.[9] Such ballads
helped to confirm the gentry's contempt for radical intellectuals like
James Harrington and his friends, but it is unlikely that they made any
impact on the common people.

Regular exposure to the newsbooks may have solidified the loyalties
of some partisans of one side or the other, but it made others totally
cynical. Wealthy and educated readers could choose from among many
competing papers according to which side they were on, knowing well
enough that the news they read was often censored and no more reliable

than the output of today's journalistic gutters. One Dorset gentleman, John Fitzjames of Leweston, observed in 1648 that much of the news 'dares not at first (many times not at all) show itself in the pamphlets', instancing the absence of printed reports about the return of the presbyterian 'Eleven Members' to the House of Commons. Always hungry for news, Fitzjames asked his London correspondent to send him the Leveller *The Moderate*, the better-named *Moderate Intelligencer*, and the royalist *Mercurius Pragmaticus*; it was always his pastime, he said, 'to read what can be said on both sides'. In several other letters he expressed further doubts about the veracity of the newsbooks, asking for an account of recent events 'beyond that of the mercuries', and for 'news in writing, as well as lies in print'.[10] Yet however sceptical they may have been, country gentlemen always panted for news from London, and freely shared it with their neighbours. In September 1648 Sir John Gell sent newsbooks to his son in Derbyshire, asking him to pass them on to Sir Cornelius Vermuyden, the fen-drainage projector. In 1648 Sir Ralph Assheton of Whalley Abbey was having newsletters from Scotland sent to his steward in Lancashire, to be handed on to Assheton's cousin. He also tried to arrange for pamphlets to be sent down and sold by booksellers in Clitheroe and other small towns, commenting that if local people had no access to the news it was 'no marvel if they be ignorant of the truth of passages'. He wrote on the day of Charles I's execution; it would be nice to know if he was involved in the distribution of the King's posthumous best-seller, *Eikon Basilike*, a few weeks later.[11]

Whatever our conclusions may be about the level of the political nation to which particular pamphlets or ballads were directed, it is undeniable that many of them included elements that were common to the political culture of all classes. But it would be absurd to blur the differences between an earl at the top of the hierarchy, and a common soldier trailing a pike at the bottom, or indeed between a peer of any degree and a commoner. Let us, then, follow the old, tried and true method of analysing English society by starting at the top, with the peers: how did the civil war and revolution affect their relative position in the political nation?

The first, inescapable fact that we confront is that the House of Lords was abolished in February 1649. For months only a pathetic handful of peers had been attending, to 'sit and tell tales by the fireside', as a newspaper sarcastically reported. The bookseller George Thomason came across a mocking description of the four most regular attenders during those last days: 'Salisbury the valiant, Pembroke the witty, Denbigh the chaste, and Mulgrave the pretty'. He did the necessary decoding for us: coward, fool, whoremaster, and dwarf respectively.[12] Obviously this is not a fair estimate of the House of Lords after the second civil war. By December 1648 the Army was firmly in control, and one might equally well point out that after Pride's Purge only a tiny fraction of the members of the House of Commons attended. If we retrace our steps by a few months, before most of the parliamentarian Lords were frightened away by the Army, we may get a fairer impression. We shall be wise, though, to distinguish between the influence of the House of Lords as an institution, and that of its individual members.

In his magisterial *House of Lords During the Civil War*, C. H. Firth took the view that the House of Lords was declining in power and influence long before its abolition. Many of the peers who had not joined the King at Oxford wanted a compromise peace, but were never able to do much more than act as a brake on the more warlike Commons. In 1643 the Upper House even lost control of its own membership. When a majority wanted to readmit the Earl of Holland and other peers who had returned after defecting to the King the Commons would not allow them to do it, and a subsequent attempt to seat them in 1647 also failed. Firth recounts the Commons' repeated successes in pressuring or manœuvring the Lords into doing what they did not want to do—over the Self-Denying Ordinance, over peace negotiations, and so on. The Lords could win temporary concessions, and there was a brief recovery of the House's prestige in 1647 when some of its most active members supported the Army against the Presbyterians. But this was short-lived: after the Self-Denying Ordinance, Firth argued, 'their substantial power was gone'.[13] We now know that Firth ignored one important aspect of the House's work—its rapidly developing judicial function through its hearings of writs of error, which reached an unprecedented level of activity in the years immediately after the civil war. So important had this part of the Lords' work become that during the discussions that preceded the House's abolition it was seriously proposed that it be retained as a court of appeal. But although Firth may have presented the decline of the House of Lords as a smoother, more seamless process than it actually was, he was surely right about the institution's declining political effectiveness. It is difficult to point to a single occasion during or after the civil war in which the initiative of the Lords on a major matter of policy was decisive, or in which they did more than obstruct and delay the implementation of decisions taken elsewhere.[14]

Firth's argument may seem less convincing, though, if we shift our gaze from the House of Lords as an institution to the individual peers who were its members. Some of them still had enormous territorial power, which could help to shape the political and religious character of a whole county. The Earls of Derby in Lancashire on the royalist side, the Earl of Warwick in Essex and, to a lesser extent, Lord Brooke in Warwickshire on the parliamentarian one, spring immediately to mind. In some counties the rivalry of great aristocratic families—of the Hastings and the Greys in Leicestershire, for example—profoundly affected the course of events. Such noblemen, like the wealthy knights and gentlemen who were only a little below them in status, often raised men and money in huge quantites for the side they had espoused. The Earl of Essex had great influence in Staffordshire and the neighbouring counties, and as Lord General of the Parliament's armies he was a figure of towering stature. His funeral in 1646 was conducted with the majestic pomp normally reserved for royalty.[15]

Many of the peers still had significant electoral influence, at least in the 1640s, though their power had waned by the time of the Protectorate parliaments. Essex's interest in Herefordshire temporarily survived him—the Harleys made use of it during the recruiter elections. The royalist peers had forfeited their remaining electoral influence, but parliamentarian lords like the Earls of Pembroke and Salisbury in the southern counties, the Earl of Northumberland and Lord Wharton in the north, could still get their clients elected.[16] A few of the peers were also major players in parliamentary politics: Lord Saye is an obvious example. In 1647 he was certainly one of the leaders (though only one—the others were all commoners) of what for want of a better term we are still entitled to call the 'middle group'.[17]

But although individual peers may have retained effective power and prestige, we should not ignore the signs of more general decline, which had deeper roots than the political setbacks of the 1640s. Whatever may be our views about the pre-war difficulties described in Lawrence Stone's classic *Crisis of the Aristocracy*, there can be no denying the fact that a good many counties had become aristocratic power vacuums. In Somerset the Seymours still had lands and clients, and by Charles I's reign there was also a resident peer in the county, the newly ennobled Lord Poulett. But real power was dispersed among an oligarchy of more than a dozen governing families. When Poulett tried to compete for county pre-eminence Sir Robert Phelips ran rings round him.[18] In Dorset the Digbys, Earls of Bristol, were recent arrivals and their influence was at first no greater than that of several of the leading gentry, while the Lords-Lieutenant, the Earls of Suffolk, were usually non-resident. The second Earl was building up an interest in the county in the 1620s and '30s, but he died before the job was finished. So here too a gentry oligarchy, among whom Erle and Strangways were the most prominent, ran things without much interference. The most that can be said is that Sir John found the Digbys useful allies, just as he did other county magnates. Recent studies of other counties in this period—Kent and Sussex, for example—tell much the same story.[19]

The influence of individual lords, though real, should not be exaggerated. I am not convinced, for example, that it required the superior intellect of a peer to draft the Heads of the Proposals. An I should not want to make too much of statements like Lord Conway's description of the Earl of Holland in 1640 as 'the invisible head of the Puritan party'. If Conway was right, Holland was extremely clever in protecting his invisibility, because nobody outside the Court seems to have noticed it. The context of Conway's statement, however, clearly shows that he was talking only about Holland's leadership of a Court 'cabal' to which the puritan label had rightly or wrongly been attached. It is true, of course, that Holland had puritan sympathies, and as Chancellor of Cambridge took it upon himself to protect some of the godly ministers of that university. When John Stoughton was summoned before High Commission in 1635 he was soon let go and, John Rous reports, 'returned with credit, in the Earl of Holland's coach'. His brother Warwick might have had better claims to leadership of a national faction, as Conway's letter perhaps implies, but the supposition that 'the Puritans' or 'the Puritan party' had any single leader is really not very plausible.[20]

We should be equally cautious about drawing conclusions from patron–client relationships among the laity. If we look in the House of Commons for the clients of noblemen we can easily find a few who were clients and nothing else: Michael Oldisworth, secretary to the Earl of Pembroke, or Hugh Potter, servant to the Earl of Northumberland, for example. But this kind of one-dimensional dependency is unusual. The more typical clients were men like Robert Scawen, who was also in Northumberland's service, but had a career of his own—and an important one when he was chairman of the Army Committee—in which he did much more than parrot the opinions of his employer. There were very few Hugh Potters—total, one-hundred-per-cent, rubber-stamping clients —in the House of Commons.[21] Samuel Pepys's career after the Restoration is a sufficient reminder that people who started out as dependants, as Pepys did of Edward Mountagu, might in the end carve out careers of their own. We should also be careful not to assume that just because a peer or other great man used his electoral influence on behalf of a particular candidate, that person automatically became his client. Lord Wharton may have used his influence on behalf of Henry Ireton in the recruiter election for Appleby, but Ireton was soon to be one of the organizers of Pride's Purge, which Wharton certainly opposed.[22]

The Dorset parliamentarian, John Fitzjames, is another whose electoral experiences suggest that we always need to be suitably cautious before we draw too many facile conclusions about patron–client connections. Fitzjames was a client of the Earl of Salisbury, whom he served as Overseer of Cranborne Chase. However, when he was angling for a parliamentary seat at Shaftesbury, a borough in which Salisbury had some influence, the connection did him no good, because another of the Earl's dependents, William Hussey, was also a candidate. Hussey also had the support of the Earl of Pembroke, who as lord of the manor had even more influence in Shaftesbury than Salisbury, so if patronage was the critical factor, his election ought to have been assured. Alas, the town elected a third candidate, a local parliamentarian gentleman named George Starre.[23]

Besides trying to use Salisbury's electoral influence, Fitzjames also sought the help of less exalted people. When he was negotiating for his arrears of pay, and for other debts owed him by the state, the people he turned to were not peers, but the MPs Denis Bond and Thomas Erle, Sir Walter's son. Erle had promised Fitzjames 'to have a care of [him]', either with a Army commission or in some other capacity, and Fitzjames relied on these 'noble promises'. Erle, who was well connected both through his father and his father-in-law, Lord Saye, looked after Fitzjames's interests at Westminster and supported him in the Shaftesbury election, though to no better effect than Salisbury. A hostile pamphleteer claimed that the younger Erle was more interested in local than in national influence, reporting that he 'seldom attended the House, but followed his business in the Country, where he was a great Committeeman, helping himself and friends'.[24] After 1646 Fitzjames's dependency on the Earl of Salisbury became less apparent. He made his alliances as it suited him—with his old friends in Massey's brigade during the Army–Parliament conflict in 1647, with Sir Anthony Ashley Cooper in the 1656 election, and with the Protector's chief newswriter, Marchamont Nedham, whom he supplied with local news for *Mercurius Politicus*, a few years later.[25]

Attempts to portray the parliamentarians as an old-fashioned baronial faction are thus not very convincing.[26] If we are searching for the survival of aristocratic power during the civil war, the place to look is in the King's camp, where the likes of Newcastle, Hertford, and Bristol continued to exercise their talents. Even on the royalist side their leadership was being challenged by the 'swordsmen'—Rupert, Maurice, Goring, and their friends. On the Parliament's side, although individual peers retained a good deal of influence—Essex, Brooke, Warwick, and Manchester during the war, Saye down to 1648 in alliance with other leaders of the middle group—they were far from being the only leaders of the parliamentary cause. In 1649, with Parliament purged, the King executed, and the middle group in ruins, even Lord Saye fled the scene; in the words of a 1659 ballad, 'stole[n] away to Lundy', his island fastness in the Bristol Channel.[27]

There was another, albeit temporary, shift in the balance of power within the political nation during the revolution. The civil war led to a significant decline in the authority of the gentry as a class, through the exclusion of the royalists from the commissions of the peace and other local offices, and the voluntary withdrawal of many neutrals and moderate parliamentarians. The undermining of traditional local institutions like quarter sessions by the new county committees also encouraged an influx of lesser people—minor gentry and townsmen—into what had hitherto been a level of government reserved for the upper gentry. Even after the dismantling of the committees in 1650, the newcomers were still prominent in the militia and other local commissions, and by now they had gained a foothold in the revived commissions of the peace. Alan Everitt has argued that the failure of the republican regimes to put down durable roots was the result of the almost unanimous opposition of the traditional rulers of the shires. It has generally been accepted that the lesser men who filled their places lacked the authority to make county government work efficiently, and were fatally tarred with the brush of centralization, being perceived as agents of an unpopular national state.[28]

Legitimate questions have been raised about the extent to which the Interregnum regimes were in fact more hostile to local interests than earlier ones, as well as about the conventional equation of localism with political moderation. But it cannot be disputed that the revolution did lead to a displacement of the old magnate families in most English counties. Although representatives of a few of them reappeared in commissions of local government during the latter part of the Protectorate, this was only possible when members of the older generation had been replaced by sons who were too young to have fought for the King.[29] Among the moderate parliamentarians, the leading families went out in stages. In some places they were kicked out of the county committee soon after the war, but managed to hold on as JPs until the purges of 1648–9. In others there was little change in the composition of the governing élite until well into the 1650s, the same families controlling both the county committee and the commissions of the peace. In some places the fragmentation of the parliamentarian cause led to repeated purges: of Presbyterians by Independents; of Commonwealth-men by Cromwellians; of Cromwellians by 'Good Old Cause' republicans. We ought not to exaggerate the extent to which local government was politicized—there were plenty of neutrals and opportunists, as well as genuine localists, everywhere. But whenever there was a shift in the national balance of power it was eventually reflected in the shires, as one minority of committed partisans was replaced by another. Some of those newcomers certainly did come from lower down the social scale, and it was to protect himself from such people that Fitzjames sought a seat in Parliament: 'to keep myself from being trampled upon by such kind of——things as the spirit of a gentleman can never brook', he told his father-in-law.[30]

One obvious result of the revolution was that no one could pretend any longer that there was a unified political culture to which everyone, deep down, subscribed, or that disagreements were merely the result of unfortunate misunderstandings. In the early months of 1641 there were many who, like Edward Pitt in Hampshire, could still utter the conventional platitudes of consensus politics. Pitt rejoiced that the Long Parliament had been summoned, for the 'better ordering of the affairs both of the church and state, whereof we have of late so much complained'. Parliament, he reminded the county's subsidy commissioners, was 'the ancient and laudable way that hath ever made the kingdom . . . happy'. But however passionately gentlemen of Pitt's moderate stamp might wish to preserve the old community harmony, they were inexorably driven into taking sides, and even those who managed to avoid doing so had only to look around them to see the lamentable results of strife and division. Moderates might maintain old friendships across the political divide—the correspondence between Sir Roger Burgoyne and Sir Ralph Verney provides a striking example—but although they might deplore the intolerance that surrounded them, they could not escape it.[31]

Let us again retrace our steps and explore the origins of these divisions. Much has been written on the subject of how Charles I got a party, but it may also help us to look at the process again as it affected a minor gentleman in the country. Ralph Ashton of Kirkby Hall in Yorkshire was one such minor gentleman, otherwise unremarkable, who left a few traces of his opinions in a commonplace book. We ought not to assume without reflection that just because he copied a text into his notebook he necessarily agreed with it. But when the overwhelming preponderance of entries in a given period clearly points in the same direction, I think it is reasonable to conclude that they reflect the general drift of the copyist's thinking. So what do we find in Ralph Ashton's commonplace book?[32]

What we find is someone who in the 1620s shared the anti-Court outlook that we have earlier encountered in Thomas Scott of Canterbury, but who by 1642 had become openly disenchanted with Parliament. In the early '20s Ashton copied down the famous pamphlet *Vox Populi*, by the other Thomas Scott (the puritan minister, not the Canterbury MP), as well as verse libels on the Spanish Match, and Eliot's speech in the stormy debate of 2 March 1629. Ten years later the entries suggest that Ashton was still hostile to the Court, but by now was blaming the bishops for the recent troubles. In October 1639 a Wakefield friend lent him a printed ballad, 'The Bishops' Bridles', which denounced the prelates' arrogance, oppression, and popish sympathies, and looked forward to the downfall of Laud ('your Lambeth lad'). Other anti-episcopal ballads follow in the commonplace book, as well as one attacking the abuses of the ecclesiastical courts. Entitled 'A dismal summons to the Doctors' Commons', this surveys the 'cageful of foul birds and beasts', the notaries, registers, and other such officials who 'match Machiavel in evil' and 'make God's house a den of thieves', and warns them that their days are numbered. Ashton also copied down the well-known 'God a-mercy, good Scot', and another violent libel against the bishops which began:

> Remember, brave Britons, the canons and the oath,
> The plots and the projects of the men of the cloth.
> Their tampering with Rome, and episcopal pride,
> Their speaking to alter religion beside.[33]

He also transcribed parliamentary speeches by Pym and Sir Benjamin Rudyard.

But Ashton lived in Yorkshire, in close proximity to the invading

Scots army, and this certainly affected his outlook. In 1640, alongside 'God a-mercy, good Scot', he also entered an anti-Scottish poem, and a list of Scottish demands on the inhabitants of County Durham for bread, meat, and other supplies. Ashton's distaste for the Scots appears to have made him rethink his position on the relationship of King and Parliament. His book contains the distinctly ambivalent poem (probably by John Cleveland) on Strafford's execution—'Here lies wise and valiant dust'—with its balanced lines, 'The prop and ruin of the state, | The Country's violent love and hate'.[34] By 1642 Ashton regarded Parliament, not the bishops, as the chief threat to stability and order. Some clever anagrams on the word 'Parliament' include 'I part al men', 'I trap al men', and 'A Pim rent al', and a mock petition to the King has the lines 'In all humility we crave | Our sovereign to be our slave'. Another verse libel satirizes recent parliamentary demands:

> Let us a consultation call
> Of able men, yet Roundheads all,
>   God knows wherefore . . .
>
> Let him be hanged that surplice wears
> Or tippet on their shoulders bears
>   The rags o' the Whore . . .
>
> Reform each University
> And therein let no learning be,
>   A great eyesore.

The libel continues with jabs at Calvinist intolerance ('shall any have free will but we?'), at root-and-branch enemies of the hierarchy ('Oh, that word sounds so servilely, | Let's have't no more'), and mechanic preachers ('Lest the Elect should go astray | Let cobblers teach the upright way'). It then suggests that the only obstacle to a political settlement is Pym's poverty:

> Next for the State, we think it fit
> That Mr Pym should govern it,
>   Were he not poor.

But the libellist quickly solves this problem: 'The money that's for Ireland writ, | Let him have it, every bit.' Finally, the King is told that Sir John Hotham will be ordered to give up Hull to him as soon as Charles 'please to resign your crown'. Reading Ashton's commonplace book makes it easier to understand the process by which former critics of the Court turned into royalists in 1642.[35]

Disenchantment with Parliament did not, however, turn Ashton into
a Cavalier firebrand. Like so many other rural gentlemen, he strove to
find a middle way, eagerly grasping at every possible sign of compromise. In the autumn of 1642 he wrote down the articles of the Yorkshire
pacification agreement, and after this had collapsed he added, in December, speeches by the Earl of Pembroke and Lord Brooke, for and
against accommodation. But as in so many of the other counties where
neutrality agreements were attempted, it was to no avail. In January
1643 Kirkby was plundered by the Roundheads and Ashton was briefly
imprisoned at Wakefield. After this experience his commonplace book
contains little more than the warrants of both sides for men and money,
along with occasional accounts of the fighting in Yorkshire.[36]

Ashton's apparent neutralism again reminds us that there always remained a large body of ideas shared by the gentry, even when they
found themselves on opposite sides. Earlier in this chapter we observed
the two Dorset knights, Sir Walter Erle and Sir John Strangways, going
off to prison in 1627 because of their resistance to the Forced Loan.
When war came in 1642 two things divided them: religion, and their
views about the nature of monarchy. The two problems were, of course,
closely connected: whether or not God's commands might be sufficiently compelling as to override even the sacred duty of obedience was
for them, as it was for so many others, the crucial issue. By the early
months of the Long Parliament, Erle's hatred of the Arminians had
become opposition to episcopacy itself. He seems to have taken literally
the recurrent alarms about popish conspiracies, and he supported the
Root-and-Branch petition. He was 'seldom out, when controversies in
religion were named', Edward Nicholas noted.[37] By 1645 he had become
a firm supporter of a Presbyterian establishment, regularly voting against
both Erastians and Independents, and supporting the motion that the
Presbyterian form of church government existed *jure divino*. He also
presented a succession of Presbyterians to Dorset livings.[38] Strangways,
on the other hand, while supporting the outlawing of Ship Money and
other illegalities of the Personal Rule, remained firmly attached to episcopacy and Common Prayer, and blamed Parliament for undermining
the whole frame of order when it abolished them. 'If we made a parity
in the church we must at last come to a parity in the Commonwealth',
he told the Commons in February 1641. Imprisoned in the Tower for
almost three years after the first civil war, he passed the time writing

some not very distinguished, yet still interesting, poetry, and making detailed notes on his readings in politics and religion.[39]

Strangways's commonplace book and poems suggest that he was a man of genuine, conventional, uncomplicated piety. He took copious notes on the Bible, recorded divine portents and prodigies from his readings in Sir Richard Baker's *Chronicle*, and composed his own prayers and precepts for the service of God. Early in his imprisonment he turned to the Book of Job for consolation, and did a verse rendering of the sixth chapter. Facing trial for treason, he brooded on his probable fate ·('And I myself foredoomed am to die'), and wrote another poem entitled 'A Meditation of Death'. The war had taught him some lessons about tolerance: only an 'ill cause' needed to be sustained by persecution, whereas 'truth upholdeth itself by mildness'. But his views on church government were at the opposite pole from Erle's. 'Novelty and alteration doth engender discord', he reflected, so episcopacy had to be preserved. It was 'an apostolical institution', justified by four General Councils, upheld by statute, and endorsed by respected continental divines of the reformed religion. He also defended ceremonies ('the hedge which guardeth the garden') and the observance of traditional holy days. Finally, although certainly no friend of the Catholics, he may have been less obsessed than Erle was by the alleged popish conspiracies of 1641.[40]

But for these profound religious differences accommodation between men like Erle and Strangways must surely have been possible, as many in Dorset thought it was going to be in the truce negotiations during the first winter of the war. Erle was an energetic, though not very successful, military commander in his county, and was also very active in the House of Commons, in which he supported the middle group policies of negotiations from strength. After the war, though, he became less militant, and by 1646 he was associated with the peace, or 'Presbyterian' faction.[41] Erle wanted a settlement that would establish presbytery, but also one that would preserve the authority of county magnates like himself. He was one of Parliament's commissioners to Charles I in 1647, stayed at Westminster when the Speakers and the 'Independents' fled to the Army at the end of July of that year, and was appointed to the Presbyterian Committee of Safety. In the following year he supported the negotiations with the King in the Isle of Wight and was imprisoned at Pride's Purge; although released after a fortnight, he never resumed his seat in the House.[42] On 12 December 1648, while he was in custody,

Sir William Waller and several other imprisoned members issued a statement of the secluded members' beliefs, the *Protestation at the King's Head*, so named for the inn in the Strand in which they had been confined. Erle undoubtedly endorsed its ringing platitudes about the rights and liberties of 'free born subjects of England', and its protests against the way those rights and liberties were now being violated by the Army; its invocation of the privileges of Parliament, the 'fundamental laws of the land', the subject's right not to be imprisoned without due process of law; and its rejection of any 'arbitrary and unlawful power', whether exercised by a king or an army.[43]

Except in the one respect already mentioned—the nature of monarchy—Strangways's views on politics and government do not appear to have been very different. At the heart of his position was a belief in the sanctity of English law. 'That person who keeps his oath, and obeys the law', he declared, 'is no delinquent', and, experienced Parliament-man that he was, he had no difficulty in marshalling an array of citations of statutes and other legal authorities to justify taking up arms for the King. He took particular pleasure in quoting his old parliamentary colleague Sir Edward Coke, 'the oracle of the law as they call him', whose works, he noted with equal relish, had been printed by order of the same Parliament that was now unjustly imprisoning royalists like Strangways. His jottings contain frequent reminders of the old debates of the 1620s; the familiar appeals to Magna Carta and assertions of immemorial custom. 'And so it hath been done in all parliaments from the beginning of parliaments', he says of the King's veto power; to support the King's authority over the militia he cites 'many statutes . . . and the practice of all times'. Again and again Strangways returns to the point that the royalist case rested on the sanctity of English law: 'For the maintenance of these laws we have fought and will fight again.' What other guide, he asks, 'had the subjects . . . to direct them, but the laws?'[44]

Strangways was well known before the wars as a defender of a lawful royal prerogative, but he was certainly not an advocate of absolute monarchy. He thus summed up the position of moderate royalists: 'We of the King's party do detest monopolies and Ship Money, and all the grievances of the people, as much as any man living. We do well know that our estates, lives, and fames are preserved by the laws, and that the King is bound by his laws.' The issues in 1645 were the same as in the pre-war years, except that it was now Parliament that was violating liberty and property, imprisoning people without due process, and imposing new and arbitrary taxes. Strangways's memory was sometimes curiously selective, as when he complained about the excise, loans, and the 'new impositions upon merchants' that Parliament had inflicted. These, he said, were 'monies raised several ways never used in this kingdom', conveniently forgetting that all three had already been used by the Stuart kings (Charles I had resorted to the excise in 1644), and that he had himself been imprisoned for resisting the 1627 Loan.[45] But he was deeply troubled by the possibility that a royalist victory might have led to absolute monarchy. 'If the King regain his crown by arms', he reflected in November 1646,

> Then we may thank ourselves for all our harms.
> For having so got all into his hands,
> He is made lord of all our lives and lands.
> And we our laws and liberties (which cost
> Our fathers so much English blood) have lost.

The only solution was a compromise settlement, though the war had made that virtually impossible. Strangways's poems contain many references to the horrors of war (his house at Abbotsbury had been blown up in one particularly bloody incident), and he notes how the royalist cause had been sullied by its leaders' inability to control plundering soldiers:

> Thus a good cause ill managed gets the name
> Of a bad cause; and merits equal blame.
> And justly so. For in conclusion
> Twas this brought England to confusion.[46]

So Strangways was no absolutist—'we love parliaments', he said with perfect sincerity—and his position in the 1640s closely resembled the stance he had taken twenty years earlier. Yet at the end of the day he took the opposite side from Erle, partly, as we have seen, because of his religious loyalties, but also because he had a very different conception of monarchy from the one held by his Dorset rival. Erle believed in monarchy too, but his religious views made it possible for him to use force against the King, on the argument that a ruler who had fallen into the hands of papists and malignants had to be rescued from them, if necessary by violent means. For Strangways there could be no such justification for rebellion, primarily because he did not accept the theory of the separation of the King's two bodies. 'The body politic', he declared, 'cannot operate but by the body natural'; the King's 'politic capacity is not to be severed from the natural'.[47] The King's powers resided in a person, not an institution, and this invalidated Parliament's claim to be fighting 'for King and Parliament' even when fighting against him. Summarizing the essential difference between the two sides, Strangways stressed the conventional royalist claim that 'the King is king by inherent birthright', not by his holding the office in trust for the people. His version of the royalist case includes all the standard arguments: that by law the King possesses the militia power, the negative voice, and the supreme authority over the church, and that subjects were bound to come to his assistance in time of war. Parliaments had often passed bad laws, so it was essential to preserve the royal veto to guard against parliamentary error; he noted that in one Elizabethan Parliament the Queen had refused to accept forty-eight bills that had passed both Houses.[48]

While a royalist victory might establish a monarchy with unacceptably absolute powers, a parliamentarian one threatened an unending vista of lawlessness, disorder, and the undermining of liberty and property. Parliaments, Strangways argued, ought to be held in a 'grave and peaceable manner, without tumults'. But in 1641 and 1642 the Commons had encouraged 'multitudes of the meaner sort of people to come to Westminster to cry for justice'. He had in fact himself been a victim of the mob violence in the autumn of 1641. Arriving at Westminster one November evening, he was surrounded by 'above 200 sworded and staved', who pressed him to vote 'for the putting down of the bishops'. Strangways told them he would listen only to a lawful petition, and angrily protested to the Speaker: parliamentary privilege, he declared, was 'utterly broken if men might not come in safety to give their votes freely'. Once again we are reminded that religion was not the only issue that divided the nation in 1642. The royalists were the party of episcopacy and Common Prayer, but they were also, in Brian Manning's words, the 'party of order'.[49]

When during the civil war men like Strangways complained of Parliament's violations of the ancient laws, they were in effect restating positions they had taken in the 1620s, when the crown and its ministers were the source of the threat to liberty. Constitutional royalists had no desire to repeat the mistakes of that earlier decade: forced loans and Ship Money were still repudiated, Buckingham still a figure to be execrated, not emulated. In 1652 the Somerset Cavalier, Edmund Wyndham, in exile at Boulogne, told his friend Gervase Holles a long story about the ghost of Buckingham's father, who in 1628 had appeared to an acquaintance of Wyndham's named Nicholas Towse. The ghost wanted

Towse to communicate some fatherly advice to Buckingham: he should dismiss the false friends who were leading him astray—Bishop Laud was especially named—and 'do some popular act in the ensuing Parliament'. Laud, the spectre continued, was destined to be 'the author of very great trouble to this kingdom'. Towse duly passed on these messages to Buckingham, but the Duke, as we all know, rejected them and was consequently murdered, a fate which the ghost also foretold. That Wyndham was still pondering these matters in 1652 and still lamenting Charles I's pursuit of policies pressed on him by Laud and Buckingham, is one more illustration of the constitutionalist outlook of many royalists during the Interregnum.[50]

The propaganda exchanges between royalists and parliamentarians suggest that the war had done surprisingly little to change either the conceptual framework of gentry politics, or the language in which it was expressed. Each side claimed to represent legitimate masculine authority; each denounced the other for having permitted an inverted, unnatural rule by women. There was a continuing resort to sexual metaphors. Royalists portrayed their enemies as led by cuckolds like Essex and Fairfax; parliamentarians stressed courtly effeminacy and Charles I's alleged subordination to Henrietta Maria. There was a nice exchange on this point in December 1643. 'The Parliament', the royalist *Aulicus* sneered, 'is ruled by the citizens, and the citizens by their wives': as usual, both the social and the gender hierarchies have been subverted. Not so, the parliamentarian *Scotish Dove* responded: 'the citizens obey the Parliament, and the men command their wives; at London women rule not . . . as they do at Oxford.'[51] In the political language used by the gentry this is a transitional period: both vocabulary and metaphors are less gendered than in the 1620s, but more so than they were to be after the Restoration. We shall find in the next chapter, however, that this kind of language was still much more common in propaganda directed towards the common people.

Both sides could plausibly claim to be fighting for the Ancient Constitution—for Liberty and Property—and the revolutionaries continued to make this claim even after they had purged the House of Commons, abolished the Lords, executed the King, and declared that the people were 'under God, the origin of all just power'. The well-known legend on the republic's new Great Seal, in 1649, read: 'In the First Year of Freedom, by God's Blessing *Restored*' (my emphasis). Yet on both sides the earlier idealism collapsed into cynical pragmatism and opportunism:

on the Parliament's into the self-interest and corruption of the Rump; on the royalists' into the alcoholic nihilism that prefigured the atmosphere of the Restoration Court; on both into a realistic, Hobbesian, acceptance of *de facto* power. Derek Hirst has shown that in many places even the godly's old enthusiasm for moral reformation was waning. Royalists and Presbyterians alike found themselves able to take the Engagement to the Commonwealth with the sort of mental reservations that twenty years earlier they would have believed only papists capable of. By 1655 Sir John Strangways himself was following the fashion and putting self-interest above principle. Imprisoned on suspicion of conspiring against the Protector, he wrote a poem, 'Upon a private and retired life', that is packed with moral backsliding. Having failed to turn out in Penruddock's recent rebellion, he decided that it was futile to try to regain 'lost credit' by quixotic actions that would 'greatly prejudice my ease | And might my safety hazard too, perhaps'. It was 'a safe way in this distempered time' to stay in the shadows, whereas by coming out into the sun, 'Tis ten to one, but I shall be undone'.[52]

For some members of the political and intellectual élite the English revolution led to a heightened religious consciousness, an even keener sense of their role in the great cosmic drama of good and evil. This was certainly the case with John Milton. But for every John Hutchinson or Gilbert Pickering who migrated across the entire godly spectrum and obtained spiritual sustenance at each stage of their journey, there were others like Richard Ingoldsby, Edward Mountagu, and Alexander Popham, who went the other way. Ingoldsby had been a regicide in 1649, but before the Protectorate was over he was denounced as one who could 'neither pray nor preach'. By 1660 Mountagu's views on uniformity and set forms of prayer would have endeared him to Queen Elizabeth. Politics was not about reforming society, it was about place and promotion. 'We will rise together', he told his faithful secretary, Samuel Pepys. It is the authentic voice of 1660.[53]

Mountagu's transformation from advocate of laymen's preaching to Restoration conservative is a fine illustration of how and why so many of the gentry who before 1642 had supported godly reformation had by 1660 turned their backs on it. The process was a gradual one: some, like Ashton, lost whatever earlier illusions they might have had even before war broke out; others, like Denzil Holles, did so during the fighting; yet others, like Ingoldsby, Popham, and Mountagu, at various times in the 1650s. The smouldering hostility to Parliament evident among large numbers of the country gentry in 1647 and 1648 suggests that a restoration of monarchy might well have been possible even at that time if a less duplicitous king than Charles I had been available. Mainstream parliamentarians had been just as attached to monarchy, patriarchy, and social order as their royalist enemies. At the proclamation of Charles II in May 1660 the town clerk of Presbyterian Dorchester spoke of the 'world of confusions' and 'unheard of governments' from which they had now so happily escaped. There is no doubt that he meant it.[54]

But by now many of the gentry equated even moderate puritanism with disorder and rebellion, and consequently repudiated the populism that their predecessors—Thomas Scott, for example—had adopted in the 1620s. In those far-off days they had been able to assume that their tenants and neighbours shared the same preoccupations with liberty, property, and Protestantism, and meant the same things by those terms as they themselves did. The civil war convinced them that they were wrong, and that putting arms in the hands of the common people led inevitably to the destruction of order and stability. The arguments against the wider franchise made by Ireton and Cromwell at Putney were, at bottom, the same as those of Denzil Holles in his memoirs and Sir John Strangways in his commonplace book—that only those with a significant, propertied stake in the kingdom could enjoy full membership in the political nation, could be recognized as genuinely 'freeborn English-men'. But there is a paradox here. By 1659 it was the royalists, not the parliamentarians, who were appealing to the people in the name of 'Liberty and Property'. In May 1660 it was Sir John Strangways, not Sir Walter Erle, who could ride through the streets of Sherborne and receive—and give back—the triumphant acclamations of the crowd.[55] 'Liberty and Property' would continue to be a resonant slogan for one section of the political nation long after 1660. Strangways's ruminations in the Tower on episcopacy, law, and monarchy remind us of another, equally durable one: 'Church and King'. Both were to be central components of the ideology of propertied and freeborn Englishmen for more than a century to come.

5

THE MAN IN THE MOON
LOYALTY AND LIBEL IN POPULAR
POLITICS, 1640–1660

We have been contemplating the civil war experiences of freeborn, propertied Englishmen: in short, the gentry. But what of the others? Historians have generally given us a choice between two apparently plausible, though sharply contrasting, versions of popular involvement in the troubles of 1640–60. One is a variant of the traditional 'deference' thesis about seventeenth-century popular political behaviour: that the lower orders, having no firm opinions of their own, took sides only when compelled, or paid, to do so. Armies were raised either by the nobility and gentry calling out their obedient, forelock-tugging tenants, or were recruited as mercenaries from those who, as Thomas Hobbes described the common people, 'would have taken any side for pay and plunder'. Left to themselves, ordinary folk would have been either cannon-fodder, or at best, ignorant neutrals.[1] Not so many years ago historians could still repeat without irony the story of the Yorkshire countryman crossing Marston Moor one July day in 1644 and asking 'What, be they two fallen out then?' when told to get out of the way because the armies of King and Parliament were about to fight a battle. The apparently innocent question, if it was ever uttered, surely reflects the typical lower-class mockery of pompous people in authority (army officers, for instance) rather than rustic ignorance. More recent accounts show more sophistication, but are still based on the supposition that the preferred stance of ordinary men and women was one of neutrality during the wars, and of a conservative localism both then and afterwards.[2]

Another, even more familiar, approach to the subject of popular politics during these years starts from the premiss that the common people of England *were* actively involved in the civil war, and that when they took sides they did so overwhelmingly on the parliamentarian side.[3] According to this theory, the wars released a pent-up popular demand for radical change, for religious toleration and political democracy, that had been suppressed for centuries. Historians who have espoused this view have generally assumed that popular politics after the civil war therefore primarily meant the politics of the Levellers and the radical sects. Earlier Whig historical orthodoxy paid little attention to them, but after languishing in neglect or contempt for almost two centuries, the Levellers were rediscovered in the late-Victorian period. C. H. Firth's edition of the *Clarke Papers* brought the Putney Debates to the attention of scholars, and the ideas of 'Buff Coat' and 'Bedfordshire Man'—of the ordinary, hitherto faceless Englishman—entered the mainstream of historical discourse. At about the same time G. P. Gooch and the German socialist Eduard Bernstein both gave the Levellers a prominent place in their writings, though it was not until 1916, with T. C. Pease's *The Leveller Movement*, that a whole book was devoted to them. Since the 1930s editions of Leveller tracts, general studies of the movement, and biographies of its leaders have appeared in profusion.[4] The religious sects, on the other hand, had to wait until after the upheavals of the 1960s to receive their historical due, which came in Christopher Hill's *The World Turned Upside Down*, with its brilliant evocation of the mental world of the radicals, who turned religion, law, and morality on their heads.[5]

The authors of these works have generally assumed that the Levellers and the even more radical groups that succeeded them—Diggers, Ranters, Quakers, and so on—expressed the typical aspirations of the common people when they were allowed to speak for themselves, as the disruption of government and the breakdown of pre-war censorship now enabled them to do. The aspirations of the politicized commoners, at any rate: those who were neither Levellers nor radical sectaries were generally ignored as pre-political. A distinction was usually made, however, between political and religious language. The religious language of the sects might be mystical and emotional, but the political language of the Levellers, however revolutionary their ideas, was essentially rational, stressing natural rights, religious toleration, and the historical theory of the Norman Yoke. It is therefore not surprising that in the twentieth century they have received the bulk of the historical attention.[6]

Each of these interpretations of popular politics contains important insights, but, as I have argued elsewhere, neither provides an entirely satisfactory account of the involvement of the English common people in the civil wars and revolution. We need, among other things, to recognize that the contours of political behaviour varied from region to region, and to find some satisfactory way of conceptualizing these variations, though this is perhaps not the place to reopen that particular argument.[7]

After my earlier remarks about pre-war popular politics, however, the reader may not be surprised to find that I regard the common folk as having been less apathetic about civil-war politics than historians of the former type have sometimes depicted them. It is one thing to question whether they enthusiastically welcomed the 'world turned upside down' that resulted from the revolution. It is quite another to dismiss them as apathetic neutrals, conservative localists, who as far as they could sat out the civil war. They rioted in London in 1640 and 1641 and on many later occasions; they combined in great popular uprisings like the one in north Somerset in August 1642; and thousands of them were actively involved in the civil wars, either as parliamentarians, royalists, or neutralist Clubmen.[8] During these unsettled decades the English people were neither predominately radical nor universally apathetic and conservative. Popular political culture, in fact, contained elements of both attitudes, and this fact explains both the dynamism of the sects and their eventual failure.

It would be a mistake to ignore the conservatism of the Clubmen and of the rural population even in many parts of England that were not affected by the Club outbreaks. It would be no less a mistake to deny the significance of the radical ideas of the Levellers and their successors in the sects. But something else is missing from both of the conflicting interpretations of popular politics that we have been discussing: the extent to which the thinking of virtually all English men and women was influenced by conceptions of gender. Since the publication of Phyllis Mack's *Visionary Women* we can no longer ignore the ways in which the histories of the radical sects were shaped by this fundamentally important historical category.[9] Many of the most prominent of the early Quakers were women who found the message of the 'inner light' infinitely empowering, much to the embarrassment of their male counterparts. But even those like George Fox, whose experiences with the likes of Martha Simmonds made him deeply distrustful of feminine enthusiasm, nevertheless stood for a turning of the world upside down that had disturbing implications for the relations between men and women, as well as between the propertied and the poor.

The 'visionary women' of Mack's title require us to look at the radicals of the English revolution in a new way. The vocabulary of inversion that the women prophets used reminds us that, as in the years before the civil war, there was more than one political language available to the common people. It is important to note that it was available to people on both sides of the political divide, to conservatives as well as radicals. Mack's remarkable book did not emerge from nowhere. Since the 1960s historians—often influenced by anthropologists and literary scholars—have been exploring an alternative popular vocabulary, the one so heavily infused with notions of symbolic inversion that we have encountered in earlier chapters. Being historians, they have naturally often disagreed about its meaning. Was the carnival image of a 'world turned upside down' a stimulus to rebellion, an affirmation of an alternative moral, sexual, and social order? Or was it merely a safety-valve which, by permitting a brief moment of festive licence, reinforced the very values that it pretended to subvert? We can take our pick from the functionalist interpretation of the anthropologists, the safety-valve thesis advanced by Max Gluckman in his studies of the societies of southern Africa, or from the concept of liberating revolt derived from Mikhael Bahktin's famous work on Rabelais. Not surprisingly, in the turbulent years around 1970 the latter approach predominated: a good many people felt that 'after so many centuries of praising order, [it was] time to praise disorder a little'. We are in the mental climate of Hill's *World Turned Upside Down*.[10]

It has recently been argued that the Ranters, the most notorious of the radical groups, were no more than figments of the fertile imaginations of conservative propagandists. In this view, the image of the Ranter was a cultural construction fashioned by preachers and propagandists, people who instinctively thought in inversionary terms, all the more so when overwhelmed by the atmosphere of 'moral panic' that followed the collapse of their world in 1649.[11] No doubt the importance of the Ranters was exaggerated at the time, and has been later by historians, but the argument that they did not exist at all is not convincing; nor can the Diggers, Quakers, and other sects who in one way or another tried to turn the world upside down be easily disposed of. It is true, though, that rebellion and liberation were not always the messages sent by the rituals of inversion that were so deeply embedded in popular political culture. Natalie Davis has shown that in France the charivari could convey a double message: for some of the participants or observers (particularly women) it may have had subversive implications, but for others the ritual affirmed traditional, patriarchal values.[12] It will be recalled that symbols of inversion were used in many grain and enclosure riots in early seventeenth-century England, but nearly always with a conservative purpose: to preserve an ancient, customary order threatened by greedy landlords and capitalists.[13]

Most of the pre-war disorders just referred to involved rituals, games, at worst riots—the shaming of an errant married couple, a Shrove Tuesday attack on a brothel, a few days of cheerful May Games or Christmas misrule, a more serious week of destroying hedges or sluices. Commenting on the riots in London in May 1640, Lord Conway thought that 'the prentices will make but a Shrove Tuesday business of it'.[14] But this was before things became serious. By 1649 it was clearly no 'Shrove Tuesday business': the King had been executed, monarchy and House of Lords abolished, the patriarchal order threatened, the whole society apparently sliding into chaos. How, we may ask, did people employ the familiar symbols of inversion then? Did they respond with joyful cries of Rabelaisian abandon and celebrate their release from the bondage of traditional authority, or did they pine wistfully for a restoration of the old stability? We certainly should not ignore the uninhibited rebelliousness of those depicted by Christopher Hill and, in a very different way, by Phyllis Mack. Yet the fact remains that in the end the revolution failed; throughout these years the outlook of the majority of the English people remained profoundly conservative. It is obviously time to take another look at the subject.

During the civil war metaphors of inversion, both verbal and visual, were even more commonly used than in earlier years; images of an inverted world frequently appear in woodcuts decorating the propaganda prints of both sides, almost always with negative connotations.[15] And if the political and social worlds were being turned upside down, so too, inevitably, was the sexual world. Both sides resorted to sexual slanders in their propaganda, with the intention of discrediting their enemies' claims to legitimate authority. Essex, Parliament's original commander, was an easy royalist target because of his youthful humiliation at the hands of Frances Howard: a husband who could neither satisfy nor control his wife (and was the victim of an almost classic 'woman on top' relationship) was surely disqualified from military leadership. The Parliament's journalists, needless to say, were not too scrupulous to retaliate. In January 1644 *Mercurius Britanicus* responded to a recent story in the royalist *Aulicus* about a Roundhead prisoner who had been caught committing bestiality. *Britanicus* dismissed the story, arguing that the notoriously immoral Cavaliers were far more likely to be prone to this kind of sin, and suggesting that royalists

may do it as lawfully as the Ladies of Honour may keep stallions and monkeys, and their bishops she-goats and ganymedes, for they make nothing of such prodigious fornications; they make nothing of Sodomy and Gomorrahism, especially your Italianated Lords, and your hot Privy Councillors who have seen fashions abroad, as Dorset the Earl, that hath travelled to Venice for his sins . . . But of all sinners, your Cathedral men are the worst, some of your Prebends make nothing of sinning with the little singing-boys after an Anthem.[16]

The passage nicely combines some long-standing 'Country' and puritan prejudices: against the Court, the aristocracy, and foreign countries (especially Catholic Italy) as devoted to every imaginable, and some unimaginable, kinds of vice; against Laudian clergy and their ritualistic practices as being also somehow bound up with homosexuality. So the language of sexual inversion was as common after 1640 as it had been earlier in the seventeenth century. A survey of some of the many ways in which it was used in popular journalism may suggest some further conclusions about its significance, for the authors of the newsbooks, certainly, but also possibly for the type of reader to whom the newspapers were directed.

Evidence of this kind is so plentiful that the best course is to choose one source for a case-study. Much of this chapter will therefore take the form of a reading of a weekly entitled *The Man in the Moon*, written by a certain John Crouch, though I shall also be quoting from other newsbooks of the period. As noted in the introductory chapter, we cannot take such material at face value, as direct evidence for what the people who read it thought and believed, and in due course we shall have to return to the problems that this raises. But let us first look at Crouch's newsbook, and see what we can make of it.

The first issue of *The Man in the Moon* hit the London Streets on 16 April 1649, proclaiming its intention to unmask 'a world of knavery under the sun, both in the Parliament, the Council of State, the Army, the City, and the Country, with intelligence from all parts of England, Scotland, and Ireland'.[17] During its brief lifetime of just over a year the paper did little to fulfil the second of these promises; no one can have read it for its news coverage, which was idiosyncratic in the extreme. But it certainly detected, or invented, plenty of scandals at the highest levels of the recently established republic. Its choice of targets, and the vocabulary and metaphors it employed, may perhaps help us to enter the mental world of one segment of the political nation at the middle of the seventeenth century.

The prospects for a new royalist newspaper were not very promising. The English press, as far as domestic news is concerned, had been born less than ten years earlier, when the Long Parliament's encroachments on royal power led to the virtual collapse of censorship. The outbreak of civil war soon stimulated a proliferation of weekly newspapers, as Grub Street writers eagerly responded to the insatiable appetite for news shown by literate Londoners. Thanks to the compulsive collecting habits of the bookseller George Thomason, vast numbers of these papers have been preserved. They are primitive and highly mendacious, but they cover all points of the political spectrum, from the left-wing (and strikingly misnamed) *The Moderate*, through mainstream parliamentarian papers like *The Kingdomes Weekly Intelligencer*, to royalist ones like *The Man in the Moon*. In the spring and summer of 1649 half-a-dozen clandestine Cavalier papers succeeded in defying Parliament's renewed attempts to control the press: several of them, like *Mercurius Pragmaticus*, generating pirated rivals.[18] Most were suppressed when a more stringent censorship law was passed in September, but *The Man in the Moon* survived with only a few brief interruptions, cheerfully dodging government agents until it too disappeared in June 1650.

If the publishing situation in April 1649 was fraught with danger for royalists, the political situation was worse. In January the victorious Parliament, purged by the Army of its moderate elements, had beheaded King Charles I in front of his own Banqueting Hall. The monarchy, the frame of England's government since time immemorial, had vanished at the stroke of an executioner's axe, and with it went the pathetic remnant of the House of Lords; the bishops had gone already. The hierarchies of church and state had been decapitated, all, as the regicide High Court of Justice proclaimed, in the name of 'the free people of England'. In truth, the regicides' claim to represent the people was not an impressive one: the men brought to power by the revolution were a handful of committed ideologues supported by a larger number of conforming opportunists. They had the support of radical puritans in and outside the Army—people inspired by a vision of the godly new Jerusalem which it was their duty, they believed, to impose on the unregenerate multitude. But they too were a minority, and some of them, like the Levellers, were convinced that the Parliament had betrayed the cause of religious and political liberty for which they had taken up arms. But the oligarchy at Westminster had the sword in their hands and the levers of power at their disposal. Charles I, as the 'royal martyr' now gaining an esteem he had never enjoyed in his lifetime, was dead; his son, the youthful Charles II, a penurious exile. The world of politics had indeed been turned upside down.[19]

Almost any of the royalist papers would have served my purpose, but I have chosen *The Man in the Moon* because it presents its conservative message in so conveniently extreme a form, and in somewhat more 'popular' language than its competitors. Not much is known about its author, John Crouch, but Lois Potter tells us that he was one of a large family of printers and booksellers, and that he drifted into the royalist literary underworld when opportunity beckoned after the civil war. His printer, Edward Crouch, may have been his brother, and Humphrey Crouch, a prolific ballad-maker, was probably also related.[20] *The Man in the Moon* was suppressed and John Crouch imprisoned in June 1650, but he soon got out and in 1652 began a new series of weeklies which pretended to avoid politics altogether, and were written, he said, only to 'create laughter': *Mercurius Democritus* (subtitled 'A Perfect Nocturnall', parodying the respectable *Perfect Diurnall*), *The Laughing Mercury*, and *Mercurius Fumigosus*.

Historians have generally dismissed these papers as frivolous and pornographic, which they certainly were, but they were also almost as subversive of republican respectability as the more openly political *Man in the Moon*. All of them lament that truth, honour, and morality have vanished from the earth:

> The world grows bad, as she grows old,
> Poor honesty lies a-dying;
> Plain-dealing's sick, her bell hath tolled,
> Religion faints with crying.

Everything we read is lies, so in what way are Crouch's admitted lies— about monsters and marvels, about naval battles fought miles inland— any worse than the official ones? The moral is obvious:

> Drink, swear and rant, and cast off care,
> Who knows what comes hereafter?
> 'Tis slavish gods or man to fear,
> Hang sorrow, welcome laughter.

But there is a political message here. In spite of his cynicism, Crouch's stories uphold a very traditional moral order, and his instances of sexual transgressions nearly always involve hypocritical puritans or women who have rebelled against masculine authority. He invents a new sect, the 'sisterhood of the Tumblers', who 'exercise on their backs in many obscure alleys', once again exploiting the widespread belief in the sexual duplicity of the godly, and the morally destructive consequences of toleration.[21]

The Man in the Moon was certainly more *explicitly* political than Crouch's later humour magazines. But all of them stem from an old tradition of popular literature—that of the jest-books, ballads, popular satires and anecdotes produced by such early Stuart hack writers as Samuel Rowlands and John Taylor the 'water poet'—now being given a political slant by the passions aroused during the English revolution. The ballads teem with inversion: they are full of knaves and fools, termagent and unfaithful wives and their henpecked, cuckolded husbands. These stock comic figures—the products, Jim Sharpe has suggested, of 'a patriarchal bad dream'—fight endless skirmishes in the eternal battle of the sexes.[22] In an age which made no sharp distinction between the public and the private spheres—which assumed a direct correspondence between authority in the family and authority in the state—it was easy for this mode of writing to become politicized. Indeed, in some ways it always had been: Thomas Cogswell points out that the more scurrilous pamphlets and newsbooks were in effect successors of the older manuscript libels and ballads now surfacing into print and going public.[23]

That *The Man in the Moon* was aimed at a more down-market readership than that of the other royalist weeklies is clear from both its price and its content. It sold for a penny, half the price of its competitors and well within the reach of the average craftsman. David Cressy estimates that during this period at least 70 per cent of male artisans in London were literate, so that there was always a large potential readership.[24] The paper's content was directed to a popular, male audience, emphasizing scandalous anecdotes about people in authority, and written in a familiar, conversational style. After the opening lines of doggerel verse which summarize the main themes of the issue, it is Crouch's habit to buttonhole the reader, drawing him—and it is, surely, him rather than her—into the scene of folly he is about to describe. 'Nay, faith, goodman', he begins his second issue; 'What, all mad?' he enquires at the start of a later one. His pages are sprinkled with familiar proverbs: 'many hands make light work', 'pride goeth before, and destruction follows after', for example. There are snatches of popular songs—'The Clean Contrary Way', 'Hey then, Up go we'—biblical allusions like the Gadarene swine and the writing on the wall at Belshazzar's feast. There is plenty of smut—in his study of civil war journalism Joseph Frank pronounces Crouch 'the smuttiest newsman' of his time. Crouch was evidently writing for that middling group of London artisans, journeymen, and apprentices who were part of what Peter Burke has called 'the chapbook culture': people 'who had gone to school but not for long'.[25]

Such people would have found *The Man in the Moon* easy to read and simple to understand. To begin with, they would have had no difficulty in decoding the paper's title. The Man in the Moon was a familiar figure in folklore and nursery tales, the old man banished to the moon for gathering sticks on a Sunday. So Crouch immediately announces his anti-puritan stance: puritans were notorious sabbatarians. With his lantern, dog, and bush of thorns the Man in the Moon shows up, of course, in Bottom's play in *A Midsummer Night's Dream*, and Crouch uses all these metaphorical effects. His lantern shines through the darkness of republican England, lighting the way for royalists engulfed by regicide tyranny. He also has his 'bush' (the sign outside a door that indicated an alehouse), and when government agents raid his printing premises he jeers that they have merely mistaken 'the bush for the man'. And he has his faithful dog, Towzer, who routinely lifts his leg at government proclamations, and is the source of many edifying demonstrations of loyalty, unlike the 'whelps at Westminster' who had betrayed their master, Charles I.[26]

There are, of course, many other examples of the Man-in-the-Moon theme in the literature of the earlier seventeenth century, besides those in Shakespeare's *Dream*. In some we naturally find the connection be-tween the moon and lunacy, with the Man in the Moon presiding over a world of madness and inversion. Such references were familiar, too, from traditional festivals. In the 1551 revels at Edward VI's court, the Lord of Misrule made his entrance 'as a king coming out of the moon'.[27] The Man in the Moon, then, is one of those 'things that are not' so central to irony, parody, and paradox. Crouch's readers would also have picked up the obvious echo of the most famous of all civil war songs, Martin Parker's 'When the King Enjoys His Own Again', in which there are the lines, 'The Man in the Moon may wear out his shoon | By running after Charles's Wain'. The image mixes astronomy and politics: Charles's Wain was a constellation, but no one could miss the reference to the King. So Crouch was proclaiming his allegiance in a way that everyone could recognize. He speaks of coming down from the moon to bring news from Charles's Wain, and in another issue again plays with the metaphor: it will take Charles's Wain to defeat the rebels.[28]

So, then, to the content of *The Man in the Moon*. Most of it is royalist propaganda of the crudest kind, which on the face of it tells us no more about the views of those who bought it than the political stance of the *Sun* does about those of its readers in the 1990s. The message is one of loyalty to legitimate authority mixed with violent polemic against the republican government and scandalous caricatures of its leaders. The regicides are ravening wolves, carrion crows feeding on blood, merciless cannibals. They are 'Hell's garrison at Westminster', 'Hell-hatched infidels, unparalleled inhuman monsters', 'the Devil's scullions and turnspits'.[29] They are 'Machiavellian knaves', their treasons worse than those of Judas, Nero, Ravaillac, and Guy Fawkes put together. What Fawkes had failed to do (destroy King and Parliament), Crouch notes in a scornful aside on the official ceremonies on Gunpowder Treason Day, 'they themselves had really acted'.[30]

The regicides also provided Crouch with many choice individual targets, and the way in which he attacked them may, I think, take us a bit further into the mental world of his readers. Some of his caricatures were drawn from the common stock of royalist propaganda, and would have been familiar to readers of *Mercurius Pragmaticus* and other competing Cavalier weeklies. There is the 'shit-breeched alderman', Thomas Atkin, so called from an unhappy accident that occurred when he was terrified by a volley fired by his own troops during the civil war.[31] There is Sir Henry Mildmay, a specialist in adultery, Crouch says, because he had been pimp for Buckingham in the 1620s: once again we observe the royalists' contempt for the Duke's memory. Mildmay was thought to be a particularly despicable traitor because he had served Charles I as Master of the Jewel House and then deserted him. In Crouch's pages he always seems to be giving jewels to his wenches.[32] There is the loud-mouthed Earl of Pembroke. 'Philip the fool, the Junta's jester', a splendid target for derision because he had abandoned his peerage and got himself elected to the House of Commons. Pembroke was widely ridiculed in the popular press: one of Crouch's competitors has him swearing 'God damn him, Democracy! Democracy!' more or less to order.[33] Another favourite character is the republican Henry Marten, well known for the libertine behaviour which prompted Cromwell to denounce him as a whoremaster. This 'lecherous goat' seems to spend most of his time in brothels, and in virtually every mention of him there is some obvious *double entendre*. Marten was known to have some sympathy for the Levellers, so in April 1649 he is said to 'stand up stiff' for them.[34]

Most of this is, of course, sheer invention, or coarse exaggeration of known weaknesses like Pembroke's bad language or Marten's philandering. Still, bearing in mind that several other newswriters were churning out similar stories, it suggests that there was a considerable market for this kind of thing. Occasionally Crouch borrows material from earlier sources in a way that shows how closely his paper was involved in the traditional chapbook culture. He has a funny story about the radical preacher, Hugh Peter, getting his fingers caught in a mousetrap when groping for the key under the door of a married woman he is trying to seduce. This was an old tale beloved of ballad-makers, with no previous connection to Peter, but used as recently as 1647 by Crouch's kinsman Humphrey. Crouch is particularly cruel to Peter's wife, asserting that she had kept a brothel in Amsterdam, and making several scathing references to her (real) mental illness.[35]

Two individuals receive particularly savage treatment: the generals Cromwell and Fairfax. Like any good cartoonist, and in common with other royalist writers, Crouch focuses on Cromwell's most striking physical characteristic, his prominent nose. Cromwell is 'Nose Almighty', 'his Noseship', or simply 'Nose'. Sometimes this is combined with sneers at Cromwell's allegedly plebeian ancestry, as in 'King Copper-nose, Beelzebub's chief ale-brewer'—Oliver's father was said to have been a brewer at one time, and earlier ancestors had also been in the trade.[36] The suggestion that Cromwell, like the rest of the regicides, was a social upstart occurs repeatedly, but sexual slurs are less common than for some of the others. Less common, but not entirely absent. Cromwell is said to have been run out of Ely for fathering bastards, and Crouch makes up a story of his being wounded in the groin during the fighting in Ireland, adding that Oliver was particularly vulnerable in that part of the body because he had previously had the pox. But it is Cromwell's ambition that really excites Crouch's interest, and once again he embellishes a character trait that was being regularly exploited by other royalist writers. Cromwell is repeatedly accused of aiming at the throne for himself: already he is 'King Noll', 'King Oliver the Devil's godson', even 'God Noll'.[37]

The other general, Fairfax, was nominally Cromwell's superior, but by 1649 he was becoming a mere figurehead. He had refused to have anything to do with the trial of the King, showed a conspicuous lack of enthusiasm for the republic, and in June 1650 resigned his commission rather than fight the Presbyterian Scots, who had allied themselves with the exiled Charles II.[38] Crouch at first seems unaware of Fairfax's disaffection, but a few hints of it begin to appear early in 1650; until then he regards Fairfax as no better than the regicides, likening him to the traitor Guy Fawkes and often punning on the name 'Fair-Faux'. On other matters Crouch's aim is surer. Fairfax was a good soldier, but was regarded as otherwise not being terribly bright. So he is 'Thom-ass',

'Tom Simpleton', his 'fool-ship', and 'his Oxilence'. He is said to sign anything his officers put before him—again a charge with some basis in fact—very proud of being able to write his own name.[39]

In 1650 Fairfax suddenly becomes 'Tom Ladle', or 'his Ladleship'. The nickname once more brings us back to the connection that we have often observed between familial and political authority. Disorder in the family, it was believed, would lead inevitably to disorder in the state, so there were compelling reasons to uphold the authority of parents over children, and of husbands over wives.[40] A common method of doing so in cases of marital disagreement was by the shaming ritual of the charivari, or skimmington ride. Let us remind ourselves of the central feature of the skimmington. English skimmingtons were almost invariably pro- voked by the discovery that a wife was beating her husband, thus invert- ing the proper order of authority. When one of these subversive instances of female assertiveness was uncovered, a procession making 'rough music' (by beating saucepans, ringing handbells, blowing horns, and so forth) would proceed to the offenders' house, in a procession headed by a theatrical representation of the incident. Two neighbours, carried on a horse, donkey, or pole, acted out the beating, to the accompaniment of much raucous derision from the crowd. The 'husband' rode backwards, in the position of humiliation, while the 'wife' (played by a man in women's clothes) beat him with a skimming ladle—used by women in the manufacture of cheese and butter.[41]

A ladle! The nickname 'Tom Ladle', probably already well known to many of Crouch's readers from a popular chapbook story[42] lampoons Fairfax as the metaphorical target of a skimmington ride: as a man henpecked and beaten by his wife. To make the point even clearer, Crouch invents a skimmington procession in Smithfields, in which the General and his Lady are being ridiculed by Londoners. It was generally assumed that the 'woman on top' who defied her husband's familial authority by beating him would automatically defy his sexual authority by being unfaithful, and so, sure enough, we find Fairfax described as the 'cuckold general' (just like Essex, his predecessor in command), and retiring defeated from an argument with his wife after he discovers her infidelity.[43] The story points the familiar moral that the man who can- not govern his own wife and family can have no right to authority in the state. Once again the private and the public spheres are seen as interchangeable.

As usual, Crouch was building on a certain grain of truth. Lady Fairfax was well known to be a strong-minded woman, a great patron of Presbyterian clergy, and her influence was often thought responsible for her husband's evident distaste for the radical policies pursued by the Army, against Presbyterian opposition, from 1647 onwards. This seemed to be confirmed by her famous interventions at the King's trial. Fairfax had been appointed to the High Court of Justice. He did not turn up, and when the clerk calling the roll at the opening of the trial came to his name, a masked lady in the gallery shouted: 'He has more wit than to be here.' Later, when the sentence against the King was being read 'in the name of the people of England', the masked lady cried, 'Not half, not a quarter of the people of England: Oliver Cromwell is a traitor!' She and her companion were thereupon ejected, while Roundhead soldiers shouted 'Down with the whores!' The masked lady was Lady Fairfax.[44] One might have thought that these sensational interruptions would have endeared her to Crouch, but either he did not know about them, or he may have thought that such female outspokenness, even in a good cause, was intolerable. At all events, Lady Fairfax's reputation explains why the General could so effectively be ridiculed as 'Tom Ladle'.

We are now in a better position to understand Crouch's constant resort to sexual imagery and slander. This was the metaphorical language which his readers would naturally have used when they thought about politics. It would have been thoroughly familiar to any of them who read the other Cavalier weeklies like *Elencticus* and *Pragmaticus*, or who remembered the ballads and jestbooks of earlier days. *The Man in the Moon*'s wearisome catalogue of sexual insults depicts an inverted moral order which Crouch, like other royalists, regarded as the appalling outcome of the illegalities of the new Commonwealth. Crouch surveyed a world turned upside down; he did not like it, and he did not expect his readers to like it. Government was in the hands of actual or metaphorical cuckolds and fornicators, who plundered the public purse while their wives kept brothels or slept around. The words 'Freedom' and 'Liberty', so prominent in republican rhetoric, become in Crouch's paper merely passwords for entering brothels patronized by leading Parliament-men.[45] Such cynicism might well be shared by Levellers, convinced that the Commonwealth had betrayed them, as well as by royalists. All branches of the revolutionary government, from the House of Commons to the City of London, are run by men who have forfeited their moral authority. Crouch has no time for the London aldermen—he is appealing, obviously, to readers disenchanted with the government of their city as well as their nation. London is 'Nodnol', a place where everything is backwards; it is 'the mother of rebels', whose part in the rebellion against Charles I is now being appropriately punished by its becoming the site of military occupation and republican tyranny. Crouch also follows a long tradition in popular balladry by portraying the leading citizens as, almost by definition, having been cuckolded. The Mayor and Common Council become the 'Mayor and Cuckoldry', or the 'Common Cuckolds'. He has a nice parody of the Lord Mayor's procession to Westminster to take the oath of office. A pair of horns are set up on a standard in Cheapside, and as the procession passes a trumpeter in The Man in the Moon tavern plays the popular tune 'Room for Cuckolds'.[46]

So the inversion of government is accompanied by sexual inversion. But as we might expect, it is also accompanied by social inversion. Seventeenth-century Englishmen assumed that political order rested on order in the family. But many of them also assumed, even after a revolution, that it rested on the preservation of appropriate distinctions of birth, rank, and wealth between the governors and the governed. In this respect, too, the revolution has turned the world upside down. The republic is led by pimps and fornicators, but it is also led by 'brewers, pedlars, tinkers, broom-men'. The regicides, Crouch sneers, killed the King because they wanted to be 'kings, princes, and lords themselves', to be 'as fine as apes in new coats'. Their lofty rhetoric was a cover for 'nothing but covetousness and lust'.[47]

The revolution has thus involved the total inversion of moral order. And not only for the regicides: in the terrible economic depression they had created prostitution was as necessary a trade in London as 'weaving of broadcloth'. But the example had been set by the regicides, and once again we encounter the automatic juxtaposition of family and state. The financial help granted to the family of the assassinated Isaac Dorislaus made 'many of the children of the High Court of Justice ready to cut their own fathers' throats for the like allowance'.[48] When a Smithfields butcher (a former Roundhead soldier, needless to say) stabs his mother to death, Crouch thinks he is unlucky not to get away with it: 'Ere long it will be lawful to kill one's parents, from the blessed example of the Junto's killing their King.' The introduction of the bill imposing the death penalty for adultery naturally gives him a field day. Adultery will be prohibited, we are assured, for 'all but Parliament-men, for whom 'tis lawful to commit any sin, whether deicide, regicide, parricide, murder, theft, lust, incest, or adultery'.[49]

So there is a serious purpose behind *The Man in the Moon*'s mocking laughter. This should not surprise us; as Leah Marcus observes, 'there was nothing fundamentally frivolous about the Stuart politics of mirth'.[50] Crouch and his Grub Street colleagues portray a state of 'universal Bedlam', marked by the inversion of the natural order in family, social relations, church and state. There were indeed many, as Christopher Hill has so vividly shown, for whom the world turned upside down had positive connotations, pointing to a possible end to sexual repression, religious intolerance, and capitalist greed. But the negative version was even more commonly proclaimed in the pamphlet and ballad literature of the period. Crouch and his fellow newsmen wrote primarily for a London audience, and they knew their market. Now obviously there were many people in London who welcomed the Commonwealth. But equally obviously there were many at both ends of the political spectrum (royalists and Presbyterians at one extreme, Levellers at the other) who did not, and outside London there was even less enthusiasm for the revolution. Many of the country people, John Morrill has recently shown us, clung tenaciously to traditional forms of worship rather than accept the religious liberty that became available after Parliament's victory. When, later in the 1650s, the Quakers, the most successful of the new radical sects, seemed to be turning the world upside down again by giving unprecedented freedom to women and others who had been oppressed, villagers were as likely to turn on them with violence as to welcome them.[51] It is no accident that Quakers were so often denounced as witches. Mob violence against them, and other sects in earlier years, was often provoked by their rejection of distinctions of gender and rank, and was expressed in ritual forms similar to the charivari against families in which the natural authority of males over females had been inverted. In one dramatic example, some Diggers were attacked near St George's Hill in 1649 by a crowd of local men dressed in women's clothes.[52]

Crouch's religious and moral framework is essentially the same as the one which inspired the popular violence against the sects. All the calamities of the times, he repeatedly insists, stem from the rebels' rejection of a divinely ordained frame of order. The overthrow of monarchy and church are inextricably connected: the murder of the King was inevitably accompanied by 'a chaos of sects and schisms, heresies and blasphemies, openly tolerated and taught, nay protected by these regicides'. The Rumpers, afflicted by a compulsive itch to reform, were 'of more minds than a woman, still purposing but never performing; always reforming, but never reformed'. The gendered image is significant, and so too is the religious framework. We catch metaphorical echoes of the Fall of Man:

'Our dying isle', says Crouch, was 'lately the paradise of Europe, till serpent Cromwell by subtle policy had ruined it.' And always there is the contrast between the peaceful order of monarchy and true religion and the current state of chaos and inversion. The radicals, Crouch proclaims, have eaten 'God out of his House, the King out of his Court, the noblemen out of their manors and lordships, the gentry out of their habitations, nay the poor commons out of their cottages'.[53]

Only the Devil, Crouch concludes, can have caused these disasters. Satan works through serpent Cromwell, but he has other agents too, as we might expect in an age when witchcraft beliefs were part of the mental furniture of virtually everyone, of whatever class or level of education. As we have seen in earlier chapters, one of the most pecu- liarly satanic features of witchcraft was that it inverted the entire chain of authority ordained by God, turning gender, familial, social, and political order upside down.[54] Crouch naturally shared this belief. Com- menting on a recent witch trial at Worcester, he observes that 'rebels and witches do not disagree, because their tenets hold a sympathy'. Rebels, witches, and devils, he adds, had joined forces to depose Charles I. He gleefully reports the words of a 'new prophet' who has called down destruction on London for the city's 'rebellions, witchcrafts, and whoredoms'. Behind the sinister figure of Cromwell there lurks, inevit- ably, a witch, who is needed 'to charm the affections of the people into an acknowledgement of [the regicides'] usurped power'.[55]

Once again we may recall that Quakers and other religious radicals were attacked because they turned gender, family, and social hierarchies upside down. The stereotypical unruly woman was the scold; Quaker women were often charged with scolding when they proclaimed their beliefs. One was ducked for preaching in the street at Malton, Yorkshire, in 1652; in another northern town one was subjected to the brank, the iron collar sometimes called the 'scold's bridle', as punishment for speak- ing out. Witchcraft accusations were even more common, and were levelled at male as well as female Quakers. The Quakers were not above using witchcraft themselves as a charge against their own deviants.[56] The association of witchcraft with dangerous brands of politics has, as we have seen, a long history. Buckingham's sorcerer from the 1620s, Dr Lambe, was still remembered. In 1653 an old woman was executed at Salisbury for witchcraft; she had once been one of Lambe's servants, and confessed to having learned her 'art' from him all those years before.[57]

Masculine women were routinely linked with witchcraft. In *Mercurius Fumigosus*, Crouch later promised to write

Of hags and cats, of imps and witches,
Of man-kind women that wear breeches.[58]

Any expression of female independence was liable to provoke explosions of male anger or derision. The papers were full of them in April 1649 when some Leveller women had the temerity to present the Rump with a petition demanding the release of their imprisoned husbands. The petition cleverly turned Parliament's republican rhetoric against itself, but also advanced the startling claim that women had 'an equal share and interest with men in the commonwealth'. The demonstration that accompanied its presentation sparked the usual chorus of journalistic derision: descriptions of the petitioners as fishwives and 'oyster women', gleeful accounts of the soldiers at Westminster throwing squibs under their skirts. A month later a pirate edition of *Mercurius Militaris* outdid all the others in its unrelenting sexual smears. The women, it said, would never submit to Parliament's 'proud flesh, until they untruss the great cod-piece point of government . . . and show you the naked truth'. Both men and women Levellers, it was assumed, wanted political freedom only as a means to sexual freedom. *The Man in the Moon* was, by comparison, fairly restrained, though it invented some facetious names for the petitioners, and suggested that they wanted the imprisoned Levellers released only so that they could be 'breeders, for the better propagation of the righteous'.[59]

Naturally Crouch is confident that in the end God will turn the world the right way up. *The Man in the Moon* reminds us that Puritans were not the only people in the seventeenth century who saw signs and protents of God's intentions. Its readers were regularly edified with stories of 'sad omens, apparitions, thunders, and monstrous births', reflecting God's anger at the disruption of cosmic order. Mysterious armies are heard fighting in the sky; three blood-red suns are seen at one time. A cattle plague in Essex was an obvious portent: it was being spread by mice with round heads. Even more overtly political were the signs that followed the Earl of Pembroke's death early in 1650. When the corpse was taken down to Wilton for burial its tongue swelled, its nose gushed blood, and all the dogs along the route howled piteously.[60]

Pembroke was not the only enemy to be visited with signs of divine displeasure. When some soldiers enact a blasphemous parody of the coronation ceremony, one of them is immediately struck dead. The accidental explosion of a gunpowder magazine near the Tower appropriately decapitates some Excise officials, whose heads are blown into

Barking churchyard. There are reports of the regicides' fear of assassination (one of Crouch's few truthful stories), and of their wearing protective armour under their clothing. Bradshawe, who had presided
over the King's trial, is said to awaken and shout 'Murder! Murder!'
whenever the wind rattles his bedroom window.[61] The regicides' guilty
fears presage their inevitable perdition. All who had anything to do with
the King's trial are haunted by demons, and several die horribly, scream-
ing 'The Devil! The Devil!' Other Rumpers are obsessed with thoughts
of suicide, and when one of them, Thomas Hoyle, does in fact take his
own life on the anniversary of Charles's execution, Crouch is triumphant.
It was, he points out, the fate of Judas, and altogether appropriate, 'as
they have acted High Treason against God and the King, that now . . .
they should at last act High Treason against themselves'.[62]

The incessantly reiterated remedy for all these disorders is the restoration of legitimate authority. Power, says Crouch in language that he
could have found in countless monarchist tracts and sermons, was never
justly given to a multitude. Religion, he assures his readers, 'should
unite us all in one body and one mind, to be governed by one head'—
in state as well as in family. And he warns his readers that they 'will
never have peace, never have a day of quiet in this kingdom, till God's
inheritance be restored, the King righted, and the people assured their
own'. It is the language of the 'Homily on Obedience' directed to political ends.[63]

Does this mean that Crouch was writing for readers whom he believed to want absolute monarchy? He was certainly speaking to people
who believed in patriarchal authority in the family, and saw paternal and
monarchical power as directly connected. But such beliefs were not
incompatible with a vague attachment to the 'Ancient Constitution'
protecting English liberties. Central to Crouch's condemnation of the
regicides is his contention that they are violating those liberties in ways
that the King at his worst had never done. Their soldiers are regularly
reported to be robbing and murdering all over England. The 'Egyptian
taskmasters' in Parliament are constantly inventing new taxes, of which
the 'thieving Excise' on food and drink inflicts a special burden on the
poor, and is far more oppressive than Charles I's Ship Money had been.[64]
Crouch prints every scrap of news he can find about anti-Excise riots.
'Are not thirty tyrants worse than one King?' he asks, '. . . the Council
of State more tyrannical than the Star Chamber or High Commission?'
He writes approvingly of John Lilburne's spirited defence when the
Leveller leader is tried for treason, and is delighted by his acquittal.[65]

Crouch in effect adopts the not very original argument put forward by Charles I at his trial that only a monarchy established by law can protect the rights of the English people. In *The Man in the Moon* we find a version of the myth of the 'freeborn Englishman' very different from the one being employed by the Levellers, but one that was to echo on into the next century in both Whig and Tory rhetoric. 'Be true Britons', Crouch exhorts his readers, and rise for Charles II to vindicate 'your religion, laws, liberties, freedoms and privileges.' The English are 'an heroic and free people', who can achieve their true destiny only under a monarchy that unites them.[66] But Crouch uses less of this rhetoric than some of his competitors. One of the pirate versions of *Mercurius Pragmaticus* somewhat more regularly invoked the spirit of the 'free-born English', 'the free people of this nation', and even appropriated one of the Levellers' favourite clichés, calling on the soldiers to remember that 'they were not born with saddles on their backs, to be ridden by their officers'. *Mercurius Elencticus* used the same image, asking its readers, 'Shall we endeavour to uphold those rules | which make them [the Rump oligarchy] riders, but our selves the mules?'[67] This kind of language is less common in Crouch's writings, though not entirely absent.

How in the end should we evaluate *The Man in the Moon*? Does it amount to anything more than a statement of the prejudices of John Crouch, or can we extract from it anything about the outlook of its readers? Was Crouch simply a scurrilous propagandist, trying to regain support for a lost cause by dressing up elements of élite political culture in a popular idiom? Obviously Crouch *was* a propagandist, one of the many who helped to whip up the 'moral panic' about the demonic, libertine consequences of the revolution which was such a feature of the early 1650s.[68] Yet there is no evidence that he was a mouthpiece for anyone else, no sign that he was a dependant of any of the aristocratic or clerical leaders of the royal party. Like the rest of his Grub Street colleagues he responded to the opportunities of the journalistic marketplace. Yet I think he also believed what he wrote: unlike Marchamont Nedham, he never sold his services to the other side.[69] John Pocock and others have shown us that people inhabit linguistic universes which shape the ideas they can express.[70] In Crouch we encounter an author consciously transmitting a conception of society and politics which upholds the authority of England's pre-war rulers, using a vocabulary and a system of symbols that came naturally both to him and to the

plebeian public he was addressing. The bawdy stories, the sexual slanders and metaphors which infuse Crouch's writing were part of the
popular language of his time, and they articulated a value-system which
he shared with his readers. Like other royalist newswriters of 1649–50,
Crouch had learned from the mistakes of his wartime predecessors, who
had written for people of somewhat higher status.[71] The racier, smuttier
newsbooks of the post-war years were clearly aimed at a more socially
diverse audience, though Nedham's brilliant *Mercurius Pragmaticus* and
its less lively imitators may have been too sophisticated for the more
plebeian public that read (or listened to readings of) *The Man in the
Moon*.

   This, admittedly, is speculation. If we look for positive evidence about
the kind of people who read Crouch's papers we soon draw a blank, for
such readers left no records of their purchases. We know something
about the choice of newsbooks made by people on the other side: the
pious puritan artisan, Nehemiah Wallington, for example.[72] He obviously would not have been found dead with *The Man in the Moon*. But
in spite of his diametrically opposite religious and political opinions,
Wallington's mental world nevertheless had some similarities to Crouch's.
He records the same kind of portents and apparitions, for example,
though he naturally ascribes opposite meanings to them. Another Lon-
doner whose reading habits we know something about is Elizabeth
Jekyll, wife of a middling-sort dealer and shopkeeper. She left some
jottings during the 1640s and '50s that reveal conventionally puritan
beliefs: gratitude for being one of the elect; for God's mercies to her in
childbed; for preserving her children from the usual hazards of growing
up, or her husband from less routine dangers encountered in the course
of his travels during and after the civil war. But she also often gave
thanks for the victories of Parliament's armies in language that shows
that she was an enthusiastic supporter of the godly cause and at least an
occasional reader of the newsbooks and pamphlets.[73] Wallington's and
Jekyll's processing of the information they got from the press and the
pamphlets may tell us something about the relationship between civil
war journalists and their readers. For the most part the propagandists
were obviously preaching to the converted. Their lurid atrocity stories
did not win Wallington or Jekyll to the parliamentary cause: they for-
tified the faith of two already-committed partisans. *The Man in the Moon*
probably fulfilled much the same function on the other side.

   One thing we can be fairly certain of is *The Man in the Moon*'s popularity. It had a print-run of several hundred, and its relative cheapness,

the homely idiom that Crouch employed, and the fact that it survived government harassment for over a year when other subversive papers did not, all suggest that it could count on a steady sale among the London middling sort. Better-educated royalists and people of different political persuasions had many other papers to choose from, so Crouch's success indicates the existence of a significant anti-puritan royalism even in London. There is plenty of other evidence for this: the disorderly outbreaks that repeatedly erupted on festival days, and the more explicitly political riots during the summer of 1647 and the winter of 1659– 60, for example.[74] Outside the capital, as I have already suggested, these attitudes were even more widespread. Without them there would have been no Restoration.

The Man in the Moon has introduced us to a mental world far removed from the one that generated the exciting, forward-looking radical ideas of the Levellers and the sects. Crouch presented a stock of unoriginal ideas in a vocabulary that expressed utterly conventional notions of the parallels between the state and the family, and of the connections between the public and the private spheres. He did so in the context of assumptions about an eternal, divinely ordained frame of cosmic order, at a time when those assumptions were being challenged by an armed, revolutionary minority, and by women as well as men who had broken free from traditional patriarchal constraints. I do not wish to minimize the importance of that minority: if we ignore it we miss the very essence of the English revolution. But alongside the radical, visionary conception of 'the world turned upside down' that Christopher Hill and Phyllis Mack have so vividly illuminated, there existed another, very different version. It was a version that also, in its own way, contributed to the myth of the 'freeborn Englishman'. *The Man in the Moon* may suggest that it had equally strong popular roots.

6

THE POLITICAL NATION AFTER
THE RESTORATION

In 1660 Crouch's predictions were fulfilled, and the King came home in peace again. Official policy encouraged reconciliation, yet for many people the Restoration was a time for revenge. And not just for royalists: soon after the Restoration one conservative 'Presbyterian' member of the Long Parliament, Lionel Copley, enacted a brilliantly symbolic rebuttal of the old Leveller cliché about no man coming into the world with a saddle on his back. Copley was charged with putting a bridle in the mouth of one of his neighbours, and then riding him round a field for half an hour, 'kicking him to make him move'.[1] Obviously we ought not to assume that this was a typical response to the Restoration. It remains for us to consider how the events of 1660 affected the relationship between the two segments of the political nation that we have been investigating in earlier chapters of this book: those broadly defined entities, the élite and the middle ranks of the people.

One familiar argument is that Copley *was* typical, that the years of revolution between 1640 and 1660 had deepened the gulf between the two social groups. Before the civil war the gentry had assumed that the common people shared their priorities—the freeborn Englishman's agenda of liberty, property, and anti-popery—and had either encouraged, or had at least not actively resisted, their increasing involvement in national affairs.[2] They then took fright when it became clear that many of the lower orders wanted something more than the limited changes their leaders had secured for them in 1641, or even than the more drastic ones a minority had imposed on them in 1648–9. Memories of New Model agitators, of Diggers on St George's Hill, of mechanic and women preachers, of Quakers refusing their betters the elementary marks of subservience like hat-honour, of Ranters flamboyantly drinking and fornicating, and all the other wild excesses of the 1650s, convinced them that the people were not to be trusted after all.

This conception of the Restoration period makes perfect sense if we recall the argument of Peter Burke and other historians of popular culture that the gulf between the élite and the common people was widen-

ing in the seventeenth century. Yet at the same time there is much evidence to contradict it, particularly from London during the Exclusion
crisis of 1678–81. During those turbulent years we can see the continuing interaction between the two levels of the political nation in the
capital. Shaftesbury's Whigs appealed to the people in pamphlets, in parliamentary speeches, and above all in London street politics, even more
shamelessly than Pym's Roundheads had done. And that well-known
phenomenon, the 'expansion of the electorate', continued until the
Whigs closed politics down after the Hanoverian succession. So perhaps
we should be unwise to accept too facile a picture of polarization, and
ought to take another look at the years after the Restoration in the light
of some of our conclusions about the first half of the century.

We have two alternative conceptions of the Restoration period as possible starting-points, one stressing the continuities from the earlier part
of the century, one emphasizing the growing divergence of élite from
popular politics. In choosing between them we confront that familiar
problem: the great divide of 1660. Most of us are either early Stuart or
later Stuart historians, rarely both. It is something of a shock for those
more familiar with the pre-civil war years to find that many of the
sources to which we are accustomed in the first half of the century
become much less plentiful in the second. Quarter sessions and other
local records begin a steady decline in volume; the newspapers and
pamphlets which make the Interregnum period so exciting dry up with
the return of more stringent censorship; and before the beginning of
Anchitel Grey's published *Debates* in 1667 the sources for parliamentary
history are much slenderer than they are in the earlier part of the century.[3] There is still plenty of correspondence, and a proliferation of
memoirs and diaries (including the greatest one in the English language), but the relative absence of other materials leaves us with a good
many questions still unanswered.

Happily, members of a new generation of historians—Tim Harris,
Ronald Hutton, and Paul Seaward foremost among them—have made
light of these difficulties and have embarked on an exciting reassessment
of the Restoration period. As in the earlier part of the century, so in the
later Stuart reigns the old Whig interpretation has long been under
attack. Macaulay's conception of 1660–88, repeated much later by his
great-nephew G. M. Trevelyan, and more moderately even by the best
of the mid-twentieth century historians of the period, David Ogg, was
that this was a distasteful, if necessary, prelude to the triumph of liberty

and parliamentary government in the Glorious Revolution: an attempt, doomed to failure, to put back the clock and establish a Stuart despotism. The smooth outlines of the Whig narrative were being questioned by historians like J. R. Jones and D. T. Witcombe as early as the 1960s, and it was becoming increasingly clear that there was nothing inevitable about Parliament's victory in 1688. Some scholars were asking entirely different historical questions, as J. H. Plumb did when he looked behind the noisy 'rage of party' to uncover the forces which led to the establishment of Whig stability in the next century. More recently we have been urged by Jonathan Clark not to think of the eighteenth century as Whiggish at all, but to reflect on the more enduring Tory and Anglican certainties which shaped it.[4]

All this suggests that we should be wise not to make too many sweeping generalizations about the political attitudes of the gentry or of any other segment of the political nation, at any rate in the years immediately after 1660. It used to be assumed that Restoration politics was characterized by a straightforward dichotomy between, on the one side, Cavalier-Tory gentry bent on imposing a narrowly defined Anglican settlement, and willing to give the crown extensive prerogative powers if (but only if) it would co-operate in this; and, on the other, a handful of Presbyterian survivors in alliance with largely urban, mercantile nonconformists working for religious toleration and limits on the prerogative. But all these time-honoured assumptions are now in question after the re-examination of Restoration politics that Seaward and the others have undertaken.

The Cavalier gentry, it turns out, were far from united in their attitude to dissent. Both in Parliament and at home in their shires they vigorously attacked Quakers and other radical separatists from whom, they believed, the real danger to the social order, and to their own position at the summit of it, came. But their attitude to the more mainstream dissenters, the Presbyterians who had, after all, played the crucial role in restoring Charles II, was more ambiguous. Under pressure from the Anglican high-flyers, both clerical and lay, they dutifully passed the Act of Uniformity and the other measures of what used to be called the Clarendon Code. But Seaward argues persuasively that many of them were never very enthusiastic about it, and that Commons' votes often show only narrow majorities against occasional conformity, which was after all the hallmark of moderate Presbyterianism.[5]

Outside Westminster, at least in the areas of the country I know best, much the same variations of opinion appear to have existed. There were intolerant Cavalier gentlemen like those who regularly sent the militia into Taunton to disrupt the celebrations on the anniversary of the town's relief by Fairfax's army, and who in 1683 cheered on the mobs attacking the nonconformist meeting houses there. But there were others who recognized that Presbyterians were as attached to monarchy and social stability as they were, and were not inclined to press persecution too hard. All this makes it easier to understand the continuing vitality of dissent in places like Taunton—and Dorchester—right down to 1688 and beyond. There were significant variations in the intensity of feeling, and correspondingly in the level of persecution, which reached peaks in years like 1663, after the discovery of the Northern plot, and in the early to mid-1680s.[6]

If the gentry were not universally Anglican high-flyers, neither were they supporters of any supposed Stuart scheme to establish a despotism on the French model. As Sir John Strangways's writings in the Tower in the 1640s remind us, most of the Cavalier gentry were as attached to the liberties of the Ancient Constitution as their old enemies had been. Hobbes's arguments for absolutism made few converts, and although there were people at Court—mostly in the Duke of York's circle—who hankered after a divine-right monarchy, and deeply regretted Charles I's failure to win the complete military victory that would have enabled him to impose it, they were hardly representative.[7]

What the gentry wanted was not an unregulated monarchy, but stability, an end to innovation and to the wild swings and speculations of the Commonwealth; a return instead to the old certainties of the law. Once again we may recall the tenor of Strangways's musings in the Tower: he and his country friends had fought for a monarchy supported by, but also in a sense bound by, the Ancient Constitution. Naturally they tended to equate the good old days of stability of which they nostalgically dreamed with a period in which their own power had been unchallenged, whether by corrupt courtiers, selfish urban money-grubbers, moralizing puritans, or upstart JPs from lower down the social scale. And although they were not successful in regaining their power at Westminster, where the use of place and patronage by party-managers like Arlington and Danby was too much for them, they *did* regain it in the counties. They recovered their authority as JPs, and Joyce Malcolm has shown how their control of the new volunteer militia further enhanced their local power, thus giving them additional reasons for supporting the crown. In a survey of seventeenth-century local government, Anthony Fletcher rightly characterizes this period as 'The Triumph of the Gentry'.[8]

The values of these provincial squires in Charles II's reign do not seem very different from those of their 'Country' predecessors earlier in the century. Like them, they were deeply suspicious of Court extravagance, incompetence, and corruption; like them they were fiercely patriotic but inclined to suspect those in authority of connivance in popish and foreign plots (Spanish earlier, French in the Restoration era) to undermine the kingdom's liberties and its virtuous Protestant identity. In 1678, with an unpopular Catholic as heir to the throne, Shaftesbury could use the Popish Plot to stampede many of the non-partisan, 'Country' gentry into the Exclusionist camp. But by the time of the dissolution of the Oxford Parliament in 1681, thanks partly to the government's skilful exploitation of Whig extremism, and to suspicions that some of Shaftesbury's friends really did have revolutionary intentions, that same 'Country' bloc swung back to the cause of legitimate succession and to what by this time we can surely call Toryism. However much nostalgic gentlemen might look for a return of the imagined harmony of pre-war days, political competition and division, as Mark Kishlansky has shown in his study of electoral politics, had come to stay.[9]

The increasing recognition that political conflict was inevitable, even acceptable, was accompanied after 1660 by other changes in the outlook of the upper reaches of the political nation. The civil war had made the old patriarchal language somewhat more problematic for all but the most determined of monarchist theorists. There were, of course, still plenty of those about. During the war royalist writers like the younger Dudley Digges had continued to invoke the parallel between King and people, husbands and wives: 'marriages and governments', he declared, 'both are ratified in heaven.' That political discourse still retained many of the old assumptions is evident in the fact that the Council thought it still worth reissuing Mocket's *God and the King* in 1661, and that Filmer's *Patriarcha*, written fifty years earlier, was published during the very heyday of radical politics at the time of the Popish Plot. But too much water had passed under the bridge for the patriarchal analogy to be accepted uncritically. Contrary to the expectations of 'moral panic' scribblers like John Crouch, in 1649 Charles I—the ultimate father—had been killed without either the familial or the social order collapsing. Patriarchal authority, many people were discovering, need not be any more absolute in theory than it clearly was in practice. Thomas Hobbes had argued that both the family and the state were based on contract— that both were artificial constructs—but it was left to John Locke to uncouple the public and private spheres completely. As Susan Amussen has suggested, Locke's dissolution of the link between the family and the state simply gave theoretical ratification to what was happening on the ground in communities throughout the kingdom: people were no longer as worried about the political implications of familial disorder. Locke expressed ideas whose time had come.[10]

All this was inevitably accompanied by a changed political language: both the familial and the gendered analogies which had been so dominant earlier in the century began to seem less appropriate in public discourse. That we are in a new political universe is apparent if we compare the parliamentary campaign against the first Duke of Buckingham in 1620s with the attack on Clarendon in the 1660s. Many of the charges against Clarendon resembled those levelled at Buckingham: self-aggrandizement, corruption, the sale of offices, the encouragement of popery, incompetence in foreign policy and the management of a foreign war. 'Country' attitudes were now compounded by the resentment felt by many Cavaliers at having been cheated out of the share of royal bounty they expected in return for their previous sufferings. It is the theme of many a Restoration ballad—'The Cavalier's Complaint' and 'The Cavalier's Litany' are good examples from 1661.[11] Clarendon, inevitably, became the scapegoat.

There certainly was resentment enough. But the sense that the great man and his family personified satanic powers, that his authority in some way rested on witchcraft and the evil influence of women, all that is missing. The nearest equivalent to the charge that Buckingham and his mother poisoned James I was the baseless accusation that Clarendon had been an agent for Cromwell, a story first spread by the Chancellor's enemies during the exile and resurrected by discontented Cavaliers in the 1660s.[12] If true, such behaviour would have been treasonable but it did not involve witchcraft or feminine black arts. There was a popular Cavalier story, which seems to have originated just after the Restoration, that on the eve of the Battle of Worcester Cromwell had made a pact with the devil: seven years of power in return for the devil's getting his soul at the end of it (which of course he did—Cromwell died in the middle of a great storm on 3 September 1658, seven years to the day later, when the devil came to claim his due). An atmosphere of evil pervades the story, but the devil is male, and there is no witch, nothing that feminizes evil. Another Restoration pamphlet makes a half-hearted effort to associate Cromwell with the supernatural, its title speaking of the Protector's 'monstrous witch' at Whitehall. But the 'witch' it turns

out, is only Elizabeth Poole, the female prophet who testified before
the Army Council in December 1648; an inappropriate feminine intervention in politics, certainly, but nothing to do with witchcraft in the
literal sense.[13]

There was plenty of sexual politics at Charles II's court—the use of
the royal mistresses to promote particular policies or undermine rivals
was a routine part of Restoration Court infighting. But the ultimate
authors of evil are French agents, Jesuits (in the Great Fire and the
Popish Plot), fanatics or republicans (in the Rye House and other Whig
conspiracies); we find no accusations of female supernatural powers.
Undue influence by women in the masculine sphere of politics might
be improper, but it was not by definition satanic. When the Whig-
dominated Middlesex Grand Jury brought in an indictment against
the Duchess of Portsmouth in 1680, the King's mistress was accused
of financial corruption, of treasonable correspondence with the French,
of being party to a conspiracy to introduce popery and arbitrary government, of having 'placed and displaced great ministers in church and
state', and of endangering Charles II's life, both by exposing him to
syphilis and by poisoning him with 'a mess of broth' prepared by her
servants. The echoes of the charges against Buckingham in 1626 are
obvious, but in all the twenty-two articles there are no references to
sorcery or witchcraft.[14]

While there was a decline in the use of gendered imagery in politics,
this does not mean that attitudes had totally changed. Most people still
firmly believed in the providential meaning of apparitions, monstrous
births, and other portents. There was an epidemic of them in the year
1666, which was widely believed to be the year of the apocalypse, sig-
nified by the number of the Beast. The courtier Sir Allen Apsley, a
passionate Cavalier even though he was the brother of the pious Lucy
Hutchinson, wrote a long religious epic with the title *Order and Disorder*, in which Eve's role as the source of the satanic confusion that
followed the fall of man is portrayed in a very traditional way. The
poem is in the genre of *Paradise Lost*, but a long way below Milton's in
imaginative and poetic quality. Restoration satirists like John Oldham
continued to insist on women's inconstancy and insatiable sexuality. As
in James I's reign, Court ladies were thought to be dominating their
menfolk, and to be cross-dressing into masculine attire as a symbolic
statement of this intention. But times had changed: in literary circles
women were now more likely to be blamed—as by the Earl of Rochester
in a succession of pornographic poems—for making men impotent by

natural means, rather than by sorcery and the black arts as Frances Howard was supposed to have done.[15]

There were many less-serious reflections on the evils of allowing women to step out of their properly subordinate sphere. One Cavalier ballad equated their rule with Cromwell's usurpation:

> Woman are born to be control'd,
>   Receive them as you please.
> Their long usurped monarchy
> Hath made me hate such tyranny.

Another, inspired by Venner's Fifth Monarchist revolt in January 1661, has a succession of stanzas in which a chorus of women sing the praises of disorder, anarchy, and free love, until the final stanza, when the men take over and call for order and loyalty to King Charles II.[16]

There were still plenty of allegations of witchcraft in the country, especially just before and just after the Restoration, when Quakers were especially likely to be charged with it. As late as 1675 a man at Gravesend confessed to having 'contracted with the Devil': six years during which he 'was to live idly so long without work', and after that Satan would get his soul.[17] But such preoccupations were becoming less intense at the élite than at the popular level, and were rarely injected into politics in the way they had been before the wars. People still believed that monarchs had supernatural healing powers: Charles II touched more people for the King's Evil than any other English king in history. Even in Presbyterian Dorchester public funds were promptly employed in 1660 to enable poor people to travel to London to be touched. The Duke of Monmouth and his advisers certainly saw the value of the ritual: one of the most effective means of asserting his legitimacy during the 1685 rebellion was his widely publicized exercise of the holy royal touch.[18] We are in a world of gentry politics that exhibits both contrasts and continuities with the pre-war years.

The same mixture of continuity and change is apparent lower down the social spectrum, among the common people. Before we examine in more detail the impact of the revolution on popular behaviour, it is as well to remind ourselves of the basic context of politics after 1660. The first and most obvious fact is that we are now on the other side of the great demographic watershed. After a century-and-a-half of rapid population growth, around 1650 the population of England and Wales began to stabilize. Meanwhile agricultural productivity was slowly rising,

as new methods of crop rotation and other kinds of 'improvement'
were introduced. All this reversed the most basic social and economic
trends of the previous 150 years. The lot of the consumer slowly im-
proved as cereal prices fell; the lot of the producer—the yeoman, the
more prosperous husbandman producing for the market—began to
deteriorate. The 'mere' gentleman, dependent upon the profits of his
demesne and the rents of his tenants, also began to feel the pinch.
We should not exaggerate—we are a long way from the conditions of
agricultural depression which plagued the first part of the eighteenth
century—but the secular trends are unmistakable.

The impact of these developments on the politics of the rural common people has never been sufficiently studied. London, thanks to the
work of Tim Harris and Gary De Krey, is now reasonably well understood. But much of the rest of England remains uncharted. We can find
occasional islands of relative certainty in this huge sea of obscurity: the
story of the dissenters of various denominations, and the Monmouth
rebellion, for example. But there is no recent study of later seventeenth-
century popular protest comparable to Roger Manning's *Village Revolts*
for the earlier period, nothing to link the studies of forest violence
between the periods covered by Buchanan Sharp's *In Contempt of All
Authority* and Edward Thompson's *Whigs and Hunters*.[19]

It has been plausibly argued that during this period the rural middling sort—yeomen, clothiers, better-off husbandmen, in other words—
were sufficiently alarmed by the disorders that had recently afflicted
them to decide that their interests were bound up with the gentry and
aristocracy rather than with those beneath them in the social scale.[20] As
usual a sweeping generalization of this kind needs many qualifications,
and the most obvious one is that religious loyalties often cut across class
interests. In the small towns and villages, the dissenting congregations
attracted people from a fairly wide social spectrum; once again, local
culture was often more decisive than class in determining where people
stood. Anne Whiteman's work confirms that the Compton Census of
1676, the old stand-by for quantifying the geography of religion, under-
estimates the numbers of dissenters in many places because of the
absence of a consistent overall definition of just what the term meant.
In some parishes occasional conformists are included; in others they
are not.[21] But with all its deficiencies the Census confirms that dissenters were thickest on the ground in most of the places where we
should expect to find them—in towns with a strong puritan tradition,
in centres of the cloth industry, and in places where the social and

residential structures created conditions favourable to religious individualism (the cheese country of north Wiltshire, for example).[22]

The subject of Restoration popular politics outside London and the history of dissent have often been regarded as virtually identical. Thanks to Christopher Hill we know a good deal about the behaviour of John Bunyan and other former radicals as they faced the 'experience of defeat'; Richard Greaves has told us much about the extent to which dissenters were or were not involved in conspiraces against the state; and Richard Ashcraft has explored the links between republican radicalism and the politics of the Whig élite, through Locke and Shaftesbury.[23] Most dissenters were not involved in plots, though it was easy to assume that logically they ought to be if they still hankered after the freedoms they had enjoyed under the Commonwealth and under Oliver Cromwell; zealous government officials thus had few scruples about framing them, or smearing them with guilt by association. There were always some unrealistic extremists about who could be relied on to talk rashly and implicate others. If they did not, double agents and *agents provocateurs* could easily be found to embroil them.[24]

To concentrate on the activist minority, however, gives a misleading impression of political realities. There were marked variations in the intensity of persecution, Quakers and other separatists being the most consistently harassed, mainstream Presbyterians inclined to occasional conformity suffering least. There were also striking alternations between periods of severity and of relative quiet. And there were quite marked geographical variations: even in some rural areas, like that old stronghold of puritanism the eastern counties, many of the gentry did little more than occasionally enforce the law against the most provocative opponents of the established church. How enmeshed dissent was in the conduct of local government sometimes becomes apparent only when it comes to light during one of the periods of severity. At East Knoyle in Wiltshire, for example, it was revealed during the 1683 crack-down that both the constable and tithingman were dissenters who had been absent from their parish church for years.[25]

Corporate towns exempt from the authority of vindictive Anglican JPs were best equipped to protect their dissenters from the full rigour of the law. Dorchester sheltered an array of ejected ministers in the 1660s, provoking loud complaints from the local royalists. In 1665 Charles II made a special journey to the town so that he could publicly give the royal assent to the Five Mile Act which theoretically kicked them out from such places. It was a nice piece of political theatre, but after a brief period of compliance the town returned to its old ways. In the 1670s most of its mayors, and a good many other local officeholders, including several churchwardens, were Presbyterians who qualified through the practice of occasional conformity.[26]

Historians have told us a good deal about religious dissent and republican survival. But they have told us much less about other kinds of popular politics, in the provinces, at any rate. There were, in fact, fewer grain riots than before the wars during this period of marginal surplus in food production, though they occasionally erupted in bad harvest years like 1662–3, and more seriously in the 1690s. They do not seem to have been very different in character from the ones before 1640.[27] The nature of enclosure riots, however, changed quite perceptibly in this period. There were few of the traditional kind in the arable regions, though discontent in the fen and forest areas continued, and there were occasional disorders over rights of common elsewhere. In 1670, near Kempsey in Worcestershire, a band of 'rude and dissolute people' were calling themselves Levellers, under the leadership of a 'Robin Hood' and a 'Little John'. They broke down the fences of more-reputable inhabitants, 'exposing their grounds to the cattle of the commons', it was reported, and if their accusers are to be believed also did other 'exploits of villainy and roguery', including a lot of thieving and inflicting malicious damage on the property of their enemies. Other outbreaks also suggest the existence of political undercurrents. In 1671, in the Forest of Dean, enclosures belonging to Charles II's mistress the Duchess of Cleveland were thrown down. A decade later riots in Wentwood Forest in Monmouthshire were aimed partly at undermining the local hegemony of the Tory Duke of Beaufort, as well as rectifying more specifically 'forest' grievances. In the fens there were several serious explosions against the drainage works—in Hatfield Chase, Wildmore and Peterborough Fens, and elsewhere. A new feature was the increasing number of attacks on the deer parks of the great landowners. These had not been unknown before 1642, but they became more common after the Restoration. Royal property was not exempt. In 1663, for example, rioters at Windsor broke down the gates and fences of the 'little park'. In the following decade well-organized poaching gangs were operating in Dorset; they made a particular target of the Whig Earl of Shaftesbury's park at Wimborne St Giles.[28]

We can unearth a few instances of this kind of rural unrest after the Restoration, but the subject has been insufficiently studied for us to know how typical they were. The scattered evidence that exists suggests that although the English rural population continued to defend their common rights when they were threatened, they did so less often and with less determination. There are two possible explanations for this. Perhaps there were fewer enclosures of the kind that aroused strong feelings of injustice; or perhaps, as Keith Wrightson has suggested, many of the sort of people who had provided leadership in earlier riots—yeomen and better-off husbandmen—had been drawn off by fears of lower-class disorder and were now identifying themselves with the men of property.

In some respects, though, popular disorder actually suggests that there may have been *more* political independence on the part of the lower orders than had been common before the civil war. We should not make the mistake of assuming that the authority of the aristocracy and gentry was reimposed after 1660 without effort. At Newbury, for example, the townsmen demanded a say in the election of churchwardens, causing a local JP to go on about 'the multitude upon all occasion flying as high as they dare against the King and the church'. The townspeople of Marlborough vigorously resisted the attempt of Lord Herbert (later the first Duke of Beaufort) to regain political control of the borough in the early post-Restoration years. Herbert used the Corporation Act to exclude his enemies from power and bring the town to heel, but this aroused such antagonism that he and two of his aristocratic friends were savagely assaulted by some of the townsmen after a convivial evening in Marlborough.[29]

Direct violence against a peer was, no doubt, unusual, but on some issues ordinary Englishmen certainly appear to have been more willing than they had been before the civil wars to take physical action to defend their rights without waiting for leadership from their superiors. This is particularly obvious in their resistance to collectors of oppressive taxes like the excise and the Hearth Tax. Riots against the Hearth Tax were particularly widespread in 1666–7, and there were further outbreaks during the following years. A Hearth Tax collector was murdered by 'a rude multitude assembled together' in Bridport, another died in the notoriously Roundhead town of Wellington, and in the early 1670s three others were killed in Herefordshire. Women were prominent in a riot at Cambridge. Some of these incidents may have been encouraged by members of the local élite—Lord Lovelace's son was involved in one incident in Wiltshire, and in another, in Yorkshire, the JPs arrested a collector, in effect giving the crowd licence to attack him—but most of them appear to have been spontaneous.[30]

Thanks to Tim Harris, Gary De Krey, and others, we know a good deal more about popular politics in London than in the provinces. De Krey has argued, contrary to some earlier historians, that a strong radical movement survived in London between the Restoration and the Exclusion crisis.[31] Meanwhile Harris has exploded several widely held myths about the London crowd: that it was a mindless mob manipulated by unscrupulous élite politicians, for example, and that it was a unilaterally populist Whig force. The study of popular journalism undertaken in the previous chapter must surely remind us that during the mid-century revolution there was a wide spectrum of lower-class politics, running all the way from Levellers and other assorted radicals at one end to lowbrow traditionalists who read *The Man in the Moon* at the other. Although the newsbooks disappeared with the return of censorship after the Restoration, the same contrasts in popular attitudes still endured. Harris suggests that in the hectic years around 1680 members of the Tory mobs were of somewhat higher social status than the typical Whig rioter, but it would be unwise to be too dogmatic about this. The Tory Roger L'Estrange was certainly pitching his argument to a less respectable segment of the populace when he denounced the Whigs for intending to ban 'comedies, interludes, wrestlings, football play, May-games, Whitsun-ales, morris-dances, bear-baitings', and suchlike plebeian amusements. Besides the Whig crowds who joyfully burned popish effigies in raucous Queen Elizabeth's Day processions, there were also anti-Exclusionist Tory riots in which the mythic Jack Presbyter was incinerated with equal fervour.[32]

There were, of course, some elements common to the political culture of all crowds of whatever persuasion. Protestant Londoners were usually bigotedly anti-Catholic, xenophobic (particularly towards the French), and instinctively inclined to smell conspiracies in times of danger. Charges of treason against Catholic, Court, and in the early 1680s, Whig scapegoats, were credulously swallowed, and public calamities ranging from trade depression to the Great Fire of 1666 and the Dutch in the Medway blamed on them, with or without supporting evidence. Other things united them; a tenacious belief in patriarchal order, for example. This, as we might expect, underlies much of the debate over the succession, in which both Whigs and Tories used the most readily available vocabulary, the language of patriarchy. The Tories had their Filmer, but in their efforts to prove Monmouth's legitimacy the Whigs also resorted to patriarchal arguments. Confronted by Charles's statement that he had *not* married Lucy Walters, the Whigs adopted a variety of ingenious tactics. In 1681 a Tory JP complained of a book by the old Cromwellian William Lawrence, entitled *Marriage by the Moral Law of God Vindicated*. Lawrence argued that Monmouth was Charles II's rightful heir, having been born in 'the moral way of matrimony', a state defined not by a religious ceremony, but by the sexual union of the partners.[33] Other Whig pamphleteers fell back on the 'evil councillors' argument. Charles's denials, they declared, had been extorted from him by the Duke of York and his clique. When 'rescued out of ill hands, and left to himself', one asserted, Charles would naturally acknowledge Monmouth's legitimacy. By the dangerously polarized early 1680s a few people in taverns were even accusing Charles II himself of being illegitimate.[34]

The Monmouth rebellion of 1685 serves as a fitting conclusion to this book. It illustrates several points that are central to this chapter, but it also encourages us to look back over the rest of the century to review the terrain over which we have travelled. I realize that as a Somerset man I shall be thought incapable of treating the rebellion with becoming judiciousness, just as historians from the Southern states are thought to be incapable of objectivity about the American Civil War. But why is it that only descendants of the victors are believed to be immune to bias?

For our purposes, the most important feature of the 1685 rebellion is that it was a genuinely popular uprising, with very little participation by the aristocracy and gentry. How do we explain this? Only a few years earlier Shaftesbury's Whigs had been encouraging popular involvement in elections and enlisting plebeian Londoners in what seemed to some like a revival of the Good Old Cause. But the fact is that ideologically motivated Whigs were always a small minority among the gentry. They had temporarily achieved a dramatic broadening of their base of support during the Popish Plot, but as the anti-Catholic hysteria subsided, the gentry's fears of popular upheaval provoked by Leveller-sounding rhetoric from the Green Ribbon Club were reawakened. Of course Monmouth had always courted the people. When he visited Oxford in 1680 the university pointedly ignored him; but in the town a Whig-organized banquet and races were attended by 'an enthusiastic rout of bargemen'.[35] In some parts of the kingdom—for example, Somerset, Monmouth's heartland, where a strong dissenting presence confronted an intransigant Cavalier governing class—the gulf between élite and popular politics had been widening ever since the Restoration. The Tory reaction of the early 1680s completed this process.

These generalizations apply, of course, only to regions where there was a serious Whig dissenting interest. In towns and villages where traditional culture, including traditional political culture, remained strong, there was little change either before or after the 1680s: popular loyalty to the old order of monarchy and deference, and to the restored Church of England, was still deeply entrenched. We may recall the overwhelming monarchist enthusiasm of places like Bruton and Sherborne in 1660, and with all due allowance for the fact that Monmouth's recruiting was heaviest within ten miles of his line of march, it is still striking how few of his men came from south-east Somerset and Blackmore Vale, always regions in which traditional culture flourished.[36]

But in the places from which Monmouth gained most of his recruits the divorce between the élite and the people, evident in the almost total absence of gentry participants, is strikingly apparent. 'We will do the work without them, and then we will have their estates', rebels were alleged to have said. Such open acknowledgements of class feeling were rare (and we may be sure that the government would have made the most of them for propaganda purposes if it had found them), yet all historians concur on the predominately lower-class character of the rebellion, even if they disagree over precisely which sections of the lower orders were most involved.[37] The rising was in many respects a replay of the civil war in the western counties, but without the gentry, and the rebels suffered the same fate at the hands of a professional army as the Clubmen had suffered in 1645 from Cromwell's men in the much smaller affair at Hambledon Hill. But they were much more explicitly politicized, much less localist than the Clubmen.

Monmouth got good support in decaying clothing towns and villages like Colyton, where something like a quarter of the adult male population were rebels.[38] But he did just as well in the old centres of a passionately puritan and parliamentarian culture—Wellington (the term 'Wellington Roundhead' was proverbial); Lyme Regis, with its memories of heroic siege in 1644; Taunton, with its memories of even more bloody resistance in 1645. These were, of course, places that were on the line of march; but the invasion route was not accidental, and was chosen partly because that was where the most potential recruits were likely to be found. At Taunton memories of the ruined town's last-minute relief by the New Model Army in 1645 were kept alive by the annual 11 May celebrations. As Robin Clifton has pointed out, these were often far from the staid and sober celebrations that we might expect from such a bastion of puritan nonconformity: in some respects they were substitutes for the ungodly May Day festivities which they replaced. There were bells and bonfires, much drinking, and on occasions, even dancing in the streets, to supplement the uplifting sermons by the great dissenting minister, George Newton. In 1682, it was reported, 11 May was kept up 'higher than Christmas'. The day was an occasion for reinforcing Taunton's civic, protestant, parliamentarian identity. Both in Taunton and in other Somerset towns and villages nostalgic memories of the civil war often surfaced in seditious tavern talk. Clifton's careful search through the sessions rolls has found people singing Roundhead songs ('Essex's March', for example) in a Taunton alehouse, and numerous other signs that Cromwellian sentiment in Somerset had not vanished at the Restoration.[39]

Whether we agree with Clifton that a more broadly diffused anti-popish feeling was at the heart of the Monmouth rebellion, or with Peter Earle that it was essentially a nonconformist affair, a rebellion of the 'people of God', it is clear that religious dissent played a major part in it. Many of the earlier conflicts in Taunton revolved around the defiant Presbyterian congregation at the St Paul's meeting-house, one of the biggest sites of nonconformist worship in the country, and the local struggles repeatedly illustrate the interaction of religion and politics. It was the county's grand inquest at the assizes, dominated by the gentry, which declared that the new meeting-house had been erected 'to the encouragement of faction'; it was the local bishop who drafted in rural constables to try to stop the 11 May celebrations in 1676; it was the Presbyterians who threw 'libels' into the houses of members of the hostile new corporation shortly afterwards. Bishop, militia, and JPs all tried and failed to stop the dissenters' meetings, until during the Tory reaction of the 1680s a new mayor organized the virtual demolition of the Whig-supported meeting-house, turning the attack on it into a festive occasion with free beer, bells, and bonfires. At Bridgwater there were similar scenes, and the Tory mayor, who obviously knew his Elizabethan church history, described the town's nonconformists as 'Grindallizing self-willed humourists'. Bridport and Lyme Regis, two other strongly nonconformist and pro-Monmouth towns, also lost their meeting-houses during this period of Tory violence.[40]

The rebels were cut down by a professional army at Sedgemoor. Yet their actions during the previous six weeks show how violently the civil war had intensified the politicization of many of the English people, and enabled them, when their interests—in this case their interest in a protestant succession—were threatened, to act without the leadership of their gentry superiors. And this is obviously true of many places outside the west country. Monmouth's presence there enabled people to come out of political hiding, so to speak, but it seems extremely likely that the same thing would have happened wherever there was a strong parliamentarian, nonconformist tradition, if Monmouth's small band had landed in the midst of it instead of at Lyme. As early as 1683 there were reports in Norfolk of seditious statements on Monmouth's behalf; among other examples, Robert Bottulph of Shipdham was already urging his neighbours to 'fight for the Duke of Monmouth'. Whig propaganda had convinced quite a lot of people that the Duke was indeed the legitimate son of Charles II: we find repeated statements of this belief by ordinary folk in both London and the provinces.[41] It took another three years of experience to persuade most of the gentry that a Catholic king was unacceptable. There was enough mob violence during the revolution of 1688 to show that the English common people generally supported it—that it was not, as some historians have argued, a mere palace coup. In comparison with Monmouth, however, the Glorious Revolution was so overwhelmingly an élite affair that it only confirms my general point about the divergence between the cultures of the two levels of the political nation.[42]

This division between the élite and the populace is surely the most striking change in the political nation during the seventeenth century. The country had been relatively united before 1640: united in opposition to both religious and constitutional innovation. At both the élite and the popular levels we can find disagreements over the nature of the church and its ceremonies, but even non-puritan moderates could join with puritans in opposing Laudian rituals. Gentry and plebeians shared many elements of a common political language, one based on a widespread acceptance of theories of patriarchal authority in the family, hierarchal authority in the community, and legitimate monarchical authority in the state, all, however, bound by law and custom. When things went wrong evil influences were blamed and scapegoats found: assertive women upsetting order in the household; greedy middlemen subverting the equitable distribution of food guaranteed by the rules of the old 'moral economy'; rapacious landlords and fen-drainers depriving villagers of age-old rights of common; wicked councillors like Buckingham misleading a supposedly virtuous, well-intentioned King. Often, it was suspected, there might be unseen, sinister forces behind the culprits. The habits of thought which led to the assumption that satanic inversion was at work in such matters, and could only be countered by the use of corresponding inversion rituals, were stronger among the lower orders than among the élite, but at no social level were they completely absent. Witchcraft beliefs, with their underlying identification of disorder with unruly women, were held as strongly by educated people as by their inferiors, and as in the impeachment proceedings against Buckingham, could be easily injected into politics.

The civil war changed much, though not all, of this. Liberty and Property; the Ancient Constitution; Protestant nationalism: these are among the great continuities of the whole century. But John Aubrey was right in seeing the Interregnum years as a great cultural divide: 'when I was a boy, and so before the civil wars', was his regular refrain when he reflected on the disappearance of ancient superstitions and rituals. The popular belief in witchcraft certainly did not vanish in these years—it was, after all, in the 1640s that the witch-finder Matthew Hopkins was conducting a veritable reign of terror in the eastern counties. But by the 1650s the cultural apparatus that had sustained this acceptance of supernatural intervention in mundane affairs began to weaken. Even among the common people, Aubrey reflected, literacy and printing—and in a roundabout way the civil wars—'frighted away Robin Goodfellow and the fairies'.[43] Skimmington rituals did not disappear either—there was one of the old-fashioned kind in Dorchester as late as 1707—but by the time of the Restoration people seem to have been less worried about the danger to society posed by unruly women than they had been before the wars.[44] This did not happen overnight, of course. John Crouch's *Man in the Moon* shows that in 1649 the old cultural universe was still alive and well for many of the London middling and lower sort. But this was during the 'moral panic' that followed the execution of the King, and by the later 1650s it was clear that the symbolic beheading of patriarchy in the state had not, after all, led to its overthrow in the family. After the Restoration, although some of the older vocabulary and symbolic structures survived among the common people, they were less evident in élite political discourse. Clarendon could be attacked on many other grounds, but not for using sorcery or the black arts to advance his political interests.

Instead, the civil war brought new kinds of division. People became accustomed to them: in regions which had experienced severe internal conflict (which had not happened everywhere) terms like 'Cavalier dog' and 'Roundheaded rogue' were for a time almost as common in popular abuse as traditional epithets like 'whore' and 'cuckold'.[45] For the gentry the older, vaguer divisions of Court and Country were in the end over-laid and complicated by the politics of Whig and Tory. But long before this happened we can observe an even more important development arising from the civil wars: the gentry's growing distrust of the common people. They had always feared 'the rabble', of course; but before 1640 they could rightly assume that the middle levels of the political nation shared their priorities: the defence of the Ancient Constitution, resist-ance to popery and foreign influences. After 1660 they became much more suspicious, using the militia to break up their conventicles, rather than encouraging their political independence, as they had done before 1640. By the later 1670s Shaftesbury's Whigs were appealing to the people again, but when the hysteria of the Popish Plot subsided it was clear that they had overreached themselves and raised the very spectre of civil disorder that the restoration of monarchy in 1660 had been intended to avert.

There is much that we still do not know about the political outlook of the common people after the Restoration. Richard Gough gives us some marvellous insights into the mental world of a Shropshire yeo-man, but we search in vain for a few successors to Nehemiah Wallington, a few lower-class equivalents of Samuel Pepys.[46] And we still know far too little about the political outlook of seventeenth-century women below the level of the gentry and aristocracy. Both before and after 1660 some of them undoubtedly took a strong interest in public affairs. Whoever it was who, in the later seventeenth century, added an entry to the now-deceased Elizabeth Jekyll's commonplace book did something very inter-esting. The entries stop after Jekyll's death early in 1653 and there is then a long silence. But eventually there is one more entry: a copy of Dame Alice Lisle's speech on the scaffold in 1685.[47]

Alice Lisle was the first and one of the most celebrated victims of the Bloody Assizes that followed the Monmouth rebellion. Widow of the regicide John Lisle, she had been living quietly in Hampshire and was over 70 when she sheltered two of Monmouth's adherents, in flight after Sedgemoor, unaware (she claimed) that they had been in the rebellion. With some difficulty Jeffreys managed to get her convicted for treason, and she was executed at Winchester early in September 1685, the first act of the judicial terrorism that was soon in full flood all over the West Country. The speech she tried to make on the scaffold—real or invented by the pamphleteers—soon became a favourite of Monmouth martyrologists.[48] It is interesting that somebody should have chosen to record it in Elizabeth Jekyll's commonplace book after the book had been silent and abandoned for so long. Was it because it was a statement of beliefs by a woman? Was it because it showed Lisle's willingness to die for the Protestant cause which Jekyll had supported all those years before in the civil war? Whoever the copyist (perhaps one of Jekyll's children), it was an appropriate memorial to her political beliefs, and perhaps to those of many others of her less articulate contemporaries, male and female.

This chapter began with Lionel Copley riding his tenant around the field; it nears its end with speculation about the Jekyll family's possible response to the execution of Alice Lisle. Both incidents illustrate some of the interactions between popular and élite political culture that we have been exploring in this book. In spite of the growing gulf between the two levels of the political nation, there are some striking continuities throughout the seventeenth century, and even beyond. The Leveller cliché that Copley was theatrically rebutting had a venerable ancestry, and had often surfaced during the revolution of the 1640s; the rebel Richard Rumbold (himself an old Leveller) repeated it on the scaffold before his execution in 1685; and Thomas Jefferson quoted it in the famous letter he wrote a few days before his death in 1826 on the fiftieth anniversary of the Declaration of Independence. The people, said Mr Jefferson, adapting Rumbold's famous last words, had not been 'born with saddles on their backs, nor a favoured few booted and spurred . . . to ride them'.[49]

One last anecdote, easily dismissed by the cynical as Whiggish; but then, by the eighteenth century people would be Whigs, wouldn't they? In 1712 the mayor of Lyme Regis issued a warrant for the imprisonment of a poor vagrant named William Powell. The warrant was challenged by a local lawyer who obviously had the language of the Ancient Constitution at his fingertips. As it showed no cause for Powell's committal, he pointed out, the warrant was 'expressly against the Petition of Right'; it was also contrary to Magna Carta, which declared 'that no freeman be imprisoned but by the law of the land'. The author of these comments also drew on his knowledge of ancient history: 'the taking away the liberty of one mean person once endangered the government of Rome.' The right to liberty, he concluded, was 'great, just and inviolable'.[50] We have heard a lot recently about clientage and deference in the seventeenth and eighteenth centuries. Important as those notions undoubtedly were, it does us no harm, I think, to remind ourselves that both branches of the political nation were inspired by other ideas as well: by ideas stemming from the myth of the Ancient Constitution. Embedded in the vocabulary of law and liberty that survived in the gentry's political culture was the concept, which when they were honest about it extended even to the poorest vagrant, of the freeborn people of England.

NOTES

PREFACE

1. Patrick Collinson, *De Republica Anglorum: Or, History with the Politics Put Back* (Cambridge, 1990).
2. After completing a lengthy book about Parliament, G. R. Elton, for example, concluded that 'the customary concentration on it as the centre of public affairs ... is entirely misleading': *The Parliament of England 1559–1581* (Cambridge, 1986), p. ix.

ACKNOWLEDGEMENTS

1. It should perhaps be noted that in 1915 Arthur T. Hadley, at that time president of Yale University, published *Undercurrents in American Politics*, whose title-page contains the statement: 'Comprising the Ford Lectures, delivered at Oxford University, and the Barbour-Page Lectures delivered at the University of Virginia in the Spring of 1914.' However, Ford's Lecturer in 1914 was Peter Hume Brown, whose lectures were delivered in Hilary Term, and later published as *The Legislative Union of England and Scotland*. See Arthur T. Hadley, *Undercurrents in American Politics* (New Haven, Conn., 1915); Morris Hadley, *Arthur Twining Hadley* (New Haven, Conn., 1948), 194–5; and P. H. Hardacre, 'The Ford Lectures: A Bibliography', *Bulletin of Bibliograhy*, 38: 1 (1981), 1.
2. 'The Language of Popular Politics in the English Revolution', in Alvin Vos (ed.), *Place and Displacement in the Renaissance* (Medieval and Renaissance Texts and Studies, Binghamton, NY, 1995), 107–31.

CHAPTER I

1. J. R. Tanner, *English Constitutional Conflicts of the Seventeenth Century 1603–1689* (Cambridge, 1928). By 1971 the book had been reprinted ten times.
2. R. H. Tawney, 'The Rise of the Gentry, 1558–1640', *Economic History Review*, 11 (1941); 'Harrington's Interpretation of his Age', *Proceedings of the British Academy*, 27 (1941). For the subsequent controversy, see Lawrence Stone, *The Causes of the English Revolution 1529–1642* (rev. edn., 1986), ch. 2; and R. C. Richardson, *The Debate on the English Revolution* (1977), 89–95.
3. Romney Sedgwick (ed.), *Letters from George III to Lord Bute, 1756–1766* (1939), Introduction, p. viii.
4. The most obvious applications of Namierite methods in early Stuart history are Mary Frear Keeler, *The Long Parliament, 1640–1641: A*

Biographical Study of its Members (Philadelphia, 1954); and D. Brunton and D. H. Pennington, *Members of the Long Parliament* (1954). My *Pride's Purge: Politics in the Puritan Revolution* (Oxford, 1971) has sometimes been seen as another Namierite work; it is in fact methodologically similar, but is based on very different political and philosophical assumptions.

5. Wallace Notestein, 'The Winning of the Initiative by the House of Commons', *Proceedings of the British Academy*, 11 (1924–5), 125–75.

6. This is still apparent in the revised, 1986, edition of Stone's *Causes of the English Revolution*.

7. These historians have often correctly denied that they form anything like a monolithic school, and they have often disagreed with each other. Nevertheless, it is possible to extract a more or less coherent interpretation from their work.

8. Conrad Russell (ed.), *The Origins of the English Civil War* (1973), Introduction, 7.

9. Conrad Russell, *The Fall of the British Monarchies 1637–1642* (Oxford, 1991). Russell is of course in good company: both C. V. Wedgwood, *The King's Peace 1637–1641* (1955), and Anthony Fletcher, *The Outbreak of the English Civil War* (New York, 1981) choose the same starting date. Russell's *The Causes of the English Civil War* (Oxford, 1990), does range further back in time in its search for causes, though in rather narrowly defined terms.

10. Elton, 'A High Road to Civil War?', in Charles H. Carter (ed.), *From the Renaissance to the Counter-Reformation: Essays in Honour of Garrett Mattingley* (New York, 1965), 325–47.

11. See e.g. Conrad Russell, *Parliaments and English Politics 1621–1629* (Oxford, 1979); Kevin Sharpe (ed.), *Faction and Parliament: Essays on Early Stuart History* (1978), Introduction; Mark Kishlansky, *Parliamentary Selection: Social and Political Choice in Early Modern England* (Cambridge, 1986); and Russell, 'The Nature of a Parliament', in Howard Tomlinson (ed.), *Before the English Civil War* (1984), ch. 6.

12. Russell, *Parliaments and English Politics*, 343, 396, 403.

13. Russell, *Fall of the British Monarchies*, 1. For a convenient summary of the revisionist version of the 1630s, see Kevin Sharpe, 'The Personal Rule of Charles I', in Tomlinson, *Before the English Civil War*, ch. 3. For a longer one, see Sharpe, *The Personal Rule of Charles I* (1992). On Ship Money, see also J. S. Morrill, *The Revolt of the Provinces: Conservatives and Radicals in the English Civil War 1630–1650* (rev. edn., 1980), 24–8.

14. Russell, *Causes of the English Civil War*, 27. See also Russell, *Fall of the British Monarchies*, ch. 2; and John Morrill, *The Nature of the English Revolution* (1993), chs. 5, 12, 13.

15. Russell, *Fall of the British Monarchies*, 27.

16. By Kevin Sharpe, for example, in *Faction and Parliament*, 5–14.

17. David Hume, *The History of England from the Invasion of Julius Caesar to the Revolution in 1688* (New York, 1879), v. 31. The most accessible version of the interpretation summarized in this paragraph is in Russell, *Causes of the English Civil War*. But for a different, though still revisionist, interpretation, see now Sharpe, *The Personal Rule of Charles I*.

18. e.g. by J. H. Hexter, 'Power Struggle, Parliament and Liberty in Early Stuart England', and Derek Hirst, 'Unanimity in the Commons, Aristocratic Intrigues, and the Origins of the English Civil War', *Journal of Modern History*, 50 (1978), 1–71; and by Theodore K. Rabb and Derek Hirst, 'Revisionism Revised', and Christopher Hill, 'Parliament and People in Seventeenth-Century England', *Past and Present*, 92 (Aug. 1981), 53–124.

19. Richard Cust and Ann Hughes (eds.), *Conflict in Early Stuart England: Studies in Religion and Politics 1603–1642* (1989). See also Thomas Cogswell, *The Blessed Revolution: English Politics and the Coming of War, 1621–1624* (Cambridge, 1989); Richard Cust, *The Forced Loan and English Politics 1626–1628* (Oxford, 1987); J. P. Sommerville, *Politics and Ideology in England, 1603–1640* (1986).

20. Russell, *Fall of the British Monarchies*, discusses political opinion in the later 1630s almost entirely in these terms: see esp. 1–4, 20–2, 83. For examples of localist historians who have used a broader socio-political catchment area, see Ann Hughes, 'Local History and the Origins of the Civil War', in Cust and Hughes, *Conflict in Early Stuart England*, 240–3. For the 'public transcript' (which he contrasts with the 'hidden transcript' of the common people), see James C. Scott, *Domination and the Arts of Resistance: Hidden Transcripts* (New Haven, Conn., 1990).

21. See esp. Hill, *Society and Puritanism in Pre-Revolutionary England* (2nd edn., New York, 1972), esp. ch. 4; also 'The Poor and the People', in *The Collected Essays of Christopher Hill*, vol. iii, *People and Ideas in 17th Century England* (Brighton, 1986), 247–73.

22. Among all of Hill's vast output, perhaps the most convenient summary of this position can be found in his *The Century of Revolution 1603–1714* (New York, 1961). See also Brian Manning, *The English People and the English Revolution 1640–1649* (1976). Robert Brenner's *Merchants and Revolution: Commercial Change, Political Conflict, and London's Overseas Traders, 1550–1653* (Princeton, NJ, 1993) presents a modified version of the same argument.

23. The classic expression of this view is, of course, Christopher Hill, *The World Turned Upside Down: Radical Ideas During the English Revolution* (1972).

24. J. C. D. Clark, *English Society 1688–1832: Ideology, Social Structure and Political Practice During the Ancien Régime* (Cambridge, 1985). Other works emphasizing the stability/consensus theme in social history include

Peter Laslett, *The World We Have Lost* (1965); and Ralph A. Houlbrooke, *The English Family 1450–1700* (1984).

25. See e.g. John Walter and Keith Wrightson, 'Dearth and the Social Order in Early Modern England', *Past and Present*, 71 (May 1976), 22–42; Wrightson, *English Society 1580–1680* (1982); Walter, 'Grain Riots and Popular Attitudes to the Law: Maldon and the Crisis of 1629', in John Brewer and John Styles (eds.), *An Ungovernable People: The English and their Law in the Seventeenth and Eighteenth Centuries* (1980), 47–84; Peter Clark, 'Popular Protest and Disturbance in Kent, 1558–1640', *Economic History Review*, 2nd ser., 29 (1976), 365–82; Buchanan Sharp, *In Contempt of All Authority: Rural Artisans and Riot in the West of England, 1586–1660* (Berkeley and Los Angeles, 1980); and Roger Manning, *Village Revolts: Social Protest and Popular Disturbances in England, 1509–1640* (Oxford, 1988).

26. I have discussed these matters in my *Revel, Riot, and Rebellion: Popular Politics and Culture in England 1603–1660* (Oxford, 1985), 144–5, 156–9; and in 'The Chalk and the Cheese: Contrasts Among the English Club-men', *Past and Present*, 85 (Nov. 1979), 25–48.

27. David Underdown, *Fire From Heaven: Life in an English Town in the Seventeenth Century* (1992), 46–59; *William Whiteway of Dorchester: His Diary 1618 to 1635*, Dorset Record Soc., 12 (1991), Introduction.

28. Peter Burke, 'Popular Culture in Seventeenth-Century London', in Barry Reay (ed.), *Popular Culture in Seventeenth-Century England* (1985), 31–2.

29. Carlo Ginzburg, *The Cheese and the Worms: The Cosmos of a Sixteenth-Century Miller*, trans. John and Anne Tedeschi (New York, 1982), Preface, pp. xv–xvii. See also Bob Scribner, 'Is a History of Popular Culture Possible?', *History of European Ideas*, 10 (1989), 173–91. See also Tim Harris, 'The Problem of "Popular Political Culture" in Seventeenth-Century London', Ibid. 43–58; and for a recent discussion, Tessa Watt, *Cheap Print and Popular Piety 1550–1640* (Cambridge, 1991), 2–6.

30. The story is recounted in notes entitled 'A view of Ecclesiastical history', in Beinecke Library, Osborn MS fb 41 (anon. commonplace book, 1640), fo. 51^v. The old version of the ideology of order is outlined in E. M. W. Tillyard, *The Elizabethan World Picture* (1943). Tillyard has been the target of much criticism by 'new historicists' and others: for a useful brief discussion, see Michael D. Bristol, *Carnival and Theater: Plebeian Culture and the Structure of Authority in Renaissance England* (New York, 1989), 9–13. For catechizing, see Gordon Schochet, *Patriarchalism in Political Thought: The Authoritarian Family and Political Speculation and Attitudes Especially in Seventeenth-Century England* (New York, 1975).

31. For a reading of the iconography of the royal and other early Stuart families, see Jonathan Goldberg, 'Fatherly Authority: The Politics of Stuart Family Images', in Margaret W. Ferguson, Maureen Quilligan,

and Nancy J. Vickers (eds.), *Rewriting the Renaissance: The Discourses of Sexual Difference in Early Modern Europe* (1986), 3–32.

32. Quotations from *1614*, 263, 350; Winthrop, *History of New England*, ed. James K. Hosmer (New York, 1908), i. 239. See also Charles H. McIlwain (ed.), *The Political Works of James I* (Cambridge, Mass., 1918), *passim*; Foster, *1610*, i. 31, 46, 187; ii. 24, 50, 59–60, 202. See also HMC, *Ninth Report*, ii. 497: Diary of Robert Woodford, 9 Oct. 1638.

33. Grosvenor, quoted in Richard Cust and Peter Lake, 'Sir Richard Grosvenor and the Rhetoric of Magistracy', *BIHR* 54 (1981), 42. Thomas Beard, *The Theatre of God's Judgements* (1648 edn.), 160 (the work was first published in 1597). 'Homily on Obedience': 'An Exhortation Concerning Good Order, and Obedience to Rulers and Magistrates', in *Certaine Sermons appoynted by the Queenes Majestie* (1574). Sir Robert Filmer, *Patriarcha and Other Writings*, ed. Johann P. Sommerville (Cambridge, 1991), 38–9. For a general discussion, see Sommerville, *Politics and Ideology in England 1603–1640*, 35–42.

34. Foster, *1610*, ii. 104.

35. Quoted by Linda Levy Peck, *Court Patronage and Corruption in Early Stuart England* (1990), 198.

36. Gardiner, *1610*, 138; *1625*, 199.

37. Foster, *1610*, i. 31; ii. 50, 191.

38. Susan Dwyer Amussen, *An Ordered Society: Gender and Class in Early Modern England* (Oxford, 1988), esp. ch. 2. See also Amussen, 'Gender, Family and the Social Order, 1560–1725', in Anthony Fletcher and John Stevenson (eds.), *Order and Disorder in Early Modern England* (Cambridge, 1985), 196–200.

39. Northbrooke, *Distractions of the Sabbath* (1579), 12.

40. G. M. Young, 'Some Wiltshire Cases in Star Chamber', *Wiltshire Archaeological Magazine*, 50 (1942–4), 451. PRO, STAC 8/34/6: Attorney-General vs. John Jennyns, 1621. Bodleian, Rawlinson MS C 764 (Dorset sermons, 1613–40), fo. 94ᵛ.

41. For a general discussion of this subject, see Joy Wiltenburg, *Disorderly Women and Female Power in the Street Literature of Early Modern England and Germany* (Charlottesville, Va., 1992), 7–20. Scott's statement comes from his answer to a 1627 divine-right sermon by Isaac Bargrave, Dean of Canterbury: KAO, U 951/Z10.

42. Natalie Davis, 'Women on Top', in her *Society and Culture in Early Modern France* (Stanford, 1975), ch. 5. Lisa Jardine, *Still Harping on Daughters: Women and Drama in the Age of Shakespeare* (2nd edn., New York, 1989), 39, 57–8, 70–7, 93–8, 161–2. I have suggested some additional reasons for these anxieties in my essay 'The Taming of the Scold: The Enforcement of Patriarchal Authority in Early Modern England', in Fletcher and Stevenson (eds.), *Order and Disorder*, 116–36. Martin Ingram has recently

argued that there were no unusual strains in gender relations in this period: '"Scolding Women Cucked or Washed": A Crisis in Gender Relations in Early Modern England?', in Jennifer Kermode and Garthine Walker (eds.), *Women, Crime and the Courts in Early Modern England* (Chapel Hill, 1994), 48–80. The evidence he deploys totally refutes his own conclusions.

43. For a fine discussion of this subject, see Jodi Mikalachki, 'Taking the Measure of England: The Poetics of Antiquarianism in the English Renaissance', unpublished Ph.D thesis (Yale University, 1990), esp. ch. 4.

44. Jardine, *Still Harping on Daughters*, esp. ch. 3.

45. The literature on witchcraft is, of course, endless. The chronology is conveniently summarized in A. D. J. Macfarlane, 'Witchcraft in Tudor and Stuart Essex', in J. S. Cockburn (ed.), *Crime in England 1550–1800* (Cambridge, 1977), ch. 3. See also Clive Holmes, 'Popular Culture? Witches, Magistrates and Divines in Early Modern England', in Steven L. Kaplan (ed.), *Understanding Popular Culture: Europe from the Middle Ages to the Nineteenth Century* (Berlin, 1984), 85–111.

46. *Certaine Sermons*, 104–5. *The Lancashire Witches* is in Thomas Heywood, *Dramatic Works* (1874), iv. See also Underdown, *Revel, Riot and Rebellion*, 38.

47. *1626*, ii. 137. Foster, *1610*, i. 50–1. Thomas Tuke, *A Treatise against Painting and Tincturing of Man and Women* (1616), 42. Thomas Adams, *Mystical Bedlam, or The World of Mad-Men* (1615), 51. 'A Pittilesse Mother..?' (1616); selections printed in Katherine U. Henderson and Barbara F. McManus (eds.), *Half Humankind: Contexts and Texts of the Controversy about Women in England, 1540–1640* (Urbana and Chicago, 1985), 361–7.

48. *Certaine Sermons*, 104. *Holinshed's Chronicles of England, Scotland, and Ireland* (1807–8), iv. 909; quoted by Annabel Patterson, *Reading Holinshed's Chronicles* (Chicago, 1994), 213. [Alexander Cooke], *The Weather-cocke of Romes religion: With her severall changes. Or: The World Turn'd Topsie-Turvie by Papists* (1625).

CHAPTER 2

1. See e.g. Sharpe, *Faction and Parliament*, 7–10.

2. Cogswell, *The Blessed Revolution*; Cust, *The Forced Loan and English Politics*. See also the essays by these two authors in Cust and Hughes (eds.), *Conflict in Early Stuart England*.

3. *1626*, ii. 430; iii. 288–97; iv. App. II E, 2, 11 (c), 14 (a). Richard Cust, 'News and Politics in Early Seventeenth-Century England', *Past and Present*, 112 (Aug. 1986), 60–90. See also Foster, *1610*, ii. 170. Cogswell shows that the government was also conscious of the need to defend its point of view: 'The Politics of Propaganda: Charles I and the People in the 1620s', *JBS* 29 (1990), 187–215.

4. Foster, *1610*, ii. 168. On the libels attacking Salisbury, see Pauline Croft, 'The Reputation of Robert Cecil: Libels, Political Opinion and Popular Awareness in the Early Seventeenth Century', *TRHS*, 6th ser., 1 (1991), 43–69. For libels more generally, see Alastair Bellany, '"Rayling Rymes and Vaunting, Verse": Libellous Politics in Early Stuart England, 1603–1628', in Kevin Sharpe and Peter Lake (eds.), *Culture and Politics in Early Stuart England* (1994), 285–310. Ben Jonson had been summoned before the Council in 1604 for his play *Sejanus*, but not, apparently, for any specific parallel between Sejanus and Salisbury. It may have been the play's coded allusions to the trial of Ralegh that got him into trouble: Ben Jonson, *Sejanus His Fall*, ed. Philip J. Ayres (Manchester, 1990), 17.

5. G. E. Aylmer, *The King's Servants: The Civil Service of Charles I 1625–1642* (1961). Peck, *Court Patronage and Corruption*.

6. Susan Amussen, 'A Norfolk Village', *History Today*, 36 (Apr. 1986), 16–20; I am indebted to Dr Amussen for further information about the Saw[y]ers. P. Eden, 'Land Surveyors in Norfolk, 1550–1850', *Norfolk Archaeology*, 36: 2 (1975), 142.

7. Madeleine Gray, 'Exchequer Officials and the Market in Crown Property, 1558–1640', in R. W. Hoyle (ed.), *The Estates of the English Crown, 1558–1640* (Cambridge, 1992), 113, 122, 125–6. Aylmer, *King's Servants*, 187–8. *CSPD*, *1611–18*, 98, 388; *1623–5*, 397; *1633–4*, 362.

8. VCH, *Berkshire*, iii. 500. Norfolk Record Office, NRS Accn. 1.8.63 (P186D).

9. *CSPD*, *1631–3*, 536, 574. Foster, *1610*, ii. 344. William A. Shaw, *The Knights of England* (1906), ii. 188. Sawyer's acquisitions in Berkshire (where he had connections with the Craven family) can be followed in VCH, *Berks.*, iii. 173–4; iv. 181; and W. Berry, *County Genealogies: Pedigrees of Berkshire Families* (1837), 104–5. See also Christopher G. Durston, 'Berkshire and its County Gentry, 1625–1649', unpublished Ph.D thesis (Reading University, 1977), 62, 93; I am grateful to Dr Durston for his help with Berkshire local politics.

10. *APC*, *1627–8*, 473. *1628*, vi. 198. Gray, 'Exchequer Officials', 125. Aylmer, *King's Servants*, 157.

11. *1628*, ii. 418; iii. 447; iv. 392, 406.

12. *1628*, iv. 393, 404, 406, 408–9, 412–13; vi. 119.

13. *1628*, iv. 188, 415, 419. Basil D. Henning, *The House of Commons, 1660–1690* (1983), iii. 401.

14. *1626*, iii. 351.

15. Hoyle (ed.), *Estates of the English Crown*, Introduction, 46. Sawyer was already a JP in Berkshire by 1624, and served on many other local commissions there: Durston, 'Berkshire and its County Gentry', 84–5, 96, 99–103, 119, 121, 123–5. He was an apparently tepid royalist in the civil war. See ibid. 155, 157, 166; M. A. E. Green (ed.), *Calendar of the*

Proceedings of the Committee for Advance of Money, 1642–1656 (1888), 968; id. (ed.), *Calendar of the Proceedings of the Committee for Compounding, 1643–60* (1889–92), 2939–40. His will, proved in 1676, suggests immense wealth: Gray, 'Exchequer Officials', 132–3.

16. *1626*, iii. 386.

17. *1628*, vi. 220.

18. Peter Clark, 'Thomas Scott and the Growth of Urban Opposition to the Early Stuart Regime', *Historical Journal*, 21 (1978), 1–26. But see also Cust, *Forced Loan*, 175–84. His outlook was in many respects similar to that of the other Thomas Scott, author of *Vox Populi*: Peter Lake, 'Constitutional Consensus and Puritan Opposition During the 1620s: Thomas Scott and the Spanish Match', *Historical Journal*, 25 (1982), 805–25.

19. Clark, 'Scott', 3–4. Christopher Hill, *A Nation of Change and Novelty* (1990), 42–3, 51.

20. *1628*, vi. 232.

21. MacIlwain (ed.), *Political Works of James I*, 340. *1621*, ii. 3; and cf. iv. 2.

22. Ellesmere, 'Special Observations', in Foster, *1610*, i. 276–9, 282. I am grateful to Tom Cogswell for the point that Ellesmere's views foreshadow those of later advocates of prerogative rule.

23. Foster, *1610*, ii. 404. In the draft of a letter that in the end he did not send, Sir Dudley Digges warned Charles I that the House of Commons was always likely to contain 'popular spirits': *1626*, iv. App. II F(1).

24. J. G. A. Pocock, *Politics, Language and Time: Essays on Political Thought and History* (New York, 1971), esp. ch. 1. See also John E. Toews, 'Intellectual History after the Linguistic Turn: The Autonomy of Meaning and the Irreducibility of Experience', *American Historical Review*, 92 (1987), 879–93.

25. *1628*, ii. 100–2. And cf. Thomas Hedley in 1610: Foster, *1610*, ii. 182.

26. *1628*, ii. 306–7, 333; iii. 79. On custom and the ancient constitution, see J. G. A. Pocock, *The Ancient Constitution and the Feudal Law: A Study of English Historical Thought in the Seventeenth Century* (2nd edn., Cambridge, 1987), 32–41. See also Glenn Burgess, *The Politics of the Ancient Constitution: An Introduction to English Political Thought, 1600–1642* (Houndsmills, 1992).

27. Foster, *1610*, ii. 157.

28. *1626*, iii. 276. And cf. Eliot two years later: *1628*, iii. 8. See also Thomas Hedley's explanation of this: Foster, *1610*, ii. 194–5, 197.

29. *1626*, iii. 361. *1628*, ii. 66. It was often noted that impositions had been introduced by Queen Mary's *Spanish* advisers. For Eliot, see e.g. *1628*, iv. 62, 64.

30. *1625*, 491. On Prince Henry's Arthurian role, see Nicholas Von Maltzahn, *Milton's History of Britain: Republican Historiography in the English Revolution* (Oxford, 1991), 98.

31. *1626*, ii. 150, 249. Trumbull to Carleton, 26 June 1621: PRO, SP 77/14/350 (I am grateful to Tom Cogswell for this reference and for discussion of the points made in this paragraph).

32. Barnaby Rich, *The Irish Hubbub, or, The English Hue and Crie* (2nd edn., 1619), 4, 8, and see also 11–17, 40–1. [John Rhodes], *The Spy: Discovering the Danger of Arminian Heresie and Spanish Trecherie* (Strasbourg, 1628). I have discussed this subject in my paper 'Yellow Ruffs and Poisoned Possets: Placing Women in Early Stuart Political Debate', given at the second 'Attending to Women' conference at the University of Maryland, in April 1994.

33. David Cressy, *Bonfires and Bells: National Memory and the Protestant Calendar in Elizabethan and Stuart England* (Berkeley and Los Angeles, 1989), 59–61, 132–8.

34. Beinecke Library, Osborn MS b. 197 (Commonplace Book of Tobias Alston), 225. [Rhodes], *The Spy*.

35. *1625*, 216, 278, 394, 488, 538, 546. *1626*, iii. 78. *1628*, iv. 62, 202–3, 405.

36. 'Gallants, to Bohemia', in Hyder Rollins (ed.), *A Pepysian Garland: Black-Letter Broadside Ballads of the Years 1595–1639* (Cambridge, 1922), 416–19. For examples of the paranoia in pamphlets, see [Alexander Cooke], *The Weather-cocke of Romes religion* (1625), and Lewis Owen, *The Unmasking of All popish Monks, Friers, and Jesuits* (1628).

37. *1628*, iv. 239. *1629*, 16. The result was to make people who a few years earlier would have indignantly rejected it find positive qualities in the term 'puritan': see the verse satire 'The Interpreter' (1622), in C. H. Firth (ed.), *Stuart Tracts 1603–1693* (repr. New York, 1964), 233–46. By 1627 Thomas Scott was using the term in a neutral, non-pejorative way: Clark, 'Thomas Scott', 18.

38. Foster, *1610*, ii. 328. Archbishop Bancroft admitted that he was suspected 'to incline too much to . . . the King's authority'; the suspicions were heightened by John Cowell's dedication of his much-criticized law-dictionary *The Interpreter* to him: ibid. 79.

39. *1614*, 349, 350–1, 365, 372, 380. Scott to Knatchbull, 14 July 1612: Bodleian, Ballard MS 61, fo. 82. *1625*, 533.

40. *1625*, 331, 333, 337–8, 517. *1629*, 13. Cf. also *1628*, iv. 313. It has been argued that Arminianism was a 'minority issue' even in 1626 and 1628, and that its alleged relevance to the coming of the civil war is a myth: Peter White, 'The Rise of Arminianism Reconsidered', *Past and Present*, 101 (Nov. 1983), 50–4. This, along with the rest of White's argument, has been effectively demolished by William Lamont, Peter Lake, and Nicholas Tyacke, in contributions to *Past and Present*, 107 (May 1985), 114 (Feb. 1987), and 115 (May 1987).

41. *1626*, iii. 355–6, 438. *1628*, iv. 116. *1629*, 15, 52.

42. Stuart Clark, 'Inversion, Misrule and the Meaning of Witchcraft', *Past*

and Present, 87 (May 1980), 105. Richard Cust and Ann Hughes, 'Introduction: After Revisionism', in Cust and Hughes (eds.), *Conflict in Early Stuart England*, 19–21. *1614*, 421. Cf. also Gardiner, *1610*, 11.

43. B. Anderton (ed.), 'Selections from the Delaval Papers', Newcastle upon Tyne Records Committee, *Miscellanea*, 9 (1929), 138. George Roberts (ed.), *Diary of Walter Yonge . . . 1604 to 1628*, Camden Soc., 1st ser. (1848), 98. Cf. also *1614*, 423.

44. Underdown, *Revel, Riot, and Rebellion*, 127. A good example of the genre is Nicholas Breton's 'The Court and the Country' (1618), in A. B. Grosart (ed.), *The Works in Verse and Prose of Nicholas Breton* (1879), ii.

45. *1625*, 507, 516, 522. *1626*, iv. App. II F (1). *1628*, vi. 127, 129.

46. *1628*, ii. 60, 63, 432.

47. Beinecke Library, Osborn MS Fb. 155 (Commonplace Book of John Browne), 132. *Whiteway's Diary*, 74. *1628*, vi. 145. As Mark Kishlansky has rightly argued in 'The Emergence of Adversary Politics in the Long Parliament', *Journal of Modern History*, 49 (1977), 617–24, consensus was the ideal, and he accepts (623) that this was beginning to break down in 1626. My own view is that the breakdown began earlier, and was more complete than the revisionist position allows.

48. A convincing recent argument for this is in Sommerville, *Ideology and Politics*; also his essay, 'Ideology, Property and the Constitution', in Cust and Hughes (eds.), *Conflict in Early Stuart England*, ch. 2. For the breakdown-of-communication argument, see Kevin Sharpe, 'Crown, Parliament and Locality: Government and Communication in Early Stuart England', *EHR* 101 (1986), 321–50.

49. Foster, *1610*, i. 18; ii. 47. HMC, *Downshire*, ii. 257–8.

50. *1614*, 420. Scott thought the 1614 Parliament 'must be our making or marring': Bodleian, Ballard MS 61, fo. 89.

51. *1626*, iii. 302. However, Grosvenor's version of the speech (304) says under James and Elizabeth.

52. Gardiner, *1610*, 112. Foster, *1610*, ii. 398.

53. Grimeston's translation appeared in 1614. See also *1626*, iii. 364; and F. W. Fairholt (ed.), *Poems and Songs Relating to George Villiers, Duke of Buckingham*, Percy Soc., 29 (1850), 40. I am indebted to Adrienne Bakos, 'Hero or Tyrant: The Historical Reputation of Louis XI', Ph.D thesis (Bryn Mawr College, 1990), ch. 5, for discussion of Matthieu's work.

54. *1625*, 449. *1629*, 19.

55. *1626*, iii. 36, 66, 241–2, 353, 357, 378, 418, 440. See also Cust, *Forced Loan*, 27–30.

56. It has become much easier to do this with the recent publication of *1626*, the first full edition of the papers of the 1626 Parliament. Volume 4 of this edition, containing much important appendix material on the

impeachment, remains to be published; citations given in this chapter are to the numbered documents it contains.

57. Croft, 'Reputation of Robert Cecil', 55–60.

58. N. E. McClure (ed.), *The Letters of John Chamberlain* (Philadelphia, 1939), i. 444, 449; [Thomas Birch] (ed.), *The Court and Times of James I* (1848), i. 380. There are numerous accounts of Jacobean court scandals, of dubious accuracy: see e.g. Sir Anthony Weldon, *The Court and Character of King James* (1650); and the anonymous 'Secret History of the Reign of King James I', in J. O. Halliwell (ed.), *Autobiography and Correspondence of Sir Simonds D'Ewes* (1845), ii. 329–88. For a recent attempt to defend Frances Howard, see David Lindley, *The Trials of Frances Howard: Fact and Fiction at the Court of King James* (1993).

59. Lawrence Stone, *The Crisis of the Aristocracy 1558–1641* (Oxford, 1965), 596, 667. McClure (ed.), *Chamberlain Letters*, ii. 88–9, 132, 144–5, 214, 216–17. D. J. H. Clifford (ed.), *The Diaries of Lady Anne Clifford* (1990), 68. For the Roos and Purbeck cases, see also my 'Yellow Ruffs and Poisoned Possets: Placing Women in Early Stuart Political Debate'.

60. McClure (ed.), *Chamberlain Letters*, ii. 601. Godfrey Goodman, *The Court of King James the First*, ed. J. S. Brewer (1839), ii. 377. HMC, *Mar and Kellie*, suppl., 220. W. Scott and J. Bliss (eds.), *Works of . . . William Laud, D. D.* (Oxford, 1847–60), iii. 154–7. Roger Lockyer, *Buckingham: The Life and Political Career of George Villiers, First Duke of Buckingham, 1592–1628* (1981), 285–6. [Rhodes], *The Spy*.

61. HMC, *Mar and Kellie*, suppl., 225–6. *CSP Venetian*, 18 (1623–5), 627. *1626*, iii. 57–8, 63–9, 73–4, 85–94; iv. App. II E, 5(a), (u), (v); E, 7(c). As the editors of the 1626 *Proceedings* point out, Thomas Birch suppressed many of the references to the poisoning charge in the letters he printed in his *Court and Times of Charles I* (1848–9), and subsequent historians have consequently been inclined to minimize its importance. It is not mentioned in S. R. Gardiner's edition of *Documents Illustrating the Impeachment of the Duke of Buckingham*, Camden Soc., new ser., 45 (1889). Russell, *Parliaments and English Politics*, 305, 315–16, mentions the accusation only in a couple of brief asides, and clearly does not take it seriously. See also Lockyer, *Buckingham*, 233–4.

62. Frederick S. Boas (ed.), *The Diary of Thomas Crosfield M. A., B. D., Fellow of Queen's College, Oxford* (1935), 7, 109. McClure (ed.), *Chamberlain Letters*, ii. 439. On the Catholic inclinations of the Duke's family, see Lockyer, *Buckingham*, 58–60, 115, 258, 358, 372, 461, 469.

63. George Eglisham, *The Forerunner of Revenge Upon the Duke of Buckingham . . .* (Franckfort, 1626), 7–22; also in W. Oldys and T. Park (eds.), *Harleian Miscellany* (1808–13), ii. 69–81. *1626*, iv. App. II F(8), G. For Dr Lambe, see below, Ch. 3, pp. 58–9. A later story says that Buckingham also consulted a conjuror or alchemist named Butler, whom he then

got out of the way by having him murdered by Jesuits: Arthur Wilson, *The History of Great Britain, being the Life and Reign of King James the First* (1653), 287–8.

64. S. R. Gardiner (ed.), *Reports of Cases in the Courts of Star Chamber and High Commission*, Camden Soc., new ser., 39 (1886), 272. For the belief system, see Keith Thomas, *Religion and the Decline of Magic* (1971).

65. See *1625*, esp. 403–6, 458–60, 540–3.

66. *1626, passim*. For details of the grants of office, see *1626*, iv. App. II. I. The sale of titles is discussed by Stone, *Crisis of the Aristocracy*, 111–15.

67. *1626*, iv. App. F(4). For the Pembroke connection, see Russell, *Parliaments and English Politics*, 12–14, 16, 281, 289.

68. *1628*, vi. 132–3. See also KAO, U951/Z17/2/11–66, pp. 76, 83–94. Scott's firm belief in the poisoning charge is also apparent in KAO, U951/Z/10.

69. *1628*, iv. 115–17, 120.

70. Both translations of Matthieu appeared with the title, *The Powerfull Favorite, or, The Life of Aelius Sejanus* (Paris [London?], 1628). The work was originally published in France in 1617 as an attack on the favourite Concini. Another translation, by Sir Thomas Hawkins, was published in 1632. See also J. H. M. Salmon, 'Stoicism and Roman Example: Seneca and Tacitus in Jacobean England', *Journal of the History of Ideas*, 50 (1989), 219–21, 225. 'Upon the Duke', BL, Sloane MS 826, fo. 174. Contemporaries were aware of the Wolsey parallel: Cogswell, 'Politics of Propaganda', 201. I am grateful to Professor Cogswell for letting me read his unpublished paper, 'Underground Verse and the Transformation of Early Stuart Political Culture', which provides convincing evidence of the increasing flood of political libels. The paper is now printed in Susan D. Amussen and Mark Kishlansky (eds.), *Political Culture and Cultural Politics in Early Modern England* (Manchester, 1995), 277–300.

71. The libel campaign against Buckingham is surveyed by Bellany, 'Rayling Rymes and Vaunting Verse', 297–308. See also Croft, 'Reputation of Robert Cecil'.

72. As noted e.g. by Bellany, 'Rayling Rymes and Vaunting Verse', 291.

73. [Rhodes], *The Spy*.

74. Cust, 'News and Politics', 66–7. Fairholt (ed.), *Poems and Songs Relating to Buckingham*, 3–4, 49. The earlier libel can be dated as 1623 from another version (with minor variants and the omissions supplied) in Beinecke Library, Osborn MS b. 197 (Alston Commonplace Book), 187–9. There is an extensive collection of libels against Buckingham in BL, Sloane MS 826, fos. 152–245, some but not all printed by Fairholt. Scott's use of the Gaveston analogy is in KAO, U951/Z/10. For the Duke's relationship with James, see Lockyer, *Buckingham*, esp. 22; and for libels on this, Bellany, 'Rayling Rymes and Vaunting Verse', 297–8.

75. Fairholt (ed.), *Poems and Songs Relating to Buckingham*, 7. For the use

of libels in aristocratic faction-fighting, see McClure (ed.), *Chamberlain Letters*, ii. 195. Pauline Croft argues that the libels against Salisbury were also aimed at a popular as well as a court audience: 'Reputation of Robert Cecil', 62–4.

76. Cambridge U. Library, MS Dd. xi. 73, fos. 67ᵛ–69. Beinecke Library, Osborn MS b. 197, pp. 187–9. BL Sloane MSS 826, fos. 152–245; 1792, fos. 5, 114ᵛ–115. M. A. E. Green (ed.), *Diary of John Rous, Incumbent of Santon Downham, from 1625 to 1642*, Camden Soc., 66 (1856), 19–22, 26, 29–31. Many of these libels are printed in Fairholt (ed.), *Poems and Songs Relating to Buckingham*.

77. *1628*, iv. 116, 119–20, 123–4, 130, 142, 316; vi. 215.

78. *1628*, vi. 235–6, 241. KAO, U 951/Z/10; U951/Z17/4, pp. 33–6, 44. There is language in Scott's account which suggests that he may have looked forward to armed rebellion in the later months of 1628: see esp. *1628*, vi. 241; and KAO, U951/Z17/4, pp. 27, 44.

79. Fairholt (ed.), *Poems and Songs Relating to Buckingham*, 52–4, 63–77. The highwayman John Clavell was one of those who secretly commended Felton: J. H. F. Pafford, *John Clavell 1601–43: Highwayman, Author, Lawyer, Doctor* (Oxford, 1993), 153.

80. *1626*, iii. 358.

81. *1628*, iv. 139, 393. For the Commons' use of this argument, see Edmund S. Morgan, *Inventing the People: The Rise of Popular Sovereignty in England and America* (New York, 1988), 25–35.

82. Foster, *1610*, ii. 190.

83. Foster, *1610*, ii. 204, 318. Gardiner, *History of England* (2nd edn., 1885), ii. 268–9.

84. *1628*, iii. 209, 275, 280.

85. *1626*, iii. 350.

86. *1628*, iv. 265.

87. *1625*, 29.

88. *1628*, vi. 134. In 1624 John Webster had celebrated Henry's memory in a civic pageant that did not mention either James or Charles, but deplored the state of the country since Henry's death: Von Maltzahn, *Milton's History of Britain*, 99–100; M. C. Bradbrook, *John Webster Citizen and Dramatist* (1980), 180–1.

89. *1628*, iv. 128, 131. Roberts (ed.), *Diary of Walter Yonge*, 114, and cf. also 110.

90. Foster, *1610*, i. 141.

91. *1626*, iii. 163.

92. Ibid. 91.

93. *1614*, 148, 150, 156, 228–32.

94. *1626*, iii. 201. *CJ*, i. 858.

95. Sharpe, 'The Personal Rule', 68–73. Sharpe has recently amplified these views in *The Personal Rule of Charles I*, without significantly changing them.

96. Sheila Lambert has argued that censorship scarcely existed in early Stuart England: 'Richard Montagu, Arminianism and Censorship', *Past and Present*, 124 (Aug. 1989), 57–62. This seems to me totally wrong. The best study of the subject is still Annabel Patterson, *Censorship and Interpretation: The Conditions of Writing and Reading in Early Modern England* (2nd edn., Madison, Wis., 1989); see esp. ch. 2, for the 'strategies of indirection' that the system required.

97. Green (ed.), *Diary of John Rous*, 79. For further examples of the divisions, see also Clark, 'Scott', 23–4; and Whiteway's Commonplace book, Cambridge Univ. Library, MS Dd. xi. 73, fo. 158ᵛ. As noted (n. 40 above), the argument that the 'rise of Arminianism' is a fiction, and that there was a 'theological consensus' in the 1630s shared by all but a handful of hard-core puritans, has been shown to be entirely without merit.

98. Esther S. Cope, *Politics without Parliaments 1629–1640* (1987), esp. ch. 2.

99. Victor Morgan, 'Whose Prerogative in Late Sixteenth and Early Seventeenth Century England?', *Journal of Legal History*, 5 (1984), 47–55.

100. Few people originally questioned the legality of Ship Money: it was the annual repetition of the writs at a time of no obviously overwhelming maritime emergency that caused the trouble. For the whole subject see Sharpe, 'The Personal Rule', 69–74; John Morrill, *The Revolt of the Provinces: Conservatives and Radicals in the English Civil War 1630–1650* (rev. edn., 1980), 24–30; Cope, *Politics without Parliaments*, 106–21.

101. Cope, *Politics without Parliaments*, 73, 117–19.

102. BL, Loan 29 (Harley Papers) /27 (5), 22 Feb. 1632/3, 24 Jan. 1633/4. See also Jacqueline Eales, *Puritans and Roundheads: The Harleys of Brampton Bryan and the Outbreak of the English Civil War* (Cambridge, 1990), 59–60, 88–9. In *The Saints Sacrifice: Or, A Commentarie on the CXVI. Psalme* (1632), dedicated to the puritan Earl of Warwick, William Gouge dutifully gave thanks for the birth of Prince Charles, but also for the Swedish victories in Germany, and for the preservation of the Dutch from both popery and Arminianism.

103. Richard Schlatter (ed.), *Hobbes's Thucydides* (New Brunswick, NJ, 1975), 12–13; see also Schlatter's Introduction, pp. xx–xxviii.

104. Cope, *Politics without Parliament*, 26. Bodleian, Ballard MS 61, fos. 79ᵛ–80. For the date of Filmer's tract, see Sommerville (ed.), *Filmer's Patriarcha*, 1.

CHAPTER 3

1. Foster, *1610*, i. 51. For the Cotswold Games, see Christopher Whitfield (ed.), *Robert Dover and the Cotswold Games: Annalia Dubrensia* (1962).

2. *1626*, ii. 53; iii. 5. Gardiner (ed.), *Star Chamber Cases*, 271.

3. *1628*, vi. 128. KAO, U951/Z/10.

4. *1625*, 545, 659–60.

5. Foster, *1610*, i. 235.

6. HMC, *Var. Coll.*, iii. 260.

7. For these and other examples, see Underdown, *Revel, Riot, and Rebellion*, 123–4; Manning, *The English People and the English Revolution*, 146–7; Underdown, *Fire From Heaven*, 151–5.

8. There are good discussions in Clark, 'Popular Protest and Disturbance in Kent', 365–81; Walter and Wrightson, 'Dearth and the Social Order', 22–42.

9. 'A Looking glasse for Corne-hoarders' (1632), in Rollins, (ed.), *A Pepysian Garland*, 370–5. There were many other ballads on this theme.

10. Walter and Wrightson, 'Dearth and the Social Order', esp. 23–4. See also Walter, 'Grain Riots and Popular Attitudes to the Law', 47–84. The classic description of the 'moral economy' is of course by E. P. Thompson, 'The Moral Economy of the English Crowd in the Eighteenth Century', *Past and Present*, 50 (Feb. 1971), 76–136.

11. For an example of collective legal action followed by later violence, see Peter Large, 'From Swanimote to Disafforestation: Feckenham Forest in the Early Seventeenth Century', in Hoyle (ed.), *Estates of the English Crown*, 403–4, 410–14. Many Wiltshire riots show similar features: Eric Kerridge, 'The Revolts in Wiltshire against Charles I', *Wilts. Archaeological Magazine*, 57 (1958–60), 65.

12. William B. Willcox, *Gloucestershire: A Study in Local Government, 1590–1640* (New Haven, Conn., 1940), 279–80. Gardiner (ed.), *Star Chamber Cases*, 95.

13. David Levine and Keith Wrightson, *The Making of an Industrial Society: Whickham 1560–1765* (Oxford, 1991), 122; and see also 117–31 for the (eventually unsuccessful) resistance.

14. Quoted in Clive Holmes, *Seventeenth-Century Lincolnshire* (Lincoln, 1980), 128. See also Gardiner (ed.), *Star Chamber Cases*, 59–65. For similar criticisms of the 'unprofitable' life of the forest-dwellers, see R. W. Hoyle, 'Disafforestation and Drainage: The Crown as Entrepreneur', in Hoyle (ed.), *Estates of the English Crown*, 360–1.

15. Quoted in Joan Thirsk, 'The Crown as Projector on its Own Estates, From Elizabeth I to Charles I', in Hoyle (ed.), *The Estates of the English Crown*, 335. This and much other evidence undermines Kevin Sharpe's attempt (*The Personal Rule*, 244–56) to absolve Charles I from responsibility for the disafforestation and drainage projects.

16. *1625*, 546. *1626*, iv. App. II F (1): Digges to Charles I (draft), Jan. 1626.

17. *1626*, ii. 137. For seditious talk see William Hunt, *The Puritan Moment: The Coming of Revolution in an English County* (Cambridge, Mass., 1983), 58–63; J. Samaha, 'Gleanings from Local Criminal Court Records:

Sedition Amongst the "Inarticulate" in Elizabethan Essex', *Journal of Social History*, 8: 4 (1975), 72–3; Amussen, *An Ordered Society*, 145–6.

18. Edwin F. Gay, 'The Midland Revolt and the Inquisitions of Depopulation of 1607', *TRHS*, new ser., 18 (1904), 215, 240. For another good example, see Willcox, *Gloucestershire*, 193–4. One early seventeenth-century ballad has the poor appealing to the shade of Queen Elizabeth: Beinecke Library, Osborn MS b. 197, p. 96. For popular historical memory, esp. the 'merry England' myth, see Keith Thomas, *The Perception of the Past in Early Modern England* (Creighton Trust Lecture, 1983).

19. Holmes, *Lincolnshire*, 11, 124. For other examples, see John Aubrey, *Three Prose Works*, ed. J. Buchanan-Brown (Carbondale, Ill., 1972), 192–4; and Thomas, *Perception of the Past*, 2–3.

20. For Cobbler, see C. S. L. Davies, 'The Pilgrimage of Grace Reconsidered', *Past and Present*, 41 (Dec. 1968), 68, 71, 74; for Poverty, M. L. Bush, 'Captain Poverty and the Pilgrimage of Grace', *Historical Research*, 65 (1992), 17–36; for Pouch, Gay, 'Midland Revolt', 217 n; for Gillingham, J. H. Bettey, 'The Revolts over the Enclosure of the Royal Forest at Gillingham 1626–1630', *Dorset Natural History and Archaeological Society Proceedings*, 97 (1975), 22.

21. Quoted in Hunt, *Puritan Moment*, 59.

22. PRO, SP 16/131, fos. 21–2; 16/132, fos. 153–4. *1628*, vi. 139–42.

23. Cogswell, 'England and the Spanish Match', in Cust and Hughes (eds.), *Conflict in Early Stuart England*, 107–33. Dorset Record Office, D1/7623 (Netherbury Manorial Presentments, 1456–1622). I am indebted to Hugh Jaques for a transcript of this document.

24. *1628*, iv. 185–6, 190; vi. 185–6, 195. See also Cressy, *Bonfires and Bells*, 85.

25. *1628*, iv. 291 n, 298, 308; vi. 117.

26. Green (ed.), *Diary of John Rous*, 12, 19, 31.

27. Ibid. 19, 52–3.

28. Cust, 'News and Politics', 65–6.

29. Douglas L. Hayward (ed.), *The Registers of Bruton, Co. Somerset*, vol. i, *1554–1680* (Parish Register Soc., 50), 81.

30. BL, Harleian MS 6715 (Casebook of Sir Francis Ashley), fo. 74. *Somerset and Dorset Notes and Queries*, 15 (1916–17), 156. It should be noted that this sermon preceded the meeting of the 1626 Parliament.

31. 'Advertisements of a Loyall Subject to his gracious Soveraigne', BL, Harleian MS 1583, fos. 60–1. Andrew Clark (ed.), 'Dr. Plume's Notebook', *Essex Review*, 14 (1905), 163; I am indebted to Tom Cogswell for this reference.

32. Mark Stoyle, *Loyalty and Locality: Popular Allegiance in Devon during the English Civil War* (Exeter, 1994), 179–80. Underdown, *Fire From Heaven*, 179–81.

33. *1628*, ii. 127–8, 168–70, 253–5, 272, 304, 361, 365, 383–5. See also Willcox,

Gloucestershire, 99–102; Underdown, *Fire From Heaven*, 181–2; Peck, *Court Patronage and Corruption*, 96–8.

34. Cust, *Forced Loan*, 153–8. Russell, *Parliaments and English Politics*, 334. Gardiner, *History of England* . . . *1603–1642* (2nd edn., 1885), ii. 264–70; iv. 295. Roberts (ed.), *Diary of Walter Yonge*, 61. Willcox, *Gloucestershire*, 116–17.

35. Willcox, *Gloucestershire*, 120–1. See also Cust, *Forced Loan*, 253–306; Hunt, *Puritan Moment*, 202–4; Holmes, *Lincolnshire*, 105–7.

36. *1625*, 475.

37. Joan Kent, *The English Village Constable 1580–1642: A Social and Administrative Study* (Oxford, 1986), 248 (and more generally, for resistance to Ship Money, 162–6, 230–2, 242–8). On the localist features of resistance to Ship Money, see Morrill, *Revolt of the Provinces*, 24–9. James Hart, *Justice Upon Petition: The House of Lords and the Reformation of Justice 1621–1675* (1991), 87, gives an example of rescue of a constable by neighbours.

38. Cust and Lake, 'Grosvenor and the Rhetoric of Magistracy', 43–52.

39. Green (ed.), *Diary of John Rous*, 12.

40. *1614*, 190. *1628*, vi. 128. Kishlansky, *Parliamentary Selection*, 14, 25–8, 74–5.

41. *1628*, ii. 428–30 (Bridport). See also Derek Hirst, *The Representative of the People? Voters and Voting in England under the Early Stuarts* (Cambridge, 1975), 63–84.

42. Wallace Notestein (ed.), *The Journal of Sir Simonds D'Ewes from the Beginning of the Long Parliament to the Opening of the Trial of the Earl of Strafford* (New Haven, Conn., 1923), 43.

43. For Kent, *1625*, 686–8. For Dorset, *1626*, iv. App. II D (3); J. K. Gruenfelder, 'Dorsetshire Elections, 1604–1640', *Albion*, 10 (1978), 3–8.

44. *1628*, vi. 138–42, 146–8.

45. Underdown, *Revel, Riot, and Rebellion*, 179, 196–8, 205–6, 230, 236. For other towns named, see Barton J. Blankenfeld, 'Puritans in the Provinces: Banbury, Oxfordshire, 1554–1660', unpublished Ph.D thesis (Yale University, 1985); Underdown, *Fire From Heaven*; Peter Clark, ' "The Ramoth-Gilead of the Good": Urban Change and Political Radicalism at Gloucester 1540–1640', in Peter Clark, Alan G. R. Smith, and Nicholas Tyacke (eds.), *The English Commonwealth 1547–1640: Essays in Politics and Society* (Leicester, 1979), 167–87; and Paul Slack, 'Poverty and Politics in Salisbury 1597–1666', in Peter Clark and Paul Slack (eds.), *Crisis and Order in English Towns 1500–1700: Essays in Urban History* (1972), 164–203.

46. Daniel Parsons (ed.), *Diary of Sir Henry Slingsby* (1836), 60.

47. Foster, *1610*, ii. 175–6, 182.

48. *1625*, 685.

49. Laud, *Works*, v. 353.

50. Judith Maltby, 'Approaches to the Study of Religious Conformity in Late Elizabethan and Early Stuart England', unpublished Ph.D thesis (Cambridge University, 1992).
51. Owen, *The Unmasking of All popish Monks, Friers and Jesuits*, p. 35.
52. Beinecke Library, Osborn MS b.197, pp. 144–6. Sharpe, *The Personal Rule*, 750–1. BL, Harleian MS 4931, fo. 39ᵛ. See also Underdown, *Revel, Riot, and Rebellion*, 54–7; id., *Fire From Heaven*, 27–30, 148–9.
53. Foster, *1610*, ii. 281. For libels against Salisbury, see Croft, 'Reputation of Robert Cecil'.
54. Rollins (ed.), *A Pepysian Garland*, 89–95. McClure (ed.), *Chamberlain Letters*, ii. 185. BL, Lansdowne MS 620 (Notes on Star Chamber cases, 1–3 Charles I), fo. 50. Bellany, 'Rayling Rymes and Vaunting Verse', 289.
55. *Whiteway's Diary*, 54.
56. Cust, 'News and Politics', 68. Green (ed.), *Diary of John Rous*, 14, 18. *1628*, vi. 185–6.
57. *CSPD, 1628–29*, 103, 149, 172–3, 180, 213, 363–4. PRO, SP 16/103, fo. 74; 16/110, fo. 22; 16/119, fos. 79–81. BL, Sloane MS 826, fos. 119ᵛ–20. The rumours repeated by Melvin clearly resemble the ones repeated by Thomas Scott: above, pp. 24–5.
58. *CSPD, 1623–5*, 90, 241, 266, 280, 474, 476–7, 485. McClure (ed.), *Chamberlain Letters*, ii. 601. *DNB*: Lambe.
59. BL, TT, E 705 (25): Edmond Bower, *Doctor Lamb Revived, Or Witchcraft condemn'd in Anne Bodenham* (1653). *1626*, iv. App. II G (Anonymous Diary), at n. 43. Fairholt (ed.), *Poems and Songs Relating to Buckingham*, 20–1.
60. 'The Tragedy of Doctor Lambe', in Rollins (ed.), *Pepysian Garland*, 278–82. An otherwise unknown play, *Dr. Lambe and the Witches*, appeared in the 1630s: Frances Dolan, *Dangerous Familiars: Representations of Domestic Crime in England, 1550–1700* (Ithaca, NY, 1994), 234 n.
61. *1626*, iv. App. III C (1). *1628*, vi. 197, 244. [Birch] (ed.), *Court and Times of Charles I*, i. 365. Fairholt (ed.), *Poems and Songs Relating to Buckingham*, Introduction, p. xv. Green (ed.), *Diary of John Rous*, 26.
62. PRO, SP 16/119, fo. 70. Beinecke Library, Osborn MS b. 32 (Commonplace Book of John Holles), 250–1. [Birch] (ed.), *Court and Times of Charles I*, i. 394–9. Green (ed.), *Diary of John Rous*, 31. Lockyer, *Buckingham*, 456–9. For Vicars, see Holmes, *Seventeenth-Century Lincolnshire*, 62–3, and Gardiner (ed.), *Star Chamber Cases*, 198–238.
63. *1621*, ii. 130, 132; v. 196–7; vi. 5. *1628*, iii. 148; iv. 28. For another example, see McClure (ed.), *Chamberlain Letters*, ii. 161. See also Underdown, *Revel, Riot, and Rebellion*, illustration 8A, facing 161.
64. Underdown, *Revel, Riot, and Rebellion*, 115–16. Keith Thomas, *Rule and Misrule in the Schools of Early Modern England* (Reading, 1976), 25. Anthony Fletcher, *Tudor Rebellions* (2nd edn., 1973), 64. Holmes, *Lin-*

colnshire, 12, 155. Holmes, 'Drainers and Fenmen', in Fletcher and Stevenson (eds.), *Order and Disorder*, 171.

65. 'A Pittilesse Mother...' (1616), in Henderson and McManus (eds.), *Half Humankind*, 363. Walter, 'Grain Riots and Popular Attitudes to the Law', 47–84.

66. PRO, STAC 5/K5/23; 5/K6/24: *Kedermister v. Hales*, etc., 1598. John Hawarde, *Les Reportes del Cases in Camera Stellata 1593 to 1609*, ed. W. P. Baildon (1894), 103–4.

67. J. W. Horrocks (ed.), *Assembly Books of Southampton*, i. (Southampton Rec. Soc., 19), 63.

68. See Jardine, *Still Harping on Daughters*, esp. ch. 1. On this subject I am also indebted to Eric Nicholson's 1990 Yale Ph.D thesis, 'Stages of Travesty: The Sexual Politics of Early Modern Comedy', and to Peter Stallybrass, 'Patriarchal Territories: The Body Enclosed', in Ferguson, Quilligan, and Vickers (eds.), *Rewriting the Renaissance*, 123–42.

69. PRO, STAC 8/16/1, *Hole v. White et al.*, 1607. There is a summary of the case in C. J. Sisson, *Lost Plays of Shakespeare's Age* (Cambridge, 1936), 162–85.

70. Underdown, *Revel, Riot, and Rebellion*, 102, 110–11. Rioters in Feckenham Forest, Worcestershire, also used ritual disguises: Large, 'From Swanimote to Disafforestation', 414.

71. Bettey, 'Revolts', 22–3. Underdown, *Fire From Heaven*, 177. *Whiteway's Diary*, 106.

72. Cope, *Politics without Parliament*, 109. *1628*, vi. 232. Scott subsequently wrote to his wife giving very detailed accounts of his examination by the Council.

73. Fairholt (ed.), *Poems and Songs Relating to Buckingham*, 8.

74. *1621*, ii. 6. See also above, Ch. 1, p. 17.

75. David Harris Willson (ed.), *Parliamentary Diary of Robert Bowyer* (Minneapolis, 1931), 58.

76. Foster, *1610*, ii. 265.

77. H. E. Rollins (ed.), *Old English Ballads 1553–1625* (Cambridge, 1920), 196–7.

78. Selections from Swetnam's pamphlet and from some of the rejoinders to it are printed in Henderson and McManus (eds.), *Half Humankind*; three of the answers are also in Simon Shepherd (ed.), *The Women's Sharp Revenge: Five Women's Pamphlets From the Renaissance* (1985). See also Constance Jordan, *Renaissance Feminism: Literary Texts and Political Models* (Ithaca, 1990), 297–307; and Diane Purkiss, 'Material Girls: The Seventeenth-Century Woman Debate', in Clare Brant and Diane Purkiss (eds.), *Women, Texts and Histories 1575–1760* (1992), 69–101.

79. Annabel Patterson, *Shakespeare and the Popular Voice* (Oxford, 1989), 17–18. Purkiss, 'Material Girls', 77, makes an interesting argument on these

lines. For Chamberlain's description of the audience, see McClure (ed.), *Chamberlain Letters*, ii. 578. See also Ann Jennalie Cook, *The Privileged Playgoers of Shakespeare's London, 1576–1642* (Princeton, NJ, 1981).

80. McClure (ed.), *Chamberlain Letters*, i. 444, 449; ii. 17, 216, 286–7. *CSPD, 1619–23*, 16. Croft, 'Reputation of Robert Cecil', 60 n.

81. McClure (ed.), *Chamberlain Letters*, ii. 289. [Birch] (ed.), *Court and Times of James I*, i. 377. *Hic Mulier*, in Henderson and McManus (eds.), *Half Humankind*, 267. 'Secret History of the Reign of James I', 348. Barnaby Rich, *The Irish Hubbub*, 4; and see also 12–17, 40–1. Linda Woodbridge, *Women and the English Renaissance: Literature and the Nature of Womankind, 1540–1620* (Urbana, Ill., 1984), 139–51. Sandra Clark, 'Hic Mulier, Haec Vir, and the Controversy over Masculine Women', *Studies in Philology*, 82 (1985), 157–83. Cristina Malcolmson, '"As Tame as the Ladies": Politics and Gender in *The Changeling*', *English Literary Renaissance*, 20 (1990), 320–39.

82. McClure (ed.), *Chamberlain Letters*, ii. 286–7, 294. *1621*, iv. 59. Cristina Malcolmson shows how 'dangerous political opinions' could be expressed in the guise of discussions of sexual politics: '"As Tame as the Ladies"', 322–3. I am grateful to Dr Malcolmson for several illuminating conversations on this subject.

83. Swetnam in *Half Humankind*, 209. *Haec Vir*, in Ibid. 286–7. Sandra Clark, *The Elizabethan Pamphleteers: Popular Moralistic Pamphlets 1580–1640* (1983), 7, 181.

84. Prynne, *The Unlovelinesse of Lovelockes* (1628), quoted in Karen Newman, *Fashioning Femininity and English Renaissance Drama* (Chicago, 1991), 121. Rollins (ed.), *Pepysian Garland*, 413.

85. Ester Sowerman, *Ester hath Hang'd Haman* (1617), in *Half Humankind*, 229–31. Mikalachki, 'Taking the Measure of England', 137–41.

86. *Muld Sacke: Or, The Apologie of Hic Mulier* (1621). *Hic Mulier*, in *Half Humankind*, 268–73.

87. *Haec Vir*, in *Half Humankind*, 288–9. For the skimmington analogy and other ideas on this subject I am indebted to Barbara M. Passman, '"Apes of the City": An Examination of the Popular Controversy over Women under James I', BA Honors thesis (Brown University, 1986).

CHAPTER 4

1. Conrad Russell, *Unrevolutionary England, 1603–1642* (1990). For a review of earlier historiography see Richardson, *Debate on the English Revolution*.

2. For Erle and Strangways, see *DNB*; Keeler, *Long Parliament*, 165–7, 353–4; Cust, *Forced Loan*, 188–9; and J. K. Gruenfelder, 'Dorsetshire Elections 1604–1640', *Albion*, 10 (1978), 1–13. Sir Thomas Aston and Sir William Brereton in Cheshire, partners in the Short Parliament election, but bitterly divided a year later, provide similar examples: J. S. Morrill,

Cheshire 1630–1660: County Government and Society during the English Revolution (Oxford, 1974), ch. 2.

3. Hyder E. Rollins (ed.), *Cavalier and Puritan: Ballads and Broadsides Illustrating the Period of the Great Rebellion, 1640–1660* (New York, 1923), 160–2. Thomas Wright (ed.), *Political Ballads Published in England during the Commonwealth*, Percy Soc., 3 (1841), 13, 223. Russell, *Causes of the English Civil War*, 16. Beinecke Library, Osborn MS b.101 (Commonplace Book of Ralph Ashton), 85–7. David Underdown, *Somerset in the Civil War and Interregnum* (Newton Abbot, 1973), 31, 182. Stoyle, *Loyalty and Locality*, 97–8.

4. Lois Potter, *Secret Rites and Secret Writing: Royalist Literature, 1641–1660* (Cambridge, 1989), 7–24.

5. Joyce Lee Malcolm, *Caesar's Due: Loyalty and King Charles 1642–1646* (1983), 131–48. BL, TT, E 279 (8): *Mercurius Aulicus*, 6–13 Apr. 1645. Walker's comment is quoted in Underdown, *Somerset in the Civil War and Interregnum*, 75.

6. Wright (ed.), *Political Ballads*, 1–8.

7. There are vast numbers of these Cavalier drinking-songs, many expressing cynical disillusion with earlier ideals: see C. V. Wedgwood, *Poetry and Politics under the Stuarts* (Cambridge, 1960), 107–10. The one quoted is in J. O. Halliwell (ed.), *The Loyal Garland: A Collection of Songs of the Seventeenth Century*, Percy Soc., 29 (1850), 84.

8. Wright (ed.), *Political Ballads*, 112–16.

9. Ibid. 215–16.

10. BL Film 330: Northumberland MS 548, Fitzjames Entry Book, ii, fos. 19–20, 27, 40, 44^v, 57^v. Underdown, *Pride's Purge*, 175.

11. Chetham's Library MS A3. 90 (Letter-book of Sir Ralph Assheton), 18 Apr. 1648; 30 Jan.; and 16 Feb. 1648/9.

12. C. H. Firth, *The House of Lords During the Civil War* (1910), 206–13. BL, TT. E 549 (5): 'A distich made vpon the Fower honble. Lrds that vsualy sate & made a house in the yeare 1648' (2 Apr. 1649); printed, without the decoding, in E 551 (5): *Mercurius Pragmaticus (For King Charles II)*, 17–24 Apr. 1649.

13. Firth, *House of Lords*, esp. 119, 132, 135–6, 150, 153–5, 171–2, 194.

14. Elizabeth Read Foster, *The House of Lords 1603–1649: Structure, Procedure, and the Nature of its Business* (Chapel Hill, 1983), 179–83, 208. For the whole subject of the Lords' appelate jurisdiction, see Hart, *Justice Upon Petition*.

15. For Derby see B. G. Blackwood, *The Lancashire Gentry and the Great Rebellion 1640–1660* (Manchester, 1978), 47–8; for Warwick, Clive Holmes, *The Eastern Association in the English Civil War* (Cambridge, 1974), 34–41; for Brooke, Ann Hughes, *Politics, Society and Civil War in Warwickshire, 1620–1660* (Cambridge, 1987), 135–56; for Essex's funeral,

Vernon F. Snow, *Essex the Rebel: The Life of Robert Devereux, The Third Earl of Essex 1591–1646* (Lincoln, Nebr., 1970), 489–93. It is an absurd overstatement to say that the war was perceived as being between the King and Essex, rather than between the King and Parliament: for this claim, see J. S. A. Adamson, 'The Baronial Context of the English Civil War', *TRHS*, 5th ser., 40 (1990), 94, 99–101.

16. David Underdown, 'Party Management in the Recruiter Elections, 1645–1648', *EHR* 83 (1968), 235–64. Underdown, *Pride's Purge*, 47–9.

17. Underdown, *Pride's Purge*, 84–6. Valerie Pearl, 'The "Royal Independents" in the English Civil War', *TRHS*, 5th ser., 18 (1968), 69–96. J. S. A. Adamson has recently unsuccessfully tried to elevate Saye into *the* effective leader of the militant group in Parliament: see his 'The English Nobility and the Projected Settlement of 1647', *Historical Journal*, 30 (1987), 567–602. This argument has been effectively demolished by Mark Kishlansky, in 'Saye What?', *Historical Journal*, 33 (1990), 917–37 (with response by Adamson in vol. 34, pp. 231–55); and 'Saye No More', *JBS* 30 (1991), 399–448.

18. Thomas G. Barnes, *Somerset 1625–1640: A County's Government during the 'Personal Rule'* (Cambridge, Mass., 1961), 36–9, 281–95.

19. J. P. Ferris, 'The Gentry of Dorset on the Eve of the Civil War', *Genealogists' Magazine*, 15 (1965–8), 105, 115. Underdown, *Fire From Heaven*, 187–8, 192–3. Brunton and Pennington, *Members of the Long Parliament*, 153–75. For other examples of gentry-run counties, see Alan Everitt, *The Community of Kent and the Great Rebellion 1640–60* (Leicester, 1966), and Anthony Fletcher, *A County Community in Peace and War: Sussex, 1600–1660* (1976).

20. *CSPD, 1640*, 278. Green (ed.), *Diary of John Rous*, 80. Russell, *Causes of the English Civil War*, 5.

21. I have listed some of these patron–client relationships in my *Pride's Purge*, 47–9.

22. Underdown, 'Party Management in the Recruiter Elections', 242–3. Id., *Pride's Purge*, 273. Wharton's attitude to the Commonwealth and the events that brought it into being are clear in Cromwell's letters to him in 1650: W. C. Abbott (ed.), *The Writings and Speeches of Oliver Cromwell* (Cambridge, Mass., 1937–47), ii. 189–90, 328–9, 453. See also G. F. Trevallyn Jones, *Saw-Pit Wharton: The Political Career from 1640 to 1691 of Philip, Fourth Lord Wharton* (Sydney, 1967), 128–37.

23. BL Film 330: Northumberland MS 547, Fitzjames Entry Bk. i, fos. 1–5, 8–9, 15–16, 26ᵛ, 49, 52–75, 80ᵛ; MS 548, Entry Bk. ii, fo. 12ᵛ. HMC, *Salisbury*, xxii. 39, 215. For the electoral character of Shaftesbury, see Keeler, *Long Parliament*, 45.

24. BL Film 330: Northumberland MS 547, Fitzjames Entry Bk. i, fos. 25–

6, 46–62, 74. *The Mystery of the Good old Cause Briefly unfolded* (London, 1660), 9.

25. BL Film 331: Northumberland MSS 551–2, Fitzjames Entry Bks. v–vi, *passim*.

26. e.g. by Adamson, 'Baronial Context of the English Civil War'. A strikingly similar argument for the peers' political influence was made earlier in James E. Farnell, 'The Social and Intellectual Basis of London's Role in the English Civil Wars', *Journal of Modern History*, 49 (1977), 641–60.

27. 'A Proper New Ballad on the Old Parliament' (1659), in Wright (ed.), *Political Ballads*, 155–6.

28. Everitt, *The Community of Kent*, esp. ch. 8.

29. Andrew M. Coleby, *Central Government and the Localities: Hampshire 1649–1689* (Cambridge, 1987), 17–27. Hughes, *Warwickshire*, ch. 6. David Underdown, 'Settlement in the Counties, 1653–1658', in G. E. Aylmer (ed.), *The Interregnum: The Quest for Settlement 1646–1660* (1972), 165–82.

30. BL Film 330: Northumberland MS 547, Fitzjames Entry Bk. i, fo. 51ᵛ. Anthony Fletcher, *Reform in the Provinces: The Government of Stuart England* (New Haven and London, 1986), 11–19, 60–1. Underdown, *Pride's Purge*, 299–318.

31. BL, Add. MS 29,975 (Pitt MSS), fo. 124. BL Film 636, 6–9: Verney MSS, 1644–9; many of these letters are printed or excerpted in F. P. and M. M. Verney (eds.), *Memoirs of the Verney Family* (1892), vols. ii and iii.

32. Beinecke Library, Osborn MS b. 101.

33. Osborn MS b. 101, pp. 13–58, 65–9, 85–9. There are several anti-episcopal libels (including a printed copy of 'The Bishops' Bridles') in BL, Harl. MS 4931, fos. 27, 80–1, 104. For 'God a-mercy good Scot', see above, p. 70.

34. Osborn MS b. 101, pp. 77–9, 81, 111–13. Wedgwood, *Poetry and Politics under the Stuarts*, 66–7; here printed as 'The People's violent love and hate'. For some other anti-Scots libels, see Sharpe, *The Personal Rule*, 912–13.

35. Osborn MS b. 101, pp. 126–9.

36. Ibid. 131–73. The Cheshire gentleman William Davenport made a similar move from an anti-Court position in the 1620s to neutrality in the civil war: Morrill, 'William Davenport and the "Silent Majority" of Early Stuart England', *Journal of Chester Archaeological Society*, 58 (1975), 115–29. For truce negotiations in other counties, see Morrill, *Revolt of the Provinces*, 36–8.

37. Willson H. Coates (ed.), *The Journal of Sir Simonds D'Ewes from the First Recess of the Long Parliament to the Withdrawal of King Charles from London* (New Haven, Conn., 1942), 234 n. See also Keeler, *Long Parliament*, 166.

38. *CJ*, iv. 336; v. 34, 332, 471. PRO, LA/1/39; LC 3/3/2/170; LC 3/3/1/94. A. G. Matthews, *Calamy Revised: Being a Revision of Edmund Calamy's Account of the Ministers and Others Ejected and Silenced, 1660–2* (Oxford, 1934), 47–8, 422. Erle's vote on 26 May 1648, for the establishment of presbyterianism for three years only (*CJ*, v. 574), is a sign that by now he was desperately anxious for a settlement with the King and was willing to make compromises for it, as he had not been as late as the previous October.

39. Notestein (ed.), *Journal of Sir Simonds D'Ewes*, 63, 339. Beinecke Library, Osborn MS b. 304. The commonplace book is at the front of the volume, the poems at the back, paginated separately.

40. Osborn MS b. 304, pp. 15–16, 35, 58–60, 73, 75; Poems, 44, 47–50, 61, 122–5.

41. Keeler, *Long Parliament*, 165–7. Valerie Pearl, 'Oliver St. John and the "Middle Group" in the Long Parliament', *EHR* 81 (1966), 494 n, 508, 513 n. For the peace moves, see Underdown, *Revel, Riot, and Rebellion*, 154.

42. *CJ*, v. 92, 101, 149, 259, 265, 293. Underdown, *Pride's Purge*, 168 n.

43. BL, TT, 669 f. 13: *A Declaration of the taking away of Sir William Waller . . . from the Kings head in the Strand, to St. James* (12 Dec. 1648). See also Underdown, *Pride's Purge*, 162–3.

44. Osborn MS b. 304, pp. 40–2, 45–8.

45. Ibid. 47. For his reputation before the war, see Coates (ed.), *Journal of Sir Simonds D'Ewes*, 47 n.

46. Strangways, Poems, 72–3.

47. Osborn MS b. 304, pp. 42, 46.

48. Ibid. 41, 46–7, 53, 56, 74.

49. Osborn MS b. 304, p. 46. Coates (ed.), *Journal of Sir Simonds D'Ewes*, 213–15. Manning, *The English People and the English Revolution*, ch. 3, esp. 53–9.

50. Beinecke Library, Osborn MS b. 230 (Commonplace Book of W. S[andys]), Wyndham to Gervase Holles, 5 Aug. 1652.

51. BL, TT, E 79 (5): *Scotish Dove*, 10 (15–22 Dec. 1643). Potter, *Secret Rites*, 45–8, 60, 182.

52. Derek Hirst, 'The Failure of Godly Rule in the English Republic', *Past and Present*, 132 (1991), 33–66. Strangways, Poems, 138.

53. For Hutchinson and Pickering, see Underdown, *Pride's Purge*, 23; for Ingoldsby, 'A second Narrative of the late Parliament (so called)' (1658), in W. Oldys and T. Park (eds.), *The Harleian Miscellany* (1808–13), iii. 482; for Popham, David Underdown, *Royalist Conspiracy in England 1649–1660* (New Haven, Conn., 1960), 117, 224, 261; for Mountagu, R. C. Latham and W. Matthews (eds.), *The Diary of Samuel Pepys* (1970–83), i. 141, 167.

54. Underdown, *Fire From Heaven*, 231.
55. Id., *Revel, Riot, and Rebellion*, 271.

CHAPTER 5

1. Thomas Hobbes, *Behemoth or the Long Parliament*, ed. F. Tonnies and M. M. Goldsmith (1969), 2. Lawrence Stone used the term 'cannon-fodder' in the first edition of his *Causes of the English Revolution 1529–1642* (1972), 145, though he has since retracted it, recognizing that ordinary people played a much more positive role: see second edition, 171–2.

2. The classic exposition of this view is John Morrill's *Revolt of the Provinces* (1976). For his later rethinking of the subject, see his *Reactions to the English Civil War 1642–1649* (1982), Introduction, and *The Nature of the English Revolution*, ch. 8.

3. See e.g. Manning, *The English People and the English Revolution*; Malcolm, *Caesar's Due*.

4. C. H. Firth (ed.), *The Clarke Papers*, Camden Soc. (1891–1901). T. C. Pease, *The Leveller Movement* (Washington, DC, 1916). There is a valuable survey of earlier historical writing on the Levellers in O. Luteaud, 'Le parti politique Niveleur et la première Révolution anglaise (Essai d'Historiographie)', *Revue Historique*, 227 (1962), 77–114, 377–414.

5. Christopher Hill, *The World Turned Upside Down: Radical Ideas During the English Revolution* (1972).

6. On the Levellers' political language, see esp. Perez Zagorin, *A History of Political Thought in the English Revolution* (1954), 28–9; and Christopher Hill, *Puritanism and Revolution* (1958), ch. 3, 'The Norman Yoke'.

7. Underdown, 'The Chalk and the Cheese: Contrasts among the English Clubmen', 25–6; id., 'The Problem of Popular Allegiance in the English Civil War', *TRHS*, 5th ser., 31 (1981), 69–73. See also my exchange with John Morrill in *JBS* 26 (1987), 451–79. An excellent recent contribution to the subject is Stoyle, *Loyalty and Locality*.

8. I have described the process of politicization in my *Revel, Riot, and Rebellion*, esp. chs. 6–9. There is much evidence about popular attitudes in Charles Carlton, *Going to the Wars: The Experience of the British Civil Wars 1638–1651* (1992). Carlton shows that some soldiers on both sides were forced to fight, and that others did so for mercenary reasons. But nothing could have made people endure the kind of carnage he describes unless at least significant numbers of them had some attachment for whichever cause it was they were serving.

9. Phyllis Mack, *Visionary Women: Ecstatic Prophecy in Seventeenth-Century England* (Berkeley and Los Angeles, 1992).

10. The quotation is from Morse Peckham (1967), quoted in Barbara A. Babcock (ed.), *The Reversible World: Symbolic Inversion in Art and Society*

(Ithaca, NY, 1978), 20. Max Gluckman, *Custom and Conflict in Africa* (Glencoe, Ill., 1959). Mikhail Bakhtin, *Rabelais and His World*, trans. Hélène Iswolsky (Bloomington, Ind., 1984).

11. J. C. Davis, *Fear, Myth and History: The Ranters and the Historians* (Cambridge, 1986).

12. Natalie Zemon Davis, *Society and Culture in Early Modern France* (Stanford, Cal., 1975), 123, and see also ch. 5, 'Women On Top'.

13. See above, Ch. 3. See also Martin Ingram, 'Ridings, Rough Music and Mocking Rhymes in Early Modern England', in Barry Reay (ed.), *Popular Culture in Seventeenth-Century England* (New York, 1985), 171; Ingram, 'Ridings, Rough Music and the "Reform of Popular Culture" in Early Modern England', *Past, and Present*, 105 (1984), 79–113; and Underdown, *Revel, Riot, and Rebellion*, 106–19.

14. HMC, *Portland*, iii. 64.

15. See e.g. the illustrations in Underdown, *Revel, Riot, and Rebellion*, following p. 160; and id., *Somerset in the Civil War and Interregnum*, 134. These represent only a small selection from the numerous instances in civil war tracts. In an article published in 1978 David Kunzle could find only one instance from the 1640s, and seemed to be unaware of the popularity of the theme in seventeenth-century England: see his 'World Turned Upside Down: The Iconography of a European broadsheet Type', in Babcock (ed.), *Reversible World*, 83. Davis, *Fear, Myth and History*, 105–7, notes the use of carnivalesque inversion in the construction of the Ranter image.

16. BL, TT, E 80 (9): *Mercurius Britanicus*, 19 (28 Dec. 1643–4 Jan. 1643/4).

17. BL, TT, E 555 (26): *The Man in the Moon*, 1 (16 Apr. 1649). Citations of *The Man in the Moon* will hereafter be given only in the form of Thomason Tracts reference numbers. Thus 551 (10) stands for BL, TT, E 551 (10).

18. For the royalist press, see Joseph Frank, *The Beginnings of the English Newspaper 1620–1660* (Cambridge, Mass., 1961), 136–45, 160–5, 193–8, 203–5. Selections from the civil war press have recently been printed in Joad Raymond (ed.), *Making the News: An Anthology of the Newsbooks of Revolutionary England* (1993).

19. For this paragraph, see Underdown, *Pride's Purge*, ch. 7; and Blair Worden, *The Rump Parliament 1648–1653* (Cambridge, 1974), chs. 1–2.

20. *DNB*: 'Crouch, John, fl. 1660–1681'. Frank, *Newspaper*, 137, 196, 203–4. Potter, *Secret Rites and Secret Writing*, 15–18.

21. BL, TT, E 660 (3): *Mercurius Democritus*, 3 (13–21 Apr. 1652); E 671 (9): no. 16 (14–21 July 1652); E 672 (2): no. 17 (21–8 July 1652). See also Frank, *Newspaper*, 229–31, 242–3, 261, 266.

22. Douglas Bush, *English Literature in the Earlier Seventeenth Century* (Oxford, 1945), 39–56. J. A. Sharpe, 'Plebeian Marriage in Stuart England',

TRHS, 5th series, 36 (1986), 88. See also Margaret Spufford, *Small Books and Pleasant Histories: Popular Fiction and its Readership in Seventeenth-Century England* (Cambridge, 1985), ch. 7; and Bernard Capp, 'Popular Literature', in Reay (ed.), *Popular Culture*, ch. 6, esp. 216–18.

23. Cogswell, 'Underground Verse and the Transformation of Early Stuart Political Culture'.

24. David Cressy, *Literacy and the Social Order: Reading and Writing in Tudor and Stuart England* (Cambridge, 1980), 154. Potter, *Secret Rites and Secret Writing*, 24–5, provides some estimates of the potential London readership of newsbooks and pamphlets.

25. Frank, *Newspaper*, 196. Burke, *Popular Culture in Early Modern Europe*, 63. For further thoughts on the readership for this kind of publication, see Sharpe, 'Plebeian Marriage in Stuart England', 72–3.

26. The lantern and Towzer both make regular appearances. For the bush, see 599 (12).

27. Bush, *English Literature*, 55, 77, 83. Jonathan Goldberg, *James I and the Politics of Literature* (Baltimore, 1983), 64–5. Enid Welsford, *The Fool: His Social and Literary History* (1935), 214. For another example, Clark, *Elizabethan Pamphleteers*, 146.

28. 554 (4); 572 (22). Parker's ballad has been often reprinted, e.g. in *The Oxford Book of Seventeenth Century Verse* (Oxford, 1934), 583–4.

29. 568 (13); 582 (2); 594 (9); 596 (3); 601 (5); 569 (14).

30. 594 (21); 558 (19); 562 (27); 578 (9).

31. 551 (10); 558 (19); 564 (3); 589 (8). For Atkin, see Valerie Pearl, *London and the Outbreak of the Puritan Revolution* (Oxford, 1961), 311–13. I am grateful to Tom Cogswell for the cause of Atkin's embarrassment.

32. 600 (11); 596 (3); 593 (8); 579 (11). For Mildmay, see Keeler, *Long Parliament*, 274; and Aylmer, *King's Servants*, 384.

33. 551 (10); 560 (2); 590 (12). BL, TT, E 556 (30): *Mercurius Pragmaticus (For King Charls II)* (22–9 May 1649). For Pembroke, see *DNB*: 'Herbert, Philip, Earl of Montgomery and fourth Earl of Pembroke, 1584–1650'.

34. 571 (18); 594 (21); 551 (10). For Marten, see C. M. Williams, 'The Anatomy of a Radical Gentleman: Henry Marten', in Donald Pennington and Keith Thomas (eds.), *Puritans and Revolutionaries: Essays in Seventeenth-Century History presented to Christopher Hill* (Oxford, 1978), 118–38.

35. 572 (11); 568 (13); 590 (12). Rollins (ed.), *Cavalier and Puritan*, 201–6. For Peter, see Raymond P. Stearns, *The Strenuous Puritan: Hugh Peter, 1598–1660* (Urbana, Ill., 1954).

36. 552 (8); 554 (4); 576 (7); 572 (22); 602 (2). On the brewing, see Antonia Fraser, *Cromwell: The Lord Protector* (New York, 1973), 14.

37. 576 (7); 578 (9); 558 (19); 593 (8); 561 (20); 582 (2).

38. Worden, *Rump Parliament*, 74.

39. 562 (27); 601 (5); 551 (10); 574 (9); 594 (9).

40. See above, Ch. 1. See also Amussen, 'Gender, Family and the Social Order'; Schochet, *Patriarchalism in Political Thought*; Sommerville, *Politics and Ideology in England*, ch. 1.
41. Underdown, 'The Taming of the Scold', 127–34.
42. Spufford, *Small Books*, 29, 59.
43. 590 (12); 575 (24); 602 (2); 601 (5).
44. C. V. Wedgwood, *The Trial of Charles I* (1964), 111, 127–8, 154–5. Underdown, *Pride's Purge*, 189–90.
45. 573 (14).
46. 587 (10); 593 (8); 575 (24); 576 (7).
47. 595 (4); 569 (14); 556 (32); 582 (2); 551 (8); 554 (4); 558 (19); 564 (3).
48. 555 (23). For Dorislaus, see Wedgwood, *Trial of Charles I*, 104, 215.
49. 576 (7); 594 (9); and cf. also 578 (9); 589 (8). For the 1650 Act, see Keith Thomas, 'The Puritans and Adultery: The Act of 1650 Reconsidered', in Pennington and Thomas (eds.), *Puritans and Revolutionaries*, 257–82.
50. Leah S. Marcus, *The Politics of Mirth: Jonson, Herrick, Milton, Marvell and the Defense of Old Holiday Pastimes* (Chicago, 1986), 23.
51. John Morrill, 'The Church in England, 1642–9', in Morrill (ed.), *Reactions*, 89–114. Barry Reay, 'Popular Hostility Towards Quakers in Mid-Seventeenth-Century England', *Social History*, 5 (1980), 387–407.
52. Underdown, *Revel, Riot, and Rebellion*, 251–5. BL, TT, E 561 (6): *A Declaration of the Bloudie and Unchristian Acting of William Star and John Taylor of Walton* ([22 June] 1649). Mack, *Visionary Women*, 70.
53. 568 (13); 575 (16); 582 (2); 573 (14).
54. As happens, for example, in the 1634 play by Heywood and Brome, *The Lancashire Witches*, in Heywood, *Dramatic Works* iv; see esp. 183.
55. 571 (18); 597 (5); 589 (8).
56. There is much evidence of witchcraft accusations by and against Quakers in Mack, *Visionary Women*; see esp. 128, 205–8, 249–50, 259. Underdown, *Revel, Riot, and Rebellion*, 254. I am not persuaded by Barry Reay's argument, in *The Quakers and the English Revolution* (1985), 68, that most of the witchcraft accusations against Quakers were made by members of the élite, though obviously some were.
57. BL, TT, E 705 (24): Edmond Bower, *Doctor Lamb Revived, or Witchcraft condemn'd in Anne Bodenham* ... ([14 July] 1653). See also BL, TT, E 707 (2): *Doctor Lamb's Darling: Or Strange News from Salisbury* ([25 July] 1653).
58. BL, TT, E 744 (5): *Mercurius Fumigosus*, 3 (14–21 June 1654).
59. 551 (10). BL, TT, E 551 (14): *The Humble Petition Of divers wel-affected Women* (1649); E 552 (12): *Mercurius Pragmaticus* (23–30 Apr. 1649); E 552 (15): *Mercurius Pragmaticus (For King Charles II)* (24 Apr.–1 May 1649); E 556 (22): *Mercurius Militaris, or Times only Truth-teller* (22–9 May 1649). The authentic *Mercurius Militaris* (17–24 Apr. 1649) gives a much more sympathetic account: BL, TT, E 551 (13).

60. 590 (3); 593 (17); 594 (21); 551 (10); 593 (8); 595 (4).

61. 572 (11); 589 (8); 589 (15); 556 (32); 560 (21); 582 (2); 594 (9); 596 (3); 594 (21). Wedgwood, *Trial of Charles I*, 110. Underdown, *Pride's Purge*, 261.

62. 551 (10); 561 (20); 589 (8); 590 (12); 593 (8); 592 (2); 594 (21). Worden, *Rump Parliament*, 224.

63. 554 (4); 601 (5); 600 (11).

64. 551 (10); 552 (8); 560 (2); 561 (20); 589 (8); 594 (9); 590 (3); 592 (4).

65. 594 (21); 595 (4); 596 (3); 602 (18); 552 (8); 555 (23); 576 (7). See also Pauline Gregg, *Free-born John: A Biography of John Lilburne* (1961), ch. 25.

66. 558 (19); 568 (13); 571 (18).

67. BL, TT, E 552 (15): *Mercurius Pragmaticus (For King Charles II)* (17–24 Apr., and 24 Apr.–1 May 1649); E 555 (37): *Mercurius Elencticus*, 4 (14–21 May 1649).

68. See Davis, *Fear, Myth and History*, ch. 5. This useful discussion of the 'moral panic' does not, however, prove Davis's argument that the Ranters therefore did not exist.

69. See Frank, *Newspaper*, 205–6.

70. Pocock, *Politics, Language, and Time,* ch. 1. And see above, ch. 2, n. 26.

71. Malcolm, *Caesar's Due*, 142–3. See also above, Ch. 4, p. 71.

72. Paul S. Seaver, *Wallington's World: A Puritan Artisan in Seventeenth-Century London* (Stanford, 1985), 156.

73. Beinecke Library: Osborn MS b. 221 (Commonplace Book of Elizabeth Jekyll). This MS appears to be a late seventeenth-century transcription. Elizabeth was the first wife of John Jekyll (b. 1611), of St Stephen's Walbrook, and mother of the divine, Thomas Jekyll (1646–98), for whom see *DNB*; after her death her husband remarried, and had another son, Joseph, later a prominent Whig lawyer. See also W. B. Bannerman (ed.), *Register of St. Stephen's Walbrook*, Pt. I, Harleian Soc., 49 (1919), 23–5. I am grateful to the Revd John Reynolds for much information about the Jekyll family.

74. Underdown, *Revel, Riot, and Rebellion*, 154, 261, 272–3. Valerie Pearl, 'London's Counter-Revolution', in Aylmer (ed.), *The Interregnum*, 42–52. Peter Burke, 'Popular Culture in Seventeenth-Century London', in Reay (ed.), *Popular Culture*, 47–8.

CHAPTER 6

1. Underdown, *Pride's Purge*, 222.

2. See above, pp. 53–4.

3. Anchitel Grey, *Debates of the House of Commons from the year 1667 to the year 1694*, 10 vols. (1763).

4. G. M. Trevelyan, *England Under the Stuarts* (21st edn., 1965); David Ogg, *England in the Reign of Charles II* (2nd edn., Oxford, 1955); J. R.

Jones, *The First Whigs: The Politics of the Exclusion Crisis, 1678–1683* (Oxford, 1961); D. T. Witcombe, *Charles II and the Cavalier House of Commons* (Manchester, 1966); J. H. Plumb, *The Growth of Political Stability in England 1675–1725* (1967); Clark, *English Society 1688–1832*; Ronald Hutton, *The Restoration: A Political and Religious History of England and Wales 1658–1667* (Oxford, 1985); Tim Harris, *London Crowds in the Reign of Charles II: Propaganda and Politics from the Restoration until the Exclusion Crisis* (Cambridge, 1987); Paul Seaward, *The Cavalier Parliament and the Reconstruction of the Old Regime 1661–1667* (Cambridge, 1989).

5. Seaward, *Cavalier Parliament*, 57–67, 193–4.

6. Underdown, *Revel, Riot, and Rebellion*, 289–90. Robin Clifton, *The Last Popular Rebellion: The Western Rising of 1685* (1984), 45. Underdown, *Fire From Heaven*, 239–43. Michael R. Watts, *The Dissenters From the Reformation to the French Revolution* (Oxford, 1978), ch. 3. Local variations in the relations between Anglicans and dissenters are examined in John D. Ramsbottom, 'Puritan Dissenters and English Churches, 1630–1670', unpublished Ph.D thesis (Yale University, 1987).

7. Seaward, *Cavalier Parliament*, 23. Tim Harris, *Politics Under the Later Stuarts: Party Conflict in a Divided Society 1660–1715* (1993), 35–6, 58.

8. Seaward, *Cavalier Parliament*, 77–130. Joyce Malcolm, 'Charles II and the Reconstruction of Royal Power', *Historical Journal*, 35 (1992), 309–15. Fletcher, *Reform in the Provinces*, ch. 10.

9. Though larger constituencies than Buckingham, with its minuscule electorate (see Kishlansky, *Parliamentary Selection*, 201–23), would make the point even more effectively. For the impact of the Exclusion crisis on politics, see Jones, *The First Whigs*; and for a good recent survey, Harris, *Politics under the Later Stuarts*, ch. 4.

10. Amussen, *An Ordered Society*, esp. 52–65. For the dating of *Patriarcha*, see Sommerville (ed.), *Filmer's Patriarcha*, pp. viii, xxxii–xxxiv.

11. Wright (ed.), *Political Ballads*, 257–65. Wedgwood, *Poetry and Politics under the Stuarts*, 129–30.

12. Eva Scott, *The King in Exile: The Wanderings of Charles II. from June 1646 to July 1654* (1904), 470–4. Underdown, *Royalist Conspiracy*, 60–1. Keith Feiling, *A History of the Tory Party 1640–1714* (Oxford, 1924), 80, 121–2.

13. BL, TT, E 1052 (4): T.M., *The History of Independency*, Pt. iv (1660), 31; E 1035 (3): *The English Devil: Or, Cromwell and his Monstrous Witch Discover'd at Whitehall* (1660), 6–7. Lawrence Echard, *History of England* (1707–18), ii. 712–13. For Poole, see Amussen, *An Ordered Society*, 61–2.

14. 'Articles of High Treason, and other high Crimes and Misdemeanors against the Duchess of Portsmouth' (1680), in Sir Walter Scott (ed.), *A Collection of Scarce and Valuable Tracts . . . [Somers Tracts]* (1809–15), viii.

137–40 (I am indebted to Nancy Maguire for this reference). See also Ronald Hutton, *Charles the Second* (Oxford, 1989), 204, 279–80, 335, 337; Hutton, *Restoration*, 249. I am grateful to Dr Hutton for confirming the absence of witchcraft charges.

15. Hutton, *Restoration*, 239, 245–6. Sir Allen Apsley, *Order and Disorder; or the world made and undone* (1679). Felicity A. Nussbaum, *The Brink of All We Hate: English Satires on Women 1660–1750* (Lexington, Ky., 1984), chs. 2, 4.

16. Halliwell (ed.), *The Loyal Garland*, 34–5. BL, TT, E 1055 (20): *The Holy Sisters Conspiracy* (26 Jan. 1661), repr. in Wright (ed.), *Political Ballads*, 250–7.

17. BL, Harleian MS 6749 (Casebook of Jonathan Dove, JP), fo. 24. The evidence for accusations against Quakers is summarized in Reay, *The Quakers and the English Revolution*, 16. See also Thomas, *Religion and the Decline of Magic*, 576–80.

18. Raymond Crawfurd, *The King's Evil* (Oxford, 1911), 105–12, 137–8. Underdown, *Fire From Heaven*, 235.

19. E. P. Thompson, *Whigs and Hunters: The Origin of the Black Act* (1975). Manning and Sharp are cited in Ch. 1, n. 25, above.

20. The argument is summarized in Wrightson, *English Society*, 226.

21. Anne Whiteman (ed.), *The Compton Census of 1676: A Critical Edition* (1986), Introduction, pp. xxxiii–xli, lxxvii–lxxviii.

22. See Donald M. Spaeth, 'Parsons and Parishioners: Lay–Clerical Conflict and Popular Piety in Wiltshire Villages, 1660–1740', unpublished Ph.D thesis (Brown University, 1985), ch. 5.

23. Christopher Hill, *A Turbulent Seditious and Factious People: John Bunyan and his Church* (Oxford, 1988); id., *The Experience of Defeat: Milton and Some Contemporaries* (1984). Richard Ashcraft, *Revolutionary Politics and Locke's Two Treatises of Government* (Princeton, NJ, 1986).

24. For the plots, see Richard L. Greaves, *Deliver Us from Evil: The Radical Underground in Britain, 1660–1663* (Oxford, 1986), *Enemies Under his Feet: Radicals and Nonconformists in Britain, 1664–1667* (Stanford, 1990), and *Secrets of the Kingdom: British Radicals from the Popish Plot to the Revolution of 1688–1689* (Stanford, 1992).

25. PRO, ASSI 24/23 (Western Circuit Order Bk., 1677–87), fo. 31ᵛ. Spaeth, 'Parsons and Parishioners', 218–30. Harris, *Politics Under the Later Stuarts*, 66–7.

26. Underdown, *Fire From Heaven*, 239–42.

27. Max Beloff, *Public Order and Popular Disturbances 1660–1714* (Oxford, 1938), 58–60. See also above, pp. 47–9.

28. Beloff, *Public Order*, 76–80. CSPD, *1663–4*, 219; *1670*, 590–1, 597–8; *1671*, 18–19. Molly McClain, 'The Wentwood Forest Riot: Property Rights and Political Culture in Restoration England', in Amussen and Kishlansky

(eds.), *Political Culture and Cultural Politics*, ch. 5. Bodleian Lib., Carte MS 79, fo. 117: [——] to W. Wharton, 19 Aug. 1677.

29. C. G. Durston, '"Wild as Colts Untamed": Radicalism in the Newbury Area During the Early Modern Period', *Southern History*, 6 (1984), 41. McClain, '"I Scorn to Change or Fear": Henry Somerset, First Duke of Beaufort, and the Survival of the Nobility Following the English Civil War', unpublished Ph.D thesis (Yale University, 1994), 106–10.

30. Beloff, *Public Order*, 92–4. PRO, ASSI 24/22 (W. Circuit Order Book, 1652–76), fos. 151ᵛ, 153ᵛ, 163ᵛ. Bodleian, Rawl. MS C 948, pp. 59x–60x; MS Don. c. 37, fo. 21ᵛ (I am indebted to Susan Amussen for this latter reference). Lydia M. Marshall, 'The Levying of the Hearth Tax, 1662–1688', *EHR* 55 (1936), 628–46.

31. Gary De Krey, 'Revolution *redivivus*: 1688–1689 and the Radical Tradition in Seventeenth-Century London Politics', in Lois G. Schwoerer (ed.), *The Revolution of 1688–1689: Changing Perspectives* (Cambridge, 1992), ch. 12.

32. L'Estrange, quoted by Harris '"Lives, Liberties and Estates": Rhetorics of Liberty in the Reign of Charles II', in Tim Harris, Paul Seaward, and Mark Goldie (eds.), *The Politics of Religion in Restoration England* (Oxford, 1990), 233. See also Harris, *London Crowds, passim*; and id., 'Was the Tory Reaction Popular?: Attitudes of Londoners Towards the Persecution of Dissent, 1681–6', *London Journal*, 13 (1988).

33. *CSPD, 1680–1*, 440–1. William Lawrence, *Marriage by the Moral Law of God Vindicated* (1680). Rachel J. Weil, 'The Politics of Legitimacy: Women and the Warming-Pan Scandal', in Schwoerer (ed.), *The Revolution of 1688–1689*, 74.

34. 'A Letter to a Person of Honour, concerning the King's Disavowing the having been married to the Duke of Monmouth's Mother' (1681), *Harleian Miscellany*, iv, 165. Harris, *London Crowds*, 161–2.

35. Mary Prior, *Fisher Row: Fishermen, Bargemen and Canal Boatmen in Oxford, 1500–1900* (Oxford, 1982), 171.

36. See the analysis of Monmouth's recruits in Clifton, *Last Popular Rebellion*, 248–52, 297–300. For the cultural and political traditionalism of the Somerset–Dorset border region, see Underdown, *Revel, Riot, and Rebellion*, 96–9, 197–8, 204–5, 271–2.

37. See esp. Clifton, *Last Popular Rebellion*, 178, 270–1; and Peter Earle, *Monmouth's Rebels: The Road to Sedgemoor 1685* (1977), 26.

38. Earle, *Monmouth's Rebels*, 17–18.

39. Clifton, *Last Popular Rebellion*, 45–8, 55. See also Underdown, *Somerset in the Civil War and Interregnum*, 194–5.

40. Clifton, *Last Popular Rebellion*, 54–6, 61–71. PRO, ASSI 24/22 (W. Circuit Order Book, 1652–76), fo. 209ᵛ. Basil Short, *A Respectable Society: Bridport 1593–1835* (Bradford-on-Avon, 1976), 20–2.

41. PRO, ASSI 16/47/4 (Norfolk Circuit bundles), Sept. 1683. For other examples, see ASSI 23/2 (W. Circuit Gaol Book, 1678–85), Lent Assizes 1685; Amussen, *An Ordered Society*, 146, n. 33; Underdown, *Revel, Riot, and Rebellion*, 290, and *Fire From Heaven*, 256.

42. William L. Sachse, 'The Mob and the Revolution of 1688', *JBS* 4: 1 (1964), 23–40. Lois Schwoerer, 'Women and the Glorious Revolution', *Albion*, 18 (1986), 201–2.

43. Aubrey, 'Remaines', 207, 290. Christopher Hill, *Intellectual Origins of the English Revolution* (Oxford, 1965), 118. Michael Hunter, *John Aubrey and the Realm of Learning* (New York, 1975), 220.

44. Underdown, *Fire From Heaven*, 264–5. Amussen, *An Ordered Society*, 130–3. Dolan, *Dangerous Familiars*, 119.

45. Underdown, *Revel, Riot, and Rebellion*, 217–18.

46. Richard Gough, *The History of Myddle*, ed. David Hey (Harmondsworth, 1981).

47. See above, Ch. 5, p. 110, for Elizabeth Jekyll's commonplace book.

48. J. G. Muddiman (ed.), *The Bloody Assizes* (London, 1929), 78–9; see also 28–9. For the trial, see Earle, *Monmouth's Rebels*, 149, 169–71; Clifton, *Last Popular Rebellion*, 233. For the speech's appeal to women, see Schwoerer, 'Women and the Glorious Revolution', 213–14.

49. Dumas Malone, *Jefferson and His Time* (Boston, 1948–81), vi. 497. Douglass Adair, 'Rumbold's Dying Speech', in Trevor Colborn (ed.), *Fame and the Founding Fathers: Essays by Douglass Adair* (Williamsburg, 1974), 192–202.

50. Dorset RO, B2/A4/7 (Lyme Regis Sessions Rolls, 1710–19), 25 October 1712. I am grateful to Susan Amussen for this reference.

INDEX